Capitalism Rebooted?

Capitalism Rebooted?

Work, Welfare and the New Economy

edited by Dave Broad and Wayne Antony

Fernwood Publishing • Halifax

Editing: Jane Butler
Printed and bound in Canada by: Hignell Book Printing Limited

Published in Canada by Fernwood Publishing
Site 2A, Box 5, 32 Oceanvista Lane
Black Point, Nova Scotia, B0J 1B0
and 324 Clare Avenue, Winnipeg, Manitoba, R3L 1S3
www.fernwoodbooks.ca

Fernwood Publishing Company Limited gratefully acknowledges the financial support of the Department of Canadian Heritage and the Canada Council for the Arts for our publishing program.

Library and Archives Canada Cataloguing in Publication

Capitalism rebooted? : work, welfare, and the new economy / edited by Dave Broad and Wayne Antony.

Includes bibliographical references.
ISBN-13: 978-1-55266-211-3
ISBN-10: 1-55266-211-X

1. Labor. 2. Globalization--Economic aspects. I. Broad, Dave, 1953-
II. Antony, Wayne Andrew, 1950-

HD4901.C245 2006   331   C2006-903780-9

Contents

About the Authors/ 8
Acknowledgements / 10

Introduction
The New Economy
Are All Our Woes Virtually Solved? / 11
Dave Broad and Wayne Antony

Chapter 1
Capitalism Rebooted?
The New Economy Might Not Be All that New / 20
Dave Broad and Wayne Antony

> What is the New Economy? / 21
> Is the New Economy New? / 24
> Work and the New Economy / 33
> The New Economy is Not a Step Beyond Capitalism / 34

Chapter 2
Where's the Work?
Labour Market Trends in the New Economy / 37
Dave Broad, Jane Cruikshank, and James P. Mulvale

> Global Employment Trends / 41
> Global ICT Trends / 44
> Quality of ICT Work / 46
> Canadian Employment Trends / 48
> Canadian ICT Trends / 51
> Knowledge Work and Productivity / 56
> Manufacturing McJobs / 59

Chapter 3
Managing Change
Organizational and Managerial
Responses to the New Economy / 63
Janice Foley

> Contemporary Organizational and Managerial Practices / 64
> The Impact of Changing Practices on Employees / 69
> Worker Protection in the New Economy / 76

Chapter 4
Lifelong Learning and the New Economy
Education or Ideology? / 78
Jane Cruikshank

> The Role of Lifelong Learning / 80
> Credentialism and Underemployment / 82
> Policy and the Skills Debate / 84
> The Role of Training Ideology / 89
> What Can We Do? / 90
> Conclusion / 92

Chapter 5
Stresses and Strains
Workers' Health and the New Economy / 93
Michael Polanyi

> The Evolving Health of Workers in the New Economy / 94
> Toward "Healthy Work" in the New Economy / 101
> Conclusion / 106

Chapter 6
From Welfare to Workfare
Public Policy for the New Economy / 108
Garson Hunter and Dionne Miazdyck-Shield

> A Brief History of Public Policy and the Economy / 110
> Third Way Welfare Policy / 115
> The New Economy and Americanization
> of Canadian Public Policy / 122
> The Future of the Welfare State / 125

Chapter 7
"Solidarity Forever" in Cyberspace?
Responses of the Labour Movement to Information and
Communication Technologies / 128
James P. Mulvale

> The Noeliberal Prescription / 146
> Assessing the Impacts of ICTs on Paid Work / 128
> The Conceptual/Strategic Level — ICTs and the Labour
> Movement's Social Vision and Broad Economic Strategy / 130
> The Practical/Organizational Level — How ICTs Change the
> Labour Movement / 131
> Conclusions / 143

Chapter 8
New Economy or New Society?
"A Change is Gonna Come" / 145
Dave Broad

> The ILO Decent Work Agenda / 148
> Labour *Is* a Commodity / 151
> Promoting Alternatives Within Capitalism / 151
> Towards a Non-Commodity Society? / 156
> Conclusion / 158

References / 161

About the Authors

WAYNE ANTONY taught sociology at the University of Winnipeg for 18 years. He is a founding member of the Canadian Centre for Policy Alternatives-Manitoba and has been on the board of directors of since its inception. He is co-author of two reports on the state of public services in Manitoba (for CCPA-MB) and co-editor (with Dave Broad) of *Citizens or Consumers? Social Policy in a Market Society* and (with Les Samuelson) of *Power and Resistance: Critical Thinking About Social Issues in Canada*.

DAVE BROAD is a Professor of Social Policy in the Faculty of Social Work at the University of Regina, Saskatchewan. His publications include (with Ron Bourgeault) *1492–1992: Five Centuries of Imperialism and Resistance*; (with Wayne Antony) *Citizens Or Consumers? Social Policy in a Market Society*; and *Hollow Work, Hollow Society? Globalization and the Casual Labour Problem*.

JANE CRUIKSHANK is a Professor at the University of Regina in the Faculty of Social Work. She holds a PhD in Adult Education. Her research interests currently focus on lifelong learning and New Economy issues, subjects on which she has presented and published widely.

JANICE FOLEY is an Associate Professor in the Faculty of Business Administration at the University of Regina. She joined the faculty in 2000, coming from the University of Winnipeg, after receiving her PhD in Organizational Behaviour from the Sauder School of Business, University of British Columbia. Her research focuses on the changing workplace environment and its impact on organizational effectiveness and employee health; and on the role of trade unions in fostering workplace democracy and equity.

GARSON HUNTER is an Associate Professor with the Faculty of Social Work, University of Regina. His publications are in the areas of poverty and social welfare. His current research focuses on the financial poverty of intravenous drug users, and the convergence of welfare policies among modern welfare states.

DIONNE MIAZDYCK-SHIELD is the Research Advocate for the Saskatchewan Association for Community Living. Her research interests are in the areas of welfare reform, guaranteed income, health care, trade relations, tax policy, deinstitutionalization, animal cruelty legislation, labour legislation and disability rights.

JIM MULVALE is a faculty member and Head of the Department of Justice Studies at the University of Regina. His areas of research include social policy innovation, work and economic security, social justice theory and Aboriginal models of justice. He has a professional background in community development work in human service organizations. His publications include *Reimagining the Welfare State: Beyond the Keynesian Welfare State.*

MICHAEL POLANYI coordinates research, education and advocacy on Canadian poverty and social justice issues at KAIROS: Canadian Ecumenical Justice Initiatives, based in Toronto. Between 2002 and 2004, he was an Assistant Professor at the University of Regina, where he conducted research on labour markets, work organization and health. He has a PhD in Environmental Studies from York University in Toronto. Over the past 15 years, he has coordinated community-based social change projects with students, low-income people, immigrants, refugees, injured workers and people of faith.

Acknowledgements

The editors thank Fiona Douglas at the Social Policy Research Unit (SPR) of the University of Regina and Lori Foster of Synthesis Research for editorial and research assistance. Our thanks also to Charlotte Yates and Errol Black who provided valuable feedback on an early draft of the manuscript. And finally, thanks to Jane Butler for editing the final manuscript, Debbie Mathers for typing the final manuscript changes and Beverley Rach for design and layout. Some of the material presented in this book is based on research funded by the Social Sciences and Humanities Research Council of Canada (SSHRC).

The New Economy

Are All Our Woes Virtually Solved?

Dave Broad and Wayne Antony

Imagine. You just finished your day's work — all three hours of it. Yesterday and today you worked at the Car Company developing software to run the latest fuel efficiency engine modules. For the next three days you will be over at the Computer Company helping to put together the latest voice command modules. The work is pleasant. After all, not only did both companies hire you based on the contract proposal you submitted for the jobs, but the work itself consists mostly of spending time with a team of other information technology professionals experimenting with various voice inflections to see if computers can accurately respond to irony. After these two jobs, you're not sure, you just might take a few days off to finish that novella you are writing. With the money from those two contracts, you won't really need to work again for a week or two. Sound impossible? Well, this scenario is not too far off in some of the more optimistic visions of the New Economy (NE).[1]

Most accounts of the New Economy say it is based on advanced information and communication technologies (ICT). Drawing on the early work of Daniel Bell (1973; see Chapter 1 below), many authors have argued that we are witnessing an industrial revolution driven by computerized production of both goods and services. The impact of computerization has without doubt been dramatic. We find computers and computer chips everywhere, from automobiles to cash registers to bank machines to musical greeting cards. Digital technology now controls television and telephone systems around the world, with cell phones multiplying exponentially. Many homes in First World countries have more than one personal computer (PC), and digital telephones and audio-visual systems on all levels.

One of the first people to use the term "New Economy" was Canadian management guru Nuala Beck (1992), who actually trademarked the term! Alan Murray (2000: 7), a leading proponent of the New Economy, has described it in glowing terms:

The New Economy… is like the Istanbul bazaar, that five-hundred-year-old covered maze where thousands of vendors sell carpets and curios, icons and samovars. The orderly world of a generation ago, with its limited choices and fixed prices and clear lines of distribution, is being transformed into a chaotic, bustling, teeming global marketplace. Countless sellers court countless buyers, with an array of merchandise. Prices aren't fixed. Each merchant tries to extract the highest price for his wares; but each customer has the power to walk to the next booth in search of a better deal.

Murray goes on to tell us approvingly that "globalization, deregulation, and digitization are turning the entire world into a modern version of the Istanbul bazaar." But unlike the old economy, "there is a new twist: pervasive information." Because of the so-called information technology revolution, both buyers and sellers are, ostensibly, much better informed about market opportunities. In his book, Murray highlights the major changes that underlie the New Economy, particularly developments in computer and information technologies, deregulation of financial and labour markets, and the dizzying expansion of market trading. Indeed, trading in shares on the technology-heavy NASDAQ Composite Index rose from less than 1000 points in 1994 to over 5000 points in 2000, but it crashed later that year and has levelled off at around 2000 points since 2001, the so-called "dot-com crash" (in reference to internet companies like Amazon.com and eBay; see below).

As Murray's definition indicates, this New Economy is, first of all, global. The ICT revolution has made possible changes in communication, production and transportation, so that economic structures are no longer constrained by geography (or political boundaries). Virtually everyone around the world is tied into one global economy. We often call this globalization.

The impact on work has been equally dramatic. ICTs and globalization have transformed work processes and created and destroyed jobs. For example, bank machines have replaced bank tellers and so on, while opportunities have opened up for computer programmers and computer tenders. Not only have the kinds of jobs changed in the New Economy, but the nature of work has also been altered. For example, we are often told that the days of having a life-long career with one employer are long gone.

Finally, the nature of government has changed with the emergence of the New Economy. Within the processes of globalization, the role of government in the New Economy is supposedly much more minimal than in the years up to the 1970s. Government is supposed to provide the conditions for international economic competitiveness, and reduce barriers to economic globalization and be less concerned about the social welfare of individual citizens (which, as we will see, will be taken care of by economic growth). That is, government is supposed to be a midwife to the New Economy.

Thus, the New Economy (NE) has three key features: a newly globalized economy, restructured — i.e., new forms of — work (both supported and driven by the new electronic technologies), and a new form of politics. Each of these key features, in turn, consists of several important elements (which are very briefly alluded to above, some of which are discussed in detail in the rest of this book). There is considerable agreement about the features of the NE, but there is equally considerable debate about the NE. In very general terms, there are two main schools of thought on the New Economy.

According to one kind of assessment and analysis, the New Economy is a good thing. It will promote economic growth in part by increasing labour productivity. Indeed, the package for the Microsoft Office program for PCs proclaims that the product is "What Productivity Means Today." New Economy growth will also be promoted because of increasing investment opportunities. Members of this school sometimes describe the New Economy as a post-industrial, post-modern, post-capitalist society — for some, capitalism has been superceded, for others, capitalism has triumphed and rejuvenated; in either case, we will all be better off than in the industrial capitalist past. As to the economic benefits overall, promoters believe that the New Economy will reboot the world economy to promote economic growth, just as rebooting our PCs will clear out all the system blocks that are impeding the workings of the system.

Very importantly (especially for this book as we are mostly concerned with the impact on the world of work and the welfare of workers), promoters state that the NE will provide new and exciting employment opportunities. There will be plenty of work for everyone, work will be flexible, well-paid and consume less and less of our time. These authors, discussed throughout the book, speak enthusiastically about the many opportunities available, especially for a growing class of "knowledge workers" — those in relatively senior positions doing primarily mental as opposed to manual work. Beck (1992: 133), for example, several years ago identified three groups: "1. Professionals, such as doctors, engineers, lawyers, accountants and actuaries... 2. Engineering, scientific and technical workers... 3. The very senior ranks of management." In particular, the term "knowledge workers" now refers to people who work with ICTs. These workers are the symbol of the NE in the world of labour.

This rebooting of the economy and work is aided by neoliberal public policy change. According to the NE'ers, and to use another computer analogy, governments will clear out system viruses like environmental, labour, and tax regulations that impede the free flow of capital. Governments that do not act in this way will be condemning their populations to the deprivations of global uncompetitiveness and, ultimately, to the dustbin of history.

Others disagree. Authors and researchers in this second school of thought argue that while ICTs have had a significant impact, a global economy is developing and governments' behaviour is changing, we are not, in fact, witnessing the emergence of a truly new economy. Rather, we are in thrall to an old economy — the same old capitalism based on fundamental social inequalities — re-developing and attempting to recharge itself. Further, proponents of the second school of thought argue that current economic restructuring is producing at least as many negative as positive results, with the positive results most often not being evenly distributed.

Regarding globalization, this line of analysis does not dispute a charged-up form of global integration — the obvious global reach of the familiar transnational corporations is clear evidence. But as many point out, capitalism has an inherent tendency to expand, and historically, capitalism has been expanding from its onset. Nor has this new globalization provided the economic opportunities promised; the ones that have emerged have often proved to be fleeting. Indeed, the dot-com crash of 2000–2001 is a clear warning sign of the fallibility of the New Economy. Interestingly, we can note that Murray's (2000) enthusiastic account of New Economy stock trading was written before the so-called dot-com crash of 2000–2001. Neither Murray nor Beck, who wrote three books on the subject in the 1990s, appear to have published any major works on the New Economy since the year 2000. (For more on the dot-com crash see Chapter 2 below.)

Not surprisingly, the world of work, while changed, is still fundamentally one in which employers have the upper hand. The NE has not opened up good jobs for all, and the ones that have been created are certainly not the high-paid, secure jobs predicted. In fact, for many, the so-called flexibility of the NE is actually insecurity in terms of pay, advancement and protection. Even in the much-touted ICT sector, the knowledge workers so loudly proclaimed do exist but are not nearly as plentiful nor as well off as predicted. In fact, many knowledge workers are simply data entry clerks and even those with interesting jobs often work in precarious circumstances.

The New Economy government is much in evidence. Those who take this second line of analysis, like their NE promoter counterparts, point out that governments in almost all industrial countries have cut back on the social safety net (witness the cutbacks to education, social assistance, health care, environmental protection and the constant drive to cut taxes). Where they do take issue is in assessing these changes. This second school regards these changes as actually making the situation worse for the majority of citizens whose lives have already been made more precarious by the economic and work changes in the NE. In fact, most in this school would argue that far from minimizing their impact on the lives of citizens and their economies, governments have been willing and necessary partners in the emergence of the NE.

New technologies, accompanied by economic globalization and the shift from social welfare to neoliberal state policies, have led to increased employer strength and weakening trade unions, to work speedup and unhealthy work environments, and to increasing unemployment and underemployment, while state regulation and provision of social welfare benefits have been eroded. In short, the capital accumulation process is being rebooted at the expense of workers, their families and their communities. This second school of thought believes it is unlikely that the global New Economy will indeed reboot the capital accumulation process in the long run. Nevertheless, its impact is significant and should be addressed by those interested in promoting social welfare and social justice.

The authors of this book subscribe to the second school of thought. We provide a critical analysis of the various trends that are being discussed in the name of the New Economy; however, our main concern is with the impact of the New Economy on work, and the implications for the welfare of workers and their families.

Chapter 1 begins by more clearly defining the NE and situates it historically and in relation to the concepts of corporate globalization and neoliberal state policy. The chapter then undertakes a discussion of views and meanings on globalization and the New Economy. To provide an understanding of these processes and a critique of globalization and the New Economy, Dave Broad and Wayne Antony review theories of economic growth, development and work. Despite broader views of social-economic development put forward in the 1960s and 1970s, the post-1980 era of neoliberalism has returned us to earlier models of development that emphasize economic growth per se as the basis for both economic and social advancement. Thus, the assumption of the New Economy is that increased productivity and economic growth will eventually benefit us all. Corresponding theories of work in the early 1970s, that presumed the coming of a post-industrial, post-capitalist society based on the new technologies from which we would all benefit, have also been revived to support the idea of a New Economy. Also in Chapter 1, we counter these assumptions about development and work with critical theories that explain how a new packaging of socio-economic structures does not alter the fact that they are capitalist in nature and, as such, will not improve the lot of the majority of humanity. In fact, the environmental and social consequences of globalization, neoliberalism and capitalist market application of ICTs have led to a deterioration of conditions for many.

In Chapter 2, Dave Broad, Jane Cruikshank and James Mulvale provide an overview of recent changes to work and the labour market in the Western countries, with a focus on Canada. The authors present information on areas of growth and decline in employment, and on the impact of ICTs on work. Of particular interest is the extent to which the so-called New Economy is producing "good jobs" or "bad jobs" with respect to the intrinsic (quality) and extrinsic (pay and benefits) characteristics of work (several aspects of which are explored in this and ensuing chapters). Available information shows that some good jobs have been created as a result of the NE, but more generally, there have been increases in global unemployment and underemployment. The Director-General of the ILO, Juan Somavia, recently announced to the World Economic Forum an "unprecedented global jobs crisis of mammoth proportions." For some years now the ILO has been saying that we are experiencing an unfair process of globalization and a "decent work deficit." Many in the Third World face unemployment and the informal economy of underground and unregulated work. And in the First World we have seen higher unemployment and a proliferation of precarious and casual work as employers attempt to construct "flexible' labour markets, notably in the much-celebrated knowledge work of the New Economy.

Janice Foley discusses how employer organizational practices have been changing in recent years as a result of advances in information and communication technologies in "Managing Change" (Chapter 3). These practices include organizational restructuring and downsizing, increased use of contingent workers, flexible work hours, lean production, high commitment human resource management practices and co-operative labour-management relations. She examines critically the outcomes of these practices in terms of their impact on organizational productivity and efficiency, and on employee growth and well-being. Foley's survey of contemporary organizational and management practices in the New Economy shows that economic restructuring has strengthened the position of employers vis-a-vis labour, often with a negative impact on job quality and employee well-being. There are some new human resource practices that could improve quality of work, but Foley finds that, with the weakening of trade union strength, most positive developments are extra-contractual and therefore subject to the whims of employers. Countering the rising vulnerability of workers in the New Economy will require input from labour and social justice organizations in workplace and industrial decision making.

Do we need lifelong learning for success in the current and emerging labour markets? This is the basic question asked by Jane Cruikshank in Chapter 4. Canadian policies on skill acquisition for the knowledge-based economy assume lifelong learning to be vital for Canada's global competitiveness. However, lifelong learning policies have failed to deal with issues of credentialism, de-skilling of work, and the underemployment of many well-educated Canadian workers. Cruikshank explains that, without dealing with these issues, government will leave workers with poor prospects regardless of their training or education. However, the role of training ideology is important to understand because it keeps people from questioning socio-economic structures and individualizes their responses to economic change. As to what can be done, Cruikshank says we need to question the rhetoric of the so-called knowledge society, and move beyond training to construct a broader and more inclusive model of lifelong education as an agent of social change.

Work free of negative health impacts was one of the promises of the New Economy. Promise broken says Michael Polanyi in Chapter 5. Job control, psychological demands, job security, work-life balance, fairness of pay and rewards, all aspects of work in the old economy are still key determinants of health in the New Economy. Polanyi explains how these health-influencing conditions have been shaped by the expansion of information technology, the rise of cost-cutting (e.g., downsizing, flexible staffing), and output-enhancing strategies (e.g., lean production). In particular, intensification of work combined with less employment security and low wages cause workers and their families greater stress. Studies show this stress has negative impacts on people's mental and physical health. These conditions affect all workers, yet women, people of colour and low-paid workers experience much more pronounced negative health effects. To deal with the negative health outcomes of the New Economy, Polanyi outlines a democratic approach for improving the health of workers. This entails promoting availability and security of work, adequacy of income and benefits, appropriateness of work arrangements and demands, active participation of workers in decision making, and demonstrating appreciation of workers. To fundamentally improve working conditions, Polanyi says we need to change power relations by creating more inclusive occupational decision making structures.

In Chapter 6, Garson Hunter and Dionne Miazdyck-Shield examine the shift in welfare program delivery from needs-based eligibility, social entitlement and labour market exclusion programs to models that emphasize selective entitlements, active programming and maximum participation in wage labour. Along with neoliberal deregulation of labour markets, national standards for social welfare have been eroded and national programs for welfare replaced by local experiments in delivery. In the United States, this is a "work-first" model for welfare programming. In England the model is viewed as "third way" policy making. This chapter argues that Canada has followed the U.S. in welfare programming but has blended the US model with ideology borrowed from Tony Blair's third-way approach to produce its own hybrid welfare programming model. The authors argue that welfare experimentation in Canada is prompted by the ongoing harmonization of social programs. This is brought about by the North American Free Trade Agreement (NAFTA) as part of economic globalization, with the result that state support for basic welfare rights is being replaced by forced "workfare," or work for welfare, programming. Hunter and Miazdyck suggest that social welfare is too important to be left to official public policy makers. Workers and community members need to be involved in social policy struggles such as those that gave us public education and public welfare, important state programs that need to be defended and advanced.

In Chapter 7, James Mulvale examines the impact of the New Economy on the labour movement. He discusses responses by trade unions to the introduction of ICTs and the struggle for social justice. Despite the neoliberal assault on labour, Mulvale shows that many unions have risen to the challenges posed by the New Economy, fighting to defend the interests of working people, and organizing workers of the new ICT sector who fall outside the traditional occupational groups represented by private or public sector unions. Labour has worked to develop new forms of "cyber-activism" using ICTs as organizing tools and means of building solidarity within the labour movement and with other social justice movements, both within Canada and internationally. Mulvale ends the chapter by arguing that the age-old labour movement goals of better working conditions and social welfare have not changed and, while new technologies can be useful to trade unions in their struggles, they will not replace the flesh and blood struggles of workers and their communities.

The evidence presented in this book tells us that the New Economy is not all that it was cracked up to be. Work is not more pleasing, healthy and well-paid for all; learning potentials are being squandered; management still aims to control rather than empower workers; and welfare policy is leaving growing numbers of working people in more precarious circumstances. The new virtual technologies will apparently not solve all our woes. Does this mean that all is lost? In Chapter 8, we tackle the thorny issues in the age-old question: what is to be done? The chapter begins with a review of the neoliberal prescription for job growth through the New Economy, then discusses the International Labour Organization's proposals for a decent work program. While the ILO's program should be supported, there are limits to labour reforms within a capitalist market economy. A more significant social transformation through social movement activism is necessary to confront problems posed by our technology-based economy. The chapter argues that the current degradation of labour, life and the environment under global capitalism cannot be sustained. A transformation of the world capitalist system must and will come about, but the final results cannot be predicted because they depend on the struggles for social change themselves. However, if we want to create a better society, social justice activists must engage in these struggles.

Note

1. Following the practice in the literature, we will use the term New Economy with capital letters to distinguish current socio-economic trends from those that might be entailed in constructing a truly new economy.

CHAPTER 1

Capitalism Rebooted?

The New Economy Might Not Be All that New

Dave Broad and Wayne Antony

For a while in the late 1990s we had a New Economy. It was the wonder of the world. Computers had unleashed a productivity miracle, recessions were a thing of the past, ideas had replaced things as the motors of economic life, the world had become unprecedentedly globalized, work had become deeply meaningful, and mutual funds had put an end to class conflict. (Henwood, 2003: 1)

*****

Since the recessions of the early 1970s, we have witnessed a global crisis of capitalism. As we do when our personal computers crash, capitalists have been trying to reboot the accumulation process through globalization and adoption of the new technologies of the so-called information age. In recent years we have been hearing a great deal about a New Economy (NE), based on information and communications technologies (ICTs) developed in the latter decades of the twentieth century. This New Economy has been touted by business and governments as the panacea for all of our economic and social ills. The New Economy is presented as a boon to all because it will increase productivity and improve our global competitiveness, bringing prosperity for everyone.

The notion of improving social welfare through new technologies is not a new one. Since at least the beginning of the Industrial Revolution in the eighteenth century, it has been the justification for applying new production methods and reorganizing work. For some, ICTs mark a third industrial revolution, the first being based on water and steam-powered machinofacture[1] and the second, in the late nineteenth century, based on electricity and rail. The third has even been presented as the beginning of a post-industrial society that will end poverty, drudgery, and social class divisions (see below and Bell 1973).

But the International Monetary Fund (IMF) (2000), for example, readily admits that the global average income rose considerably over the twentieth century, so why do we still hear that there is a problem with economic growth and labour productivity? If the global economy produces more commodities than can easily be sold on the world market, is there really a crisis of productivity? When we see cities trying to cope with the piles of garbage tossed out by our global consumer society (Brennan, 2003), what logic says we must produce even more? Why is there an incessant drive to increase productivity in the face of massive wealth alongside continuing poverty, inequality, environmental destruction and waste? A rational person might well conclude that crying "productivity crisis!" is a false alarm. And if decades, if not centuries, of global economic growth have not by now decreased social inequality, but rather the reverse, how will yet more economic growth decrease inequality?

In this chapter, we will argue that the promises of the New Economy in fact promote the profit needs and desires of capitalism, not the social welfare needs of the majority of people. The drive to increase economic growth serves an ideological argument constructed under a number of guises, most recently as part of the gospel of globalization. Teeple (2000) illustrates the two sides of this coin in the title of his book, *Globalization and the Decline of Social Reform*. Therein he documents the post-1980 neoliberal assault on social welfare and workers' rights, which contributors to this volume show to be at the heart of the New Economy. The underlying purpose of current "reforms" is to exhort more work at lower wages out of labour forces around the world — to reboot the raw exploitation of workers who had gained some degree of labour market and social security through trade union and welfare state protections.

To put it most simply, the New Economy is not really new. There have been some economic changes in recent years, and some changes that are significant to the lives of many people. But the NE is really capitalism with a new face — "version 6.0 of the American Dream" (to quote Steve Earle, 2002). All the inequalities, exploitation, and conflicts that are part and parcel of capitalism have not been superceded.

What is the New Economy?

While the term, New Economy, may be new, the idea is not. Below we will often refer to writing from the late 1960s and early 1970s, particularly that of US sociologist Daniel Bell who wrote the two influential books, *The End of Ideology* and *The Coming of Post-Industrial Society.* For Bell and other social observers, capitalism, or at least the problems of capitalism, was on the verge of ending; and a new era of massive economic growth, social peace, and unprecedented prosperity was being ushered in — an era of a new economy. In an important sense, the NE was said to be non-capitalist.

The NE is also global. What is globalization and what is behind it? In his survey of writings on globalization, Waters (2001: 1) tells us that, if post-modernism was the key concept for the 1980s, then globalization must be the key concept for the 1990s, and this much-discussed globalization is based on the celebrated New Economy. After examining a number of authors' definitions, Waters (2001: 5) defines globalization broadly as: "A social process in which the constraints of geography on economic, political, social and cultural arrangements recede, in which people become increasingly aware that they are receding and in which people act accordingly." For most authors and public policy makers, globalization is conceptualized narrowly as an economic process, as the integration of national economies and production processes into the capitalist world market.

This global economic integration is made possible by the new technologies that have impacted communications, transportation and production, in particular computer technologies that are seen to be at the heart of the New Economy. Indeed, the editorial introduction to a special issue of *ISUMA: Canadian Journal of Policy Research* (Spring 2002: 6) begins: "In its strictest sense, the 'new economy' can be defined as a series of changes in the economic landscape that resulted from industry's massive investment in new information and communications technologies (ICTs) over the past ten years or so." Thus, the NE has several new economic, work and social welfare elements, at least in the eyes of its proponents.

More specifically, proponents of the NE make several claims about its economic structure. First of all, they argue, as we said above, that the NE is not only based on global markets but that this global view and reach are new. The gigantic transnational corporations of the new millennium are a central symbol of the NE. No one would argue that economic markets have never before been international, but the NE has brought internationalism to an unprecedented position of economic centrality. More importantly, proponents argue that the focus on an integrated international market will unleash, and indeed, already has unleashed, the economic competitiveness that is the hallmark of capitalism. This, in turn, has and will produce almost unlimited economic growth and expansion, and this growth will spread throughout the world. New markets will be found or created and will expand in ways and at rates never seen before. Former Canadian prime minister Paul Martin (2000), for example, spoke of the "cascade of new industries" that would mark the NE, resulting from never-before-seen economic opportunities. Most supporters of globalization present themselves as true believers in an unfettered free-market, capitalist economy. Thomson (1999: 400) explains the "conventional economic wisdom" favouring globalization:

> In policy terms, it is widely accepted that if governments acted to ensure unimpeded free trade in goods, services, capital and technology, then an integrated capitalist global market would stimulate competition and spur productivity thus raising living standards, particularly for the aspiring citizens of the developing countries.

Neoliberal economist Easterlin (1998) favourably sees this as "growth triumphant."

Much of this expansion will result from some old economic "laws" of capitalism being superceded. Many argue, for example, that the growth potential of the new capitalism will mean that the booms and busts characteristic of decades — maybe centuries — of industrial capitalist development gone by have been ended. The growth potential of the NE is very much seen as unlimited (see, for example, Murray, 2000).

In an equal dose, this growth and expansion is driven by the spread of new technologies (ICTs) throughout the production processes of the NE. No industry will be deprived of the benefits of this technological revolution — thus, new industries and markets will emerge and expand, and old ones will be rejuvenated by the spread of ICTs. Many NE proponents claim, for example, that our economic well-being will not rest, as it has for many decades, on the old industries — manufacturing and resource extraction, to name just two, will recede into the NE sunset, as more ICTs rule the economic roost.

On the social welfare front, proponents of the NE essentially claim that the social dislocations consequent to capitalist economic development in most societies are also, or will soon be, a thing of the past. Resting largely on the claims about economic growth, the NE is said to be bringing in an era of improved living standards for everyone. The International Monetary Fund (IMF 2002: 5), for example, states:

> economic growth is the only way to improve living standards in developing countries, and that it is best achieved through globalization. [The IMF] is doing its utmost within the mandate given by its members, to safeguard the international financial system, and help its members take advantage of the opportunities offered by

integration into the world economy, while minimizing the associated risks.

By following this advice, the IMF says the poorer countries of the South will
begin to achieve the economic heights of the industrialized world, including, at least the beginning of, the end of abject poverty. The ILO (2005a),
which once had something of a social democratic orientation, has clearly
adopted the NE approach in its *World Employment Report 2004–05*, saying that
pursuing economic growth by increasing labour productivity is the best way
to overcome world poverty. In the industrialized world, the wealth created
by this new growth would also reduce the many economic inequalities with
which we were familiar. So, for example, wages will rise and the income gap
will shrink. In short, this wealth will trickle down to everyone so that the
poor become richer (even though the rich may not become poorer!).

And nowhere will the effects of the NE be more revolutionary than in
the world of work (the aspect of the NE about which most of the rest of this
book is written). Work, in the eyes of NE proponents, is to become much
less onerous and routinized. Given the expansion of the NE, jobs should
be plentiful. Given the increasing reliance on the new technologies, work,
in most industries, will be stimulating and rewarding in the kinds of tasks
people are doing (gone are the days of dirty, dangerous and highly unskilled
jobs). As it is put in Chapter 2, workers in the NE will not be "movers and
makers," as people work with information not things. Moreover, as we will
see in Chapter 2, this upgrading of work is promised to result from the
development of so-called flexible labour markets and jobs. Flexibility will
mean not only better working conditions but also much more variety on the
job and throughout people's working lives. This will draw on our entrepreneurial spirits for self-marketing and self-promotion, as is suggested by the
subtitle to Murray's (2000: 153) chapter on working in the New Economy,
"You Are Your Own Brand."

Is the New Economy New?

There is, of course, a great deal of debate about the NE, its elements and
its effects. Many social analysts argue that the NE is not really new, nor is it
as beneficial to everyone as it proponents proclaim. In short, we will argue
below that the changed economic landscape is really the new international
division of labour (NIDL) that began to emerge in the 1960s. What is being
called the New Economy is simply the now-obvious effects of the NIDL, itself only an extension of centuries-old capitalism. And just like the old capitalism, on which the NIDL is based, the NE has mainly benefited capitalists.

Is Globalization New?

There is considerable debate among observers left, right and centre as to how real and how new is the globalization element of the New Economy. British author John Gray (2002), whose work influenced Margaret Thatcher and the British New Right (avid supporters of globalization and the NE), however, is now critical of the globalization agenda: "A universal state of equal integration in worldwide economic activity is precisely what globalization *is not*" (Gray, 2002: 55–56, emphasis in original). He argues that globalization accentuates uneven development between countries, a feature of the capitalist world economy noted long ago by critical development theorists (see below and Chilcote, 2003).

Uneven development is something that can be traced back to early colonialism, but it has more recently been manifest in the so-called Third World debt crisis. Foreign investment and foreign aid to Third World countries accelerated growth of export production that tied these countries more closely to the world market, at the same time that it indebted them to foreign lending agencies. The result was that increasing amounts of government and private financial resources were flowing out of the Third World, to the point that more was going out than coming in (Ellwood 2001). After debt defaults by some countries in the early 1980s, the IMF formalized "structural adjustment" agreements for repayment of Third World debts. But, for example, "in six of the eight years from 1990 to 1997 developing countries paid out more in debt service (interest plus repayments) than they received in new loans: a total transfer from South to North of $77 billion" (Ellwood, 2001: 49). The situation was so bad in the mid 1990s that major Third World countries like Argentina were bankrupt. "So we are left with a bizarre and degrading spectacle. In Africa, external debt has ballooned by 400 percent since the [World] Bank and the IMF began managing national economies through structural adjustment" (Ellwood, 2001: 51). This situation has continued in recent years (Auer et al., 2006; Hart-Landsberg, 2006), and incited much public outcry and calls to cancel Third World debt through events such as Bob Geldof's Live 8 concerts and campaigning by organizations like Make Poverty History <www.makepovertyhistory.org>.

Globalization as Americanization

Another lesson we learn from development studies is that globalization is not exactly what it is touted to be by its supporters. Mike Mason (1997: 408) puts it succinctly: "Besides the prospects of economic growth, 'development,' as it turned out, was also 'Americanization'." Liberal economist James Thomson (1999) argues that globalization has been promoted mainly by transnational corporations, US governments, and international institutions heavily influenced by US governments. Globalization was pushed strongly by the US when Bill Clinton was President, but less so by European and Asian governments. In fact, Thomson (1999: 398) quotes former French Prime Minister Lionel Jospin as having said that "capitalism is its own worst enemy. The crises we have witnessed teach us three things: Capitalism remains unstable, the economy is political, and the global economy calls for regulation." That the symbol of globalization — the transnational corporation — is most likely US-based speaks volumes. Of the 100 largest economies in the world, over half are corporations, and some of the largest and most powerful are based in the US (Anderson and Cavanagh, 2003).

Thomson (1999: 400) asks: "What are the sources of [former US president] Clinton's globalization agenda? It's not difficult to establish the chronology. The pivotal year was 1989." With the breakup of the Soviet Union, the U., as the only remaining superpower, moved to take advantage of what Western pundits called "the triumph of capitalism." Considering this context, it becomes apparent that the US state's strong support for globalization is driven by imperialism. Observers have noted that the US, like empires before it, is in decline, economically at least, challenged especially by Europe and Asia (Du Boff, 2003).[2] Thus, promoting free market globalization is one means by which the US is trying to shore up its empire (another is by military might). In fact, the openly imperialistic, Washington-based right-wing think-tank, Project for the New American Century (PNAC), created in 1997 with a mission to "promote American global leadership," has as signatories high-level officials in the government of George W. Bush. While, as Thomson (1999) argues, former President Clinton was promoting US interests on the political-economic front, the current US regime of President Bush is taking a more openly militaristic approach to foreign policy, currently through the US assault on Iraq.

In discussing the US global position, Gray (2002) notes that the promotion of global market freedom, while until recently creating a boom for the US economy, has not benefited the majority of US citizens. The impact of promoting a war economy at the expense of social welfare was laid bare by the human devastation in the wake of Hurricane Katrina in the Gulf of Mexico. The Bush government's failure at hurricane preparation and the divisions of class and race were plain for all to see in New Orleans in 2005. Thus, globalization is not some unconscious economic evolution spreading around the world and bringing good fortune for everyone. Much of the strength of globalization derives from US imperialism, and thus will mainly benefit the US and its corporations.

Even though the 1990s saw globalization accelerate and ideas about it expand exponentially, it is a phenomenon that started before the emergence of the NE. "The early 1970s were watershed years in the shaping of the current period. To pick two events: within months of each other, the Bretton Woods agreement was dissolved and the first commercial micro-processor was introduced by a young start-up company, Intel" (Davis, 1999: 39). After World War II, the major powers of the West met at Bretton Woods, New Hampshire, under US tutelage to establish means for stabilizing the world economy. These meetings produced the major world financial institutions, the International Monetary Fund (IMF) and the International Bank for Reconstruction and Development (World Bank). They also pegged the value of gold to the US dollar, a recognition of the US post-war ascendance hegemonic imperial power. But in 1971, economic pressures arising from, among other things, the rebuilt economies of Europe and Japan, led then-US President Nixon to float the value of the US dollar, thus ending the stable convertibility of dollars for gold. This, of course, cheapened the value of dollars held by foreigners, to the benefit of the US economy. "On a separate track, the micro-processor was developed and deployed as part of the search for new tools to cheapen production and co-ordination costs to compete and profit in this environment" (Davis, 1999: 39).

So, the US infatuation with globalization did not begin in the 1990s with President Clinton. Moreover, as Davis (1999: 39) notes of the dissolution of the Bretton Woods agreement and the introduction of the micro-processor: "At a deep level, the coincidence of the events was not a coincidence at all." It was already apparent to some observers in the early 1970s (Sweezy and Magdoff, 1972) that we were witnessing the end of US hegemony in the world economy, which, as noted above, the US has been trying to regain ever since, through economic and military globalization.

Economic Growth as Development

As noted above, the phenomenon that in the 1990s came to be called globalization, with its New Economy, is not different from the new international-al division of labour (NIDL) that developed in the 1970s (Frobel et al., 1980). But historical shifts and continuities may be difficult to see because a narrow definition of capitalist economic activity and productivity continues to hold sway globally. This narrow economism results from the dominance of the classical liberal, and now neoliberal, theory of development and economic growth. As in the immediate post-World War II years, development is, in the NE view, unabashedly equated with a promised blossoming of capitalist economic growth. That is, economic growth itself is called development.

In the 1960s and 1970s, there was considerable debate of explanations for world economic development. Modernization theory predominated until the mid 1960s. Based on classical liberal assumptions about the workings of a capitalist market economy, modernization really meant capitalist development. And based on eighteenth century ideas, mainly of Adam Smith (1776), classical liberalism assumes that the capitalist market, if allowed to operate freely, would produce ceaseless economic growth. Further, we would all reap the social benefits as competition and a market based on supply and demand would assure the best use of society's resources in meeting our needs. This was what Smith (1776) called the "invisible hand of the market."

Twentieth century modernization theorists admitted that economic growth may initially benefit some countries and some groups within countries more than others, but the wealth would "trickle down" to all in the end. And one way to hasten this process was through aid and investment from developed countries to the Third World, which would produce industrial revolutions like those of Britain and the US. In practice, the modernization approach could, and often did, co-exist with both free market and interventionist state policies. Sometimes First World international policy was viewed as global Keynesianism.[3] Altvater (2001: 75) tells us: "Steady growth was indeed the backbone of the corporatist 'Keynesian class compromise' associated with the 'Fordist' mode of regulation that characterized developed capitalism during the postwar period; and it assumed to offer a remedy for backwardness in the less-developed world — the argument of 'modernization' theory."

By the mid 1960s, some students of development, particularly those from the Third World, were arguing that the assumptions of modernization theory did not hold true in the real world (Chilcote, 2003). Their critical studies showed that significant economic growth was occurring, but the benefits were not trickling down (see, for example, Frank, 1969). As they had done historically, foreign corporations and their local allies were making fortunes off the extraction and export of raw materials, such as agricultural and mineral products, while workers were being paid a pittance for their labour. The foreign connections ran so deep that companies like Anaconda and United Fruit became thoroughly enmeshed with the governments of some countries, colourfully labelled "banana republics." With the NIDL, Third World manufacturing for global markets, not just exporting natural resources, has been added to the mix (see below). That is, there was economic change and growth but not development. This second set of writers argued that inequality was in fact persisting and increasing because of the unequal economic and political structure of the international system. Rather than helping, so-called aid and investment from the First World were actually draining more wealth and resources out of the Third World than they were putting in, creating what Frank (1969) called "the development of underdevelopment." These authors showed that weak peripheries

— the Third World — were tied to strong imperial centres though chains of economic and political dependence. The new approach thus acquired the name "dependency theory" and produced the argument that, rather than more aid and investment, development requires that Third World countries attain national liberation from First World domination.

An important part of the dependency critique of modernization theory was that economic growth was being conflated with development. In his appraisal of modernization theory, Mason (1997: 407) asks: "What was development?" He answers: "'Development' was the promise of universal economic growth along the routes pioneered by the leading countries of the West. 'Growth' implied steady economic expansion and sophistication in the form of industrialization." In the late 1960s, dependency theorists had distinguished economic growth as a quantitative process from development as qualitative change, involving the creation of new economic and non-economic social structures. This distinction became important enough in critiques of development that even the World Bank began, in the 1970s, to promote its development assistance programs as being about more than just economic growth. World Bank literature adopted the terminology of a "basic needs" approach to development being advocated by many non-governmental organizations in the 1970s, defining basic needs as more than simply food, shelter and clothing. But the changes to the World Bank's programming were largely rhetorical.

The New International Division of Labour

It seemed that dependency theory had defeated modernization theory, and in academia this may have been true. But in response to the growing global crisis of profitability around 1970,[4] new strategies emerged to reboot the global capital accumulation process. Sweezy et al. (2002: 2) observe: "This notable [post-1970 economic] slowdown has also taken place alongside a major leap in technology (the so-called New Economy) and the widening globalization that increased exploitation of the third world." In the 1970s this was being called the "new international division of labour" (NIDL) (Frobel et al., 1980). With new technologies in transportation, communications and production processes, the old division between a Third World, producing primary goods in agriculture and mining and other natural resources, and an industrialized First World, producing the manufactured end goods from those resources, was breaking down.

One example of the expanding new international division of labour discussed by observers in the 1970s was the case of the "world car." Rather than being produced at one production site in one country, automobiles were increasingly being assembled from parts produced throughout the world. The average family car is now made from components produced in 20 or more countries, from Canada to India to France to Brazil (Ransom, 2001: 98). Now production processes could be parcelled across the globe and, with the new technologies, still controlled from corporate headquarters. It was this dynamic that led modernization theorists to say that the Third World was modernizing and developing. Whatever we call the process, it is now obvious that capital's increased mobility has had a dramatically negative impact on workers, their communities and governments, which are increasingly forced into bidding wars for investment (Broad, 2000).

Accompanying these economic changes came changes in public policy (see Chapter 6). The elections of Margaret Thatcher in Britain in 1979 and Ronald Reagan in the US in 1980 marked a shift in the role of states in the world economy. An open return to unfettered capitalism, a neoliberal free market approach to state policies of privatization, de-regulation and cutbacks to state welfare services (Merret, 1996; Sears, 1999; Teeple, 2000) was being espoused as a good thing by these governments. In terms of post-World War II development theory, this brought about, in official policy and practice, the resurgence of modernization theory, as evidenced in the quotes from the IMF presented above.

By the 1990s, the continuing advance of the post-1970 economic and political processes were being re-packaged. Changes that had been occurring for several decades appeared under new labels: "globalization" and "New Economy."[5]

The New Economy

World-system theorists,[6] while arguing that globalization does not mark a break with capitalism, accept that recent transformations have produced what we might call a *deepening* of the capitalist world economy (Amin, 1994; Broad, 1995; Chase-Dunn, 1999). Chase-Dunn (1999: 190) argues: "The capitalist world-economy has experienced cyclical process and secular trends for hundreds of years." Following this logic, Robertson (2003) claims that there have been three waves of globalization, the first in the early modern period (fourteenth to eighteenth centuries), the second accompanying the Industrial Revolution (eighteenth to nineteenth centuries), and a third wave of "American globalism" after World War II. From this same perspective, Chase-Dunn (1999: 190) notes that, "globalization is a long-term upward trend of political and economic change that is affected by cyclical processes. The most recent technological changes, and the expansions of international trade and investment, are part of these long-run changes." But we need to ask how the most recent changes compare with long-run trends, and what are the important continuities as well as qualitative differences.

Asking how much has really changed with globalization and the New Economy leads some observers to argue that expanded use of new technologies and the deepening integration of the global capitalist economy after 1970 are a return to raw capitalism, but at a higher stage of development. The results benefit the most powerful economies and transnational corporations, but hurt many others. The editors of the journal *Monthly Review*, for example, have argued this, though admitting that there are significant socio-economic impacts from recent global and technological developments. "The existence of the New Economy, in the sense of a dynamic information technology sector within the economy that has been a spur to accumulation, is not to be doubted. Clearly, it constitutes something distinct in the history of capitalism" (Sweezy et al., 2001: 2–3).

Others see a qualitative transformation with the new technologies that has permitted the new international division of labour. Davis (1999: 37) claims that "globalization describes capitalism in the age of electronics" and goes on to argue:

> This tack is to say that there is something new, epochal, different today from the capitalism of, say, fifty years, eighty years or 150 years ago. This is not to say that capitalism no longer operates according to the same laws. The notion that the laws of capitalism have been suspended, implicit in the talk of "the new economy," is crazy talk.

The law of value and the incessant drive to accumulate capital through maximization of profit continue to underpin the world economy. Consequently, under capitalism, there is no end to the pursuit of economic growth and ever-increasing productivity. Altvater (2001: 74) refers to this as "the growth obsession," and says: "the statement 'growth forever'... only makes sense if the growth that Easterlin (1998) and other growth-enthusiasts have in mind is mere monetary growth (known as inflation), or a purely virtual 'new' economy (without transportation, material production, and physical consumption of resources)."

The Economic Structure of the New Economy

In more specific terms, there are several economic features of the New Economy that suggest that we are not witnessing a fundamental shift from old-style capitalism. Several key predictions flowing from the economic growth claims of NE proponents do not seem to have occurred despite the NE being in place for some time. For one, NE proponents claim that we should see not just growth in the services sector — financial, information, and so on — but evidence that our economies have come to depend on these new industries. That does not appear to be the case (see Cohen and Zysman, 1987). More recently, Palley (1999) and Ryan (2000) have noted the importance of an economically healthy manufacturing sector for improving national economies and household incomes. And in the wake of the dot-com crash of 2000–2001, there has been renewed interest in the question of why manufacturing matters. Some of this interest comes from conservatives in the United States who are concerned about global outsourcing of production and foreign takeover of US manufacturing industries. The Cambridge-MIT Institute organized a conference called "Manufacturing Matters" in 2002 that highlighted the importance of manufacturing in the US economy.[7] The *National Review* published an editorial on December 8, 2003, lamenting the US' loss of its manufacturing capacity, noting that "each $1 of final manufacturing output creates another $1.43 in related manufacturing and business services," not to mention personal services and retail sales. The *National Review* concludes that "manufacturing matters to the people of the United States for it helps produce the taxes we pay, the jobs we need, the goods we consume, and the weapons for our national defense (sic)" (National Review, 2003). [8]

In fact, it is arguable that the New Economy does not constitute a technological-industrial revolution of the magnitude seen with the two historical industrial revolutions. New technologies have not spread evenly throughout the economy. "Contrary to a widespread view, computers are not used equally everywhere within business" (Sweezy et al., 2001: 4). In fact, 75 percent of computer input in business is found in finance, insurance, real estate and other services (including software, health care and legal services). Though we have heard much about the impact of computers and robotics on manufacturing, the scale of use is much smaller (10-12 percent). In fact, globalization has brought with it a revival of labour-intensive sweatshops and informal economy in both the First and Third Worlds (Sassen, 1998; Tabak and Crichlow, 2000). As to the impact on productivity growth, the service sector has contributed little. And to the overall application of ICTs to the economy, much economic research shows "that the effect of digital technology on productivity was small on the whole; such advance as there was took place almost entirely in the manufacture of durable goods" (see Sweezy et al., 2001: 6–7). In fact, we could conclude that "the digital revolution certainly is a technological revolution with widespread effects; the important thing from an economic standpoint, however, is that it is not epoch-making, as in the case of the steam engine, the railroad, and the automobile" (Sweezy et al., 2001: 7).

Nor has the New Economy attenuated or eliminated the business cycle. Again, many NE proponents such as Murray (2000), following their faith in economic growth, predicted a "taming of the business cycle" (eliminating the wild boom-and-bust swings so characteristic of capitalism), or the replacement of the business cycle by a "tech cycle." *Business Week* editor Michael Mandel suggests (cited in Sweezy et al., 2001) there are good reasons to be skeptical. Much NE investment is based on debt, and what came to be called the "millennium boom" (because it came at the turn of the millennium) was a classic speculative bubble. Recent fallout from debt financing, speculation and over-expansion of capacity have shown that business cycles are alive and well, as witnessed by the stock market crash in New Economy dot.com industries in 2000-2001 (see Sweezy et al., 2001, 2002, 2003; Magdoff et al., 2004; and Chapter 2 below). As noted above, NASDAQ trading in dot-com businesses rose from less than 1,000 points in 1994 to over 5,000 points in 2000, then crashed to 2,000 points in 2001. *Wikipedia* encyclopedia lists eight dot-com successes (like Amazon.com and eBay) that weathered the storm, but lists 35 dot-com related ventures that crashed.[9]

There was, however, economic expansion in the 1990s, based on both an increase in profit rates and investment in new information technologies. But contrary to New Economy accounts of recent economic growth, "It was the historical reversal, after 1973, of the long post-Second World War trend of rising real wages, and its replacement by a trend of declining wages, that is the main factor accounting for the long-term rise in the rate of profits in the 1990s" (Kotz, 2003: 23). Neoliberal regimes, in Britain and the US in particular, reduced the bargaining power of workers by attacking trade unions, deregulating business and lowering barriers to international trade and investment (Magdoff and Magdoff, 2004). A key piece of evidence here is the long-term unemployment rate that rose from two or three percent in the 1950s and 1960s to between seven and ten percent during the years of the NE. "This is not the aspect of neoliberalism that its advocates advertise, but it was effective in raising the rate of profit" (Kotz, 2003: 23). The profit rate increase was also assisted by cuts to business taxes, as part of the shift of state functions away from social welfare towards corporate profits.

Work and the New Economy

Complementary to debates about development and economic change, debates about work can also help us place the current situation in historical context. In the early 1970s, social changes producing what is now called the New Economy gave rise to the notion that industrial capitalism as we knew it was being superseded. Bell (1973), for example, argued that new technologies were producing a shift from a manufacturing-based society to a service society, supplanting blue-collar workers with "knowledge workers."[10] More than this, he argued that knowledge was the ascendant form of capital in this society, and that workers who possessed this knowledge capital would become the favoured class. In one sense, this was a re-packaging of a post-World War II sociological notion that the blue-collar working class was declining in numbers and we were all becoming middle class, as signalled by the growing importance of white-collar service workers.

The year after Bell's book came Braverman's (1974) *Labor and Monopoly Capital.* Braverman observed that changes in production were not yielding a qualitatively new form of society, nor was the lot of most workers becoming pleasurable and stimulating. Late twentieth century monopoly capitalism was, in fact, producing both old and new forms of what he called "degraded" labour. There are still plenty of exploited blue-collar workers about, and many of the now numerically dominant service workers find themselves in degraded and/or de-skilled job situations (Menzies, 1996; Rinehart, 2001; Lowe, 2000). One thing that Braverman noted was the continuing adaptation of the principles of so-called "Scientific Management" developed by Frederick Taylor in the late 1800s. Taylorism entails a very specific division of labour and minimization of the time and motion required for production tasks. The overall result is a generalized de-skilling of work for many workers. In discussing the growth of "second jobs," Braverman (1975) also foresaw the expansion of what has come to be called "flexible employment" and the casualization of labour (see Chapter 2 and Broad, 2000 for more on this trend). Other effects of the NE on work, labour markets and workers that lead to the same conclusion — the NE is not so new — are taken up in the rest of this book.

The New Economy is Not a Step Beyond Capitalism

Generally, we can conclude that, while producing significant effects like the recent wave of globalization and the spread of ICTs, the New Economy is not a step beyond capitalism. We must keep in mind that the world-system is still a capitalist socio-economic system, not a post-industrial or post-modern utopia. It is not human need but the incessant drive to accumulate capital that says we must continue to produce more, faster, at lower costs of labour and resources, with no apparent end in sight (Altvater, 2001). Karl Marx (1867: 742), the foremost student of capitalism, characterizes the imperative of the system thus: "Accumulate, accumulate! That is Moses and the prophets!" There are increasing signs that neoliberalism and the New Economy have already begun to run their course and will not reboot the capital accumulation process (see Chapter 2; Amin, 2004; and Henwood, 2003). And in the longer run, some economists have identified a systemic trend towards economic stagnation that will continue to plague the capital accumulation process (see Steindl, 1952; Baran and Sweezy, 1966; Foster and Szlajfer, 1984; and Chapter 8 below).

However, despite the exaggerated claims about the New Economy, we cannot simply write these trends off as pure rhetoric. Globalization and the New Economy may not really be new and New Economy industries may not have produced the sort of economic and employment growth that promoters wish us to believe they have (see Chapter 2). But they are still being promoted so strongly by business and government that their impacts on workers, their families and their communities are significant.[11] Neoliberal policy has been used to shift the role of the state away from promoting social welfare, as under Keynesianism, to promoting privatization and deregulation of the economy. We are constantly being told that we must improve our individual and collective productivity to be more competitive on the global market. In the workplace, this means constantly pushing workers to exceed production targets by "re-engineering" production processes. Meanwhile, neoliberal governments have shifted from a focus on ensuring social rights to promoting individual "responsibilities." Social assistance is being replaced by "workfare" as we are all exhorted to increase our economic productivity (see Broad and Antony, 1999; and Chapter 6 below).

In Canada and other countries, governments continue to promote investment in the New Economy. Statistics Canada, for example, continues to produce reports on economic growth and employment in the New Economy (see Chapter 2), and federal granting agencies such as the Social Sciences and Humanities Research Council of Canada (SSHRC) offer grants to academics to research the New Economy. With this continued promotion, it is worthwhile to consider how the various aspects of the New Economy agenda are affecting work and the social welfare of workers, their families and their communities.

Notes

1. At the beginning of the industrial revolution the term "machinofacture" was used to distinguish the new factory, and often mechanized, production from hand production of commodities by craftspeople in small workshops, then described as manufacture. Curiously history bequeathed the term manufacture to describe factory production, though machinofacture is more apt.
2. See various articles in the journals *Monthly Review* and *Review* since 1970.
3. Keynesianism, ascribed to John Maynard Keynes and his followers, is the term often applied to economic theories and policies of government monetary and fiscal programming to increase employment and spending. The two main goals are to deal with the crisis-prone economic nature of capitalism, and to promote social welfare spending to prevent social crisis and upheaval resulting

from economic hardship and inequality. These are social reform measures, not intended to alter the basic nature of the capitalist economic system.

4. Some observers date the beginning of global economic crises to recessions of the late 1960s, others to those of the early 1970s. Suffice to say that the changes under discussion became more and more obvious after 1970.

5. The National Film Board of Canada has produced some revealing documentaries of the process, such as *The Emperor's New Clothes* and *Turbulence.*

6. The school of world-systems theorists is often formally associated with the work of Immanuel Wallerstein and the Fernand Braudel Center at Binghamton University in Binghamton, New York. But I am referring here to world-systems studies in the broader sense of those whose work encompasses the structures and processes of the capitalist world system.

7. See <www.cambridge-mit.org/cgi-bin/default.pl?SSSID=467> for a list of presentations (on video) at this July 2002 conference.

8. <www.findarticles.com/p/articles/mi_m1282/is_23_55/ai_n1361030>.

9. <http://en.wikipedia.org/wiki:/Dot-com>.

10. One of the best-known works of this era is Bell's (1973) book, *The Coming of Post-Industrial Society.* A newer version of Bell's thesis, touting the merits of the "knowledge society," appears in Drucker's (1993) book *Post-Capitalist Society.* More recently, this discussion has focused on an ostensible shift from the old industrial society to a new "digital society" (Grantham, 2000).

11. A search of University of Regina library holdings, for example, shows recent publications with titles such as *New Economy and Macroeconomic Stability* (Togati, 2006), *Academic Capitalism and the New Economy* (Slaughter and Rhoades, 2004), *Environmental Regulation and the New Global Economy* (Bartin et al., 2004), *Female Enterprise in the New Economy* (Hughes, 2005) and *Aboriginal Economic Development in the New Economy* (Anderson, 2005).

CHAPTER 2

Where's the Work?

Labour Market Trends in the New Economy

Dave Broad, Jane Cruikshank, and James P. Mulvale

One great promise of the New Economy is that it will deliver good jobs and thereby improve living standards. What does this mean in more specific terms? The kinds of claims made by proponents of the NE can be divided into three interrelated categories. There are arguments and predictions about the labour market in general and about the quality of work in the NE, and there are claims about ICT or knowledge work and workers. Recall from Chapter 1 that most of these claims are premised on the economic growth and technological transformations that underpin the NE.

In the most general terms, proponents of the NE tell us employment should expand. As the NE grows at rates not seen before, so should the number of available jobs. In simple terms, the NE will deliver jobs to people who want to work. It follows that such large job growth in the NE should deliver decent pay to all workers as the wealth created by economic growth trickles down. As the economic pie gets bigger, everyone will get more and more, bigger and bigger slices. Along with higher wages, NE proponents — especially those in the post-industrial camp — promise that hours of work will decrease and people will have more leisure time. Moreover, as the economic "slice-per-person" grows we should also see a decline in the kinds of inequalities well known in capitalist labour markets of the past. Those who often found it hard to get work or work under decent conditions, like women, young people, people of colour and so on, will become less distinguishable in the NE labour market.

One of the most highly-touted work promises of the NE was something called labour "flexibility." Almost all NE proponents theorize a world of work quite unlike the past, when most people had one employer or one career throughout their working lives. Bridges (1994), for example, predicts a "post-job organization" that consists of four types of workers: (a) a small group of full-time, professional workers who have the core skills of the organization and are paid according to organizational performance, (b) external contractors who replace the support and staff departments of the organization and are paid in fees for service, (c) contingent or "flexible" workers who are hired for short periods and are paid by the hour, day or week, and (d) customers or clients who do the work previously done by employees, such as at automated teller machines (ATMs), self-service gas stations, cafeterias, IKEA furniture stores and the furniture departments of various store chains such as Office Depot and Staples. In the post-job organization, Bridges (1994) also claims, people will work on specific short-term projects. Some NE proponents go so far as to predict the end of paid work (see, for example, Rifkin, 1995).

Directly related to claims like those made by Bridges are hypotheses about the quality of work in the NE. Clearly, all these flexible, post-organization workers will have to call on a diverse range of work skills. No more will most or many workers carry out repetitively a very few tasks over the course of a work day. As Foot (1996: 91, 92) explains:

> the very notion of "jobs" will come to seem an anachronism during the working lives of many young Canadians. Jobs were developed during the nineteenth century, when factories required units of labour to do the same tasks over and over again. In the information age, workers will apply a wide range of skills to an ever-changing series of tasks, rather than occupying a particular job.

And of course, to keep up with rapid technological change and to reap its benefits, workers will need to continuously upgrade their skills and education throughout their lives (Chapter 4). Not only will workers use many skills, but they will be engaged in a wider variety of tasks. The now almost classic work teams of human resource management, where workers not only do modules of work instead of simple tasks but also manage their own teams, deciding on hours of work, allocation of tasks, scheduling workers and so on, exemplifies this claim (see Chapter 3 for detailed discussion of this and other new organizational management techniques). Coupled with ICTs, the new organization will drastically reduce the dull, routine, unpleasant, unsatisfying, and dangerous elements of working. This is not to say that there will not be monotonous, dangerous work in the NE, only that such work will not define the labour market.

Nowhere will these general labour market trends be more evident than in ICT or knowledge work. These industries and workers, at the centre of the new technologies, are the prototypes of the NE, leading the NE revolution. The trends predicted above apply to these situations but to a greater extent. The levels of employment in ICT work and industries will, at least, grow faster than in other, especially old, industries; and they will at some point come to dominate the labour market. These jobs will require more technical skills, be more diverse and flexible, more autonomous than the kinds of other work that dominated the pre-NE eras. Computerization will leave its mark everywhere in more interesting work (Lin and Popovich, 2002). Even the location of work can and will be flexible, no longer tied to "the shop" as it has been for centuries — the growth of telework, discussed below, being the most obvious example. The new technology promises to avoid some of the negative consequences of older technology at work. Peter Drucker (1993), a pre-eminent NEer, tells us, for example, that machines will now serve workers rather than the other way around. And given all these characteristics, the wages, pay, working conditions and job security of knowledge workers should be second to none.

Before leaving this outline of NE work, we should be clear on what knowledge or ICT work means, especially if we are to assess any of these claims. In general, knowledge work is work done with information, with people, with communication rather than with things. Knowledge workers use their heads rather their hands, doing primarily mental as opposed to manual work. To reiterate from our Introduction, Beck (1992: 133) identified the key occupations within the category of knowledge workers as professionals (doctors, engineers, lawyers, accountants and the like), engineering, scientific and technical workers, and, of course, executives and managers occupying the command posts of organizations. "Work with things" generally describes the "old" economy industries. In manufacturing, primary resource industries and transportation, we find tradespeople, like carpenters and electricians, people working at hauling things, like stevedores and truck drivers, and people making things, like the countless workers on car and household appliance assembly lines. "Work with people, information, communication and ideas" describes the new economy industries like science, research and education, and finances (where we would find what we in the past often referred to as professionals: physicists, sociologists, teachers and accountants) and those organizations that produce, distribute and service the new IC technology (computers and telecommunication being the most obvious). These could be called core ICT industries — ICT manufacturing, ICT services. They include the obvious computer programmers and systems designers but also computer assembly workers, repair technicians, call centre receptionists and the like.

But this general definition is misleading in that knowledge work is not confined to particular industries in the NE. Even in the old industries, much work also involves people, information, communication and ideas. Even in obviously pre-NE industries like manufacturing there is widespread use of new computer and robotic technologies. Generally, in manufacturing, computerized information technology is used for inventory control systems (for keeping track of products, raw materials and factory parts), for product design (for inventing computerized three-dimensional products and changing existing products; a simple example of this technology is in your local paint store, where, with the push of a button, you can see the walls of your hypothetical house painted in various combinations of colours) and in manufacturing processes themselves. Making cars, for example, requires myriad computer workers — people who design cars and car parts; people who run the machines that make the dies that cut the steel and plastic that go into making cars; people who tend the robots that weld the car frames and so on. In lumbering and mining, some employees now require the knowledge to program and run automated and robotic cutting and drilling equipment. ICTs are very evident in office work, in every industry and especially in those defined by such work. The financial sector (banks, insurance companies, investment dealers and advisors), for example, once home to the "typing pool," is now home to the desktop computerized, networked, wireless office, instantly and continuously linked to branch offices around the world. Some back office jobs like file clerking and data entry are now sourced out to the new electronic homeworkers, usually women set up in their homes with computer terminals and Internet connections to the company's main office. Such workers are generally not designated as employees but work on a contract or piece-rate basis. Many of the tasks done by front office reception workers are now often done over the phone from call centres, or perhaps at home by homeworkers.

It might seem like nothing could be wrong in the "garden of NE." But is this really the case? Certainly there are some good jobs being created, but for the last couple of decades, many labour market economists and forecasters have been pointing out greater labour market polarization rather than good jobs replacing bad jobs. In fact, there is solid evidence of an increase in bad jobs over good jobs, both in terms of their intrinsic (quality of work) and extrinsic (pay and benefits) characteristics. The Economic Council of Canada (ECC 1990, 1991) first made this observation over 15 years ago, it has since been repeated by other researchers. In fact, the Organization for Economic Co-operation and Development (OECD), in its *Jobs Study* report of 1994 and in follow-up reports (OECD 1994, 1995), clearly welcomes this phenomenon. The *Jobs Study* report not only notes the trend but actually advocates the creation of two distinct streams of jobs — high-skill, high-wage and low-skill, low-wage — and promotes regressive ways to ensure workers are desperate enough to take the low-wage jobs.[1] What are the current trends in quantity and quality of work in the world economy and in Canada?

Global Employment Trends

First let us consider the availability of employment. Promoters of the NE suggest that, for those with the proper education (see Chapter 4), there are plenty of good jobs available. Juan Somavia (2006: 1), Director-General of the International Labour Office (ILO), recently told those convened at the World Economic Forum in Davos, Switzerland "that the world is sliding into an unprecedented global jobs crisis." He informed the gathering that half the workers of the world, 1.4 billion people, live in families trying to survive on less than US$2 a day per person, and that unemployment is at its highest point ever, and continuing to rise. In its *Global Employment Trends Brief, January 2006*, the ILO (2006: 1, 10) says that, despite robust economic growth in 2005, there are more people unemployed than in 2004 (191.8 million versus 189.6 million). The level of world unemployment has increased from 157.3 million people in 1995 to the current number in 2005. The ILO (2006: 2) emphasizes that unemployment is only the "tip of the iceberg," as it does not come close to measuring "decent work deficits," which include poor quality of work and the fact that "every fifth worker in the world has to face the almost (sic) impossible situation of surviving with less than US$1 a day for each family member."

The ILO (2005b, 2006) notes a number of things that are negatively affecting global labour markets, including: high energy prices; natural disasters; the HIV/AIDS epidemic, which is especially affecting Africa; globalization-based trade policies, particularly in agriculture and textiles; the international transfer (outsourcing and insourcing) of manufacturing and service sector jobs; an ongoing "decent work deficit" in the growing informal economy in many Third World countries; global wage inequalities.

The ILO also points out, contrary to NE predictions of less disparity in the labour market, the significant problem of youth unemployment. The ILO (2006: 2) informs us: "Almost half of the unemployed people in the world are young people, a troublesome figure given that youth make up only 25 per cent of the working-age population. Young people are more than three times as likely as adults to be unemployed." Also, the fact that youth are more likely to be employed in informal, intermittent, insecure and low-paid work is a serious issue because it can create a sense of uselessness and exclusion that can encourage engagement in illegal and violent activities (ILO, 2004b, 2005b, 2006). Women as well do not seem to be benefiting from the NE labour market. They make up an inordinate number of those employed in the informal economy, but even their increasing entry into the formal labour market is for many an entry into formal unemployment, with a slightly higher unemployment rate for women than men (ILO, 2004c, 2006).

In addition to unemployment, underemployment is manifested in various ways in the world economy. If NE predictions are accurate, we should expect that workers are using their training and education at work. However, underemployment, that is work in jobs that do not require their skills and education, is becoming a problem worldwide. The ILO (2004a: 1) says: "In parallel to the deteriorating employment situation, the size of the informal economy has increased in the developing regions with low GDP growth rates." While the informal economy of underground and unregulated work is more apparent in the Third World, researchers have reported that it has been growing in both developed and underdeveloped countries (Portes et al., 1989; Tabak and Crichlow, 2000). Many of the unemployed can be found in the informal economy, but there is an increasingly obvious connection between the formal and informal economies. The revival and growth of industrial homeworking, the subcontracting of manufacturing and service work to primarily female, home-based workers in both new and old industries, reveals one bridge between formal and informal employment. The ILO (2005b: 6) suggests that linkages between the informal and formal economies should be encouraged but sees the need to create decent work for informal workers: "The challenging task ahead is to improve the conditions of work in the informal economy through the formalizing process, while at the same time maintaining its potential to create jobs for those who would otherwise be unemployed." Given current globalization trends, this would seem to be a monumental task because it runs counter to businesses' interest in accessing the informal economy to cut production costs (see Chapter 8 for further discussion of this issue).

Related to the growth of the informal economy, there have been various sorts of casual work in formal labour markets including part-time, temporary, contract and self-employment, all growing out of what are being called "flexible" labour markets (Broad, 2000). While still representing less than 10 percent of total employment in some industrialized countries, self-employment has grown faster in recent years than the overall employment rate. Temporary employment has grown rapidly in recent years as well (ILO, 2001a: 17). Particularly noteworthy has been the growth of the temporary help industry as more and more businesses attempt to reduce costs by contracting out (Vosko, 2000).

The ILO (2001a: 17) notes: "Part-time work has tended to increase as a proportion of total employment. Between 1990 and 1999 it increased from 13 percent to 16 percent in the European Union, from 13 to 15 percent in Europe as a whole, and from 14 to 16 percent in all OECD member countries." Part-time work has, in fact, grown throughout the West over the latter third of the twentieth century, though more in northern Europe, for example, than in southern Europe. The majority of part-time workers are women, who are more likely than men to work part time because of their socially constructed need to mix paid work with household responsibilities. In most industrialized countries, women constitute up to three quarters of part-time workers, with one quarter of employed women working part time (Broad, 2000; O'Reilly and Fagan, 1998).

The increasing proportion of women in the formal labour force is one of the most striking labour market features of recent decades. "More women work today than ever before: in 2003 out of 2.8 billion people that had work, 1.1 billion were women. The share of women with work in total employment has risen slightly in the past ten years to just above 40 percent" (ILO, 2004b: 1). Potentially beneficial for women, in terms of social opportunities and economic independence, ILO researchers, however, are not hopeful about women's current possibilities; improved equality in terms of quantity of male and female workers has yet to result in real socioeconomic empowerment for women: an equitable distribution of household occupations. In short, true equality in the world of work is still out of reach (ILO, 2004b: 1).

While more women in the First World are entering the formal labour market, the employment situation for the majority of the world's women is not good, with little improvement in global female unemployment rates between 1993 and 2003 (ILO, 2004b: 2). While women are less likely to be in waged or salaried employment than men, they represent a higher share of family workers in almost all countries of the world. This is because "women are more likely to find employment in the informal economy than men, outside legal and regulatory frameworks, with little, if any, social security benefits and a high degree of vulnerability" (ILO, 2004b: 3). Women aged 15 to 24 have even greater difficultly finding work, with 35.8 million of the world's young women involuntarily unemployed (ILO, 2004b: 2). As mentioned above, it appears that the NE has not been kind to women around the world. One of the age-old capitalist labour market inequalities is still very evident in most countries.

That unemployment rates and participation in the informal economy are greater in the Third World than in the industrialized world highlights another ongoing form of discrimination in the labour market: the racial and ethnic divide. But this is also evident in the First World, where unemployment rates and participation in informal economies are greater for visible minority and immigrant populations. This is especially noticeable in "global cities" where there is an obvious presence of visible minorities, and especially females, in the low-waged service sector, in manufacturing sweat-shops and in industrial homeworking (Sassen, 1994, 2000; Huws, 2003).

Global ICT Trends

One obvious issue in the New Economy is employment trends in global information and communication-sector industries. The ILO devoted its *World Employment Report 2001* to issues of work in the "information economy," which the authors of the report relate to the "digital convergence of information and communication technologies (ICT)" and to discussions of the NE (ILO, 2001a: 2). They go on to tell us that the new technologies are associated with new patterns of job creation and job loss. "The report is guardedly optimistic on the chances for employment growth where ICTs are most in use. Productivity growth is greatest in the core ICT sector itself where, in manufacturing, it has resulted in stunning increases in output with nevertheless declining employment" (ILO, 2001a: 5). Employment growth has occurred in service production, which is traditionally less unionized and lower paid than manufacturing (Huws, 2003), data entry and call centre employment being cases in point. The evidence shows a link between widespread use of ICTs and employment growth (ILO, 2001a), though this may not be a causal relationship wherein ICT use promotes employment growth. The ILO (2001a: 6) notes a rise in self-employment related to use of new technologies, with highly skilled "e-lancers" (freelance workers who work and communicate through internet and cell phone contact) constituting a new type of employee, but with self-employment growing alongside temporary and part-time work throughout OECD countries.

The ILO report also refers to an emerging era of "digital globalization," wherein some companies are relying on temporary labour as well as outsourcing to less developed countries (see as well Auer et al. 2006). There has been much discussion about job losses in the US resulting from the outsourcing of high technology jobs to "a cheap but highly educated workforce" in, for example, India and Russia. Price Waterhouse Coopers estimates that at least 75,000 Canadian information technology jobs, representing 14 percent of the current workforce, could "migrate" to low-cost countries by 2010 (Price Waterhouse Coopers, 2004).

In addition to levels of employment per se, reports on ICT employment often note the rapid growth in that sector. Rates are higher in some countries than others, with Ireland, for example, experiencing an average

Table 2.1
Employment in the ICT Sector, Selected Countries, 1999

	ICT employment (thousands)			Share of ICT employment in total employment	Share of female employment in total ICT employment	Average annual percentage growth, 1992 to 1999		
	Total	Male	Female	%	%	Total	Male	Female
Austria	132	100	32	3.6	24.2	5.4	5.8	3.4
Belgium	143	102	41	3.7	28.8	1.3	0.9	2.4
Denmark	122	85	37	4.6	30.1	4.4	6.0	1.5
Finland	118	75	43	5.4	36.6	7.0	9.2	3.7
France	905	548	358	4.0	39.5	2.5	2.8	2.1
Germany	1255	839	416	3.5	33.2	2.0	2.5	1.0
Ireland	97	64	33	7.1	34.5	18.0	18.4	17.2
Italy	632	435	197	3.1	31.1	0.9	0.8	1.3
Luxembourg	6	4	2	3.3	27.4	12.2	...	...
Netherlands	302	216	86	4.1	28.4	2.3	0.5	8.4
Portugal	68	44	24	1.4	34.8	-3.8	-2.4	-6.3
Sweden	214	136	77	5.4	36.2	5.2	5.1	5.2
United Kingdom	1338	977	361	5.0	27.0	4.0	4.4	3.1
EU15	5712	3899	1813	3.9	31.7	3.9	4.0	3.6

Source: ILO, 2001a: 118

18 percent annual ICT employment growth rate over the 1992–1999 period (ILO, 2001a: 117). The ICT employment growth rate throughout the European Union was only 3.9 percent for the same period. The share of ICT employment in total EU employment was only 3.9 percent in 1999 (see Table 2.1), ranging from 1.4 percent in Portugal to 7.1 percent in Ireland, with, in fact, declining ICT employment in Portugal. There is a divide between higher-waged "knowledge worker" ICT jobs (those involving mental as opposed to manual labour) for some countries, such as the Scandinavian countries, and lower-waged manufacturing/assembly ICT jobs in other countries, such as Ireland and Portugal, which increasingly compete with

the Third World. Ireland's case seems a curious one. Although it was one of the first sites for core corporations outsourcing to peripheral zones of the world economy, Ireland had been historically peripheral within the European economy (Frobel et al., 1980). We can also note from Table 2.1 a gender divide in ICT employment, with the female share of ICT employment in the EU being only 31.7 percent in 1999, ranging from 24.2 percent in Austria to 39.5 percent in France.

To some, ICT employment rates of around 5.0 percent appear high (ILO, 2001a), but it seems logical to suggest that if 95 percent of jobs are in non-ICT employment, the direct employment impact of ICT jobs will be small. Moreover, the growth of ICT jobs was slowed considerably by the "dot.com crash" of 2001 (see below). But there is another direct negative impact of ICTs on job growth. Because using ICTs "lowers costs and can increase productivity economy-wide, including in 'old-economy' industries" (ILO, 2001a: 3), the historical trend of machines replacing workers is continued.

Quality of ICT Work

When we look at the kinds of jobs created by the ICT revolution, the labour market picture is not nearly as rosy as painted by NE proponents. There are, without a doubt, stimulating and rewarding ICT jobs in areas such as programming. These jobs are the high-skill, well-paid, "set-your-own-agenda" jobs that figure prominently in NE discussions. However, as many or more other kinds of jobs have been created by ICTs. For every programmer, systems designer and telecommunications expert, there are hundreds of bored data entry clerks and harassed and stressed-out call centre workers. In fact, call centres and data processing operations are the "sweatshops of the digital era" (ILO 2001a: 7). Again, women are more adversely affected, though they are often thought to benefit from the new independence of working at home. So, while women in ICT jobs can sometimes find it easier to balance work and family, they can also experience isolation and exclusion (ILO, 2001a; Huws, 2003).

One result of the adoption of ICTs is the rapid growth of "telework" — paid work done in the home using electronic connections to the employer's office. On the positive side, this work arrangement is thought to give employees greater flexibility in scheduling, more free time due to eliminating the commute to the work site, and freedom from direct supervisory gaze and distracting or unpleasant office politics. On the negative side, telecommuting can isolate the worker from the stimulation of fellow workers and from opportunities to advance through direct personal contacts, and can place women workers, especially, in situations where they have to juggle child care and domestic labour while doing paid work in the home.

Huws (2003) points out that the advent of telework was seen as the death knell for trade unions by some but as a liberatory development for women by others. In fact, the wide variation in telework arrangements and the multiple and often subtle and contradictory implications of these patterns make it impossible to say in categorical terms that telework is "good" or "bad." Huws contends that analyses of telework typically "de-gender" the concept, and render it so abstract and disconnected from the actual experience of teleworkers as to be meaningless. She points out that telework can open up opportunities for women, for people with disabilities and for remote regions seeking economic regeneration. But there is also the danger that telework can become the "solution" to the "problem" of needing women to work both for pay in the labour market and for free in the home. "The teleworker is now a woman who, by implication, 'puts her family first,' the corollary of which is that her [paid] work is relatively unimportant, something to be fitted in between emptying Granny's bedpan and washing the baby's diapers" (Huws, 2003: 95).

Generally, because with the new technologies work can increasingly be done anywhere and anytime, there is a blurring of hours of work and hours of leisure, with resulting negative effects on individual and family health (Brennan, 2003). Huws (2003: 100) argues that the future of telework "will depend on the decisions taken by a range of social actors — large employers, entrepreneurs, creative individualists, women with dependents, planners. These directions will not be monodirectional; nor will they necessarily be permanent." (Missing from Huws' list of social actors are labour unions, but see Chapter 7 below.)

The ILO (2001a) suggests that there are potentials in the new technologies for welfare gains in the Third World. These would result from global dispersal of ICT jobs, from industrial "leapfrogging" potentials (skipping lower stages of national development) inherent in the new technologies, and from poverty alleviation because ICTs can improve aggregate economic growth (see also ILO, 2005a). The problem with this argument is, first of all, that economic growth is not synonymous with development (see Chapter 1). Second, as to how much this trend will benefit workers and their families in the Third World, we must remember that a majority of the world's population still does not have access to electricity, and less than "6 percent of the world's people have ever logged onto the Internet — and 85 to 90 percent of them are in the industrialized countries" (ILO, 2001a: 3). In general, there has been what Golding (1998) calls an unequal inheritance of the global communications revolution. The transfer of manufacturing jobs to low-waged workers in Third World countries after the 1960s as often as not resulted in those workers and their families experiencing superexploitation, not to mention the fact that poorly paid workers make poor consumers. The ILO does, of course, recognize that to alleviate these problems requires social action and social policy, and has thus been campaigning for decent work through a "fair globalization" (ILO, 2004c). We will return to this issue in Chapter 8.

Canadian Employment Trends

The Canadian labour market is similar to those of other Western capitalist countries. Regarding NE predictions, Canada is also very similar to the rest of the world in terms of general trends, even though in some specific senses Canadian workers are better off than many others. Much evidence indicates that youth and women fare poorly in the Canadian labour market in comparison to men aged 24 and over, with high unemployment rates for youth and lower earnings for women, partly because women are more concentrated in low-waged service sector jobs than men.

Since World War II, and especially since the 1960s, more and more women have entered the formal labour market in Canada. In 1941, only 21 percent of working-aged women participated in the Canadian labour market, constituting 19 percent of those in formal employment (Armstrong and Armstrong, 1994: 16). Women's labour market participation increased steadily throughout the post-World War II decades (Statistics Canada, 2006a). By 2004, 58 percent of working-aged women were in the labour market, making up 47 percent of the employed workforce (Statistics Canada, 2006a: 13). However, despite some gains, women are still concentrated in a small number of low-status jobs, while men are found in a wider range of employ (Armstrong and Armstrong, 1994; Benoit, 2000; Statistics Canada, 2006a). Over half of women workers are found in those areas of the service sector that contain the so-called "women's jobs." Seven out of 10 employed women, compared to only three out of 10 men, are working in teaching, nursing and related health occupations, clerical or other administrative positions and sales and service occupations (Statistics Canada, 2006a: 113). Women have made some gains in higher professions but still represented only 43 percent of those employed in professional, scientific and technical services in 2002 (Statistics Canada, 2004a). In businesses, women continue to be over-represented in the junior management and secretarial positions (Armstrong and Armstrong, 1994; Menzies, 1996; Statistics Canada, 2006a). In 2004, "37% of all those employed in managerial positions were women, up from 30% in 1987"; however, in 2004, "women made up only 22% of senior managers, compared with 38% of managers at other levels" (Statistics Canada, 2006a: 113). It would seem then that even though Canadian women might be faring better in the labour market than their sisters in other parts of the world, gender inequality has not been eradicated by the NE.

Another trend that has affected the Canadian labour market is the casualization of labour, which, again, is the reality of what NE proponents call flexibility. This aspect of the labour market may indicate flexibility for corporations and employers, but it mainly signifies poor pay, few hours and very few benefits — i.e., insecurity — for Canada's working people. In the wake of the global economic restructuring begun in the 1960s, we have seen increases in what has been variously called casual, contingent, flexible, precarious or non-standard labour in Canada. In the early 1990s, the Economic Council of Canada (ECC, 1990, 1991) estimated that one-third to two-fifths of Canadian workers were in non-standard employ, meaning other than full-time, full-year permanent paid employment, including part-time, temporary, contract and self-employment. Between 1990 and 2000, the number of part-time jobs grew by 21 percent, while full-time jobs increased by only 13 percent. Similarly, between 1997 and 2000, when the economy was supposedly strong, the number of temporary jobs in Canada grew by 21 percent, while permanent jobs increased by only 8 percent (Campaign 2000, 2002). By 2002, 11 percent of Canadian workers were temporary, up from 7 percent in 1989, and 15 percent were self-employed, up from 12 percent in 1976 (Cranford et al., 2003: 12; Fudge et al., 2002: 14).

In 2002, 560,000 new jobs were created in Canada, a number that signifies strong economic growth. However, closer examination reveals that 40 percent of these jobs were part-time and 17 percent were in self-employment, leaving only 43 percent as full-time jobs (Statistics Canada 2003a). In 2005, over 18 percent of Canadian workers were employed part time, up from less than 13 percent in 1976 (Statistics Canada, 2006b; Broad, 2000: 14). Most of these part-time jobs are in the lower paying service sector (New Jobs, 2003).

As in other countries, there are gender and racial characteristics to the casualization of labour, with women and visible minorities over-represented in the various types of casual employment (Cranford et al. 2003). A recent study on vulnerability in the labour market notes that workers holding full-time, permanent jobs represent only 63 percent of the workforce, and 37 percent of workers are either self-employed or work at part-time or temporary jobs (Saunders, 2003). Saunders argues that women are over-represented in the precarious employment category (part-time and temporary work and self-employment) and states that, in 2001, 63 percent of precarious workers were women, even though women accounted for only 46 percent of the labour force. Similarly, 65 percent of workers earning less than $10 per hour and 69 percent of those earning less than $8 per hour were women. In 2003, the average annual pre-tax income of women aged 16 and over from all sources, including employment earnings, government transfer payments, investment income, and other money income, was $24,400. This was just 62% of the figure for men, who had an average income of $39,300 that year (Statistics Canada 2006a: 133).

Overall, Canadian labour in the NE has experienced the same sort of dislocation from unemployment and underemployment that has affected other OECD countries. Nevertheless, Statistics Canada (2003b: 5) glowingly reports: "According to new data from the [2001] census, average annual earnings surpassed $30,000 for the first time in 2000, as working Canadians began reaping the benefits of globalization and the knowledge-based economy." Average earnings were $29,229 in 1980, $29,596 in 1990 and $31,757 in 2000 (Statistics Canada, 2003b: 24). Nevertheless, we are informed that the number of earners making $80,000 or more per year, and especially those earning over $100,000 per year, "soared during the 1990s," while four in 10 workers made less than $20,000 per year in 2000, the same as 1990 (Statistics Canada, 2003b: 5). "In 2000, the combined income of the 10% of Canadian families with the highest incomes accounted for 28% of total family income, up from 26% in 1990. The 10% of families with the lowest incomes made up less than 2% of all family income, similar to what was observed in 1990" (Statistics Canada, 2003c: 5). Immigrants coming to Canada in the 1990s made almost 25 percent less than Canadian-born workers. About one in five university-educated male immigrants worked in computer and information systems occupations in 2000, but "many university degree-holders who came to Canada in the 1990s worked in lower skilled jobs" (Statistics Canada, 2003b: 12-13).

A recent Statistics Canada report asks: "Are good jobs disappearing in Canada?" (Morissette and Johnson, 2005). The evidence is mixed, but three trends are clear:

> [First,] wages of newly hired male and female employees — those with two years of seniority or less — have fallen substantially relative to those of others. Second, in the private sector, the fraction of new employees employed in temporary jobs has risen substantially, increasing from 11% in 1989 to 21% in 2004.... Third, pension coverage has fallen among men of all ages and among females under 45. Taken together, these findings suggest that Canadian

firms (existing and newly-born) have responded to growing competition within industries and from abroad by reducing their wage
offers for new employees, by offering temporary jobs to a growing
proportion of them, and by offering less often pension plans that
guarantee defined benefits at the time of retirement. (Morissette
and Johnson 2005: 4)

Overall, labour market trends suggest that Canadian workers and their
families are experiencing growing economic and social polarization, with
declining economic and social well-being in the employment and welfare
conditions emergent since the 1980s. These labour market trends developed
precisely in the period in which the NE emerged and developed. It would
appear that the ICTs and so-called "flexible" labour markets, characteristic
of the NE, have not served the interests of most workers and their families.

Canadian ICT Trends

There has been an acceleration in the use of information technology in
Canadian workplaces since the 1980s. The proportion of Canadian workers who use computers in their paid jobs grew from 16 percent in 1985 to
57 percent by 2000 (Krahn and Lowe, 2002: 294). Computers and other
forms of information technology "are now linked throughout entire production and service-delivery processes, within workplaces, across multi-site
work organisations, and globally " (Krahn and Lowe, 2002: 295). While
computerization has had dramatic effects on the labour market in Canada
and elsewhere, the accelerated use of ICTs has not thus far led to apocalyp-
tic outcomes such as "the end of [paid] work" scenario advanced by writers
like Rifkin (1995). However, the advent of ICTs has,

> in some cases... led to layoffs while, in others, new jobs have been
> created, although it is evident that workers made redundant by
> new technologies are seldom first in line for new jobs.... Further-
> more, the 1990s witnessed significant job growth in the service in-
> dustries where IT has had the largest effect..., though many of
> these are non-standard [e.g., part-time or temporary] jobs. (Krahn
> and Lowe, 2002: 300)

Canadian ICT Employment Levels
As with other OECD countries, the growth rate of the Canadian ICT sector
has outpaced that of non-ICT industries in recent decades. "From 1987 to

1997, the GDP in the ICT sector increased by 96%, compared to 28% for the non-ICT, non-science industries. Firms in the ICT sector employed 44% more workers in 1997 than in 1981. By comparison, employment outside of ICT and science industries increased by 24%" (Beckstead and Gellatly, 2003: 7). As well, in terms of labour productivity measured by GDP to hours worked, from 1987 to 1997, ICT manufacturing experienced a 90 percent increase and core ICT services recorded a 27 percent increase. Meanwhile, non-ICT goods production saw a 20 percent gain and other services realized only a 12 percent increase (Beckstead and Gellatly, 2003: 52). More generally, there has been an increase in the number of knowledge workers in the Canadian labour market. This has been a steady growth rate, from a 14 percent annual increase in 1971 to 25 percent in 2001 (Baldwin and Beckstead, 2003: 5). This conclusion is reinforced by Table 2.2. The percentage change in ICT paid employment of 72.6 percent between 1990 and 2000 is noteworthy, especially in comparison to the 12.2 percent growth of paid employment in the Canadian labour market overall.

Table 2.3 shows the relative share of Canadian businesses in ICT and science-based industries in comparison to other industries as of 2001. As to the direct impact on employment, it is important to note that only 4 percent of business establishments are in the ICT sector, with 5.5 percent of total employment and 5.7 percent of revenue. Science-based industries make up only 6.9 percent of businesses, 9.6 percent of employment and 10.9 percent of revenue. "Knowledge-based firms employed about 7% of workers in 1999 — 3% of them in information communication technology (ICT) industries. Conversely, 1% were employed in ICT workplaces not belonging to knowledge-based industries" (Drolet and Morissette, 2002: 47). All told, we see that the total share of ICT and science-based paid employment in Canada in 2000 was only 8.1 percent of all paid employment (Table 2.2). Moreover, the majority of ICT employment in Canada is concentrated in four major urban centres; Montreal, Toronto, Ottawa and Vancouver (Beckstead et al., 2003).

According to Beckstead and Brown (2005: 1): "The role of the ICT sector as a source of employment growth in the 1990s cannot be underestimated. One out of every six new jobs over the decade was created in the ICT industries. Moreover, in Canada's largest cities — Toronto, Montreal, Vancouver and Ottawa — ICT firms created four out of every ten new jobs gained during the 1990s." But let us note that they are referring to new jobs, not to total employment, and as we have already noted, the total number of good full-time jobs has not kept pace with the needs of Canadian workers, as is evidenced by the growing number of casual workers. Also, because ICT jobs remain concentrated in the four major urban areas, they have had little

Table 2.2

Aggregate Measures of the ICT and Science-based Sectors in Canada

Paid Workers	1990	2000	Absolute change between periods	Percentage change between periods
ICT	324,700	560,000	235,900	72.6%
Science-based	490,800	541,100	50,200	10.2%
Canada	12,080,800	13,555,600	1,474,800	12.2%

Note: Numbers may not add due to rounding.

Source: Beckstead et al., 2003: 15.

Shares of the ICT and Science-based Sectors in Canada

Paid Workers	Share 1990	Share 2000	Change in Share
ICT	2.7%	4.1%	53.8%
Science-based	4.1%	4.0%	-1.8%

Source: Beckstead et al., 2003: 16.

Table 2.3

Share of Business Sector (%), 2001

	Establishments	Employment	Revenue
ICT Sector	4.0	5.5	5.7
ICT Manufacturing	0.2	1.2	1.5
Core ICT Services	2.8	3.0	2.3
Other ICT Services	1.0	1.3	1.9
Science-based Industries	6.9	9.6	10.9
ICT-based Science	3.1	4.3	3.9
Non-ICT Science-based Goods	0.7	3.0	5.3
Non-ICT Science-based Services	3.1	2.3	1.6
Other Industries	92.1	89.2	87.4
Goods	27.5	26.6	27.9
Services	64.6	62.5	59.4
Business Sector Total	100.0	100.0	100.0

Source: Beckstead and Gellatly, 2003: 20.

impact on the broader Canadian labour market (Beckstead and Brown, 2005: 9). The increase in numbers of knowledge workers more generally is not tied specifically to growth of the ICT sector, although a high concentration of knowledge workers are employed in these NE industries. But in fact the highest knowledge intensity is found in public-sector, non-market service employment (Beckstead and Vinodrai, 2003; Baldwin and Beckstead, 2003). Looking at the above figures, our gut response to all the hoopla about the New Economy might be to say that "the emperor wears no clothes." It is likely fair to say that the direct impact of NE employment on the majority of Canadian workers is slight.

Quality of ICT Work in Canada

The authors of one Statistics Canada study specifically ask: "Are jobs in knowledge-based firms better jobs?"; and they answer: "It depends" (Drolet and Morissette, 2002: 53). They inform us that, on average, hourly wages in knowledge-based industries are one-third higher than in other industries. When factors such as education, location, size of firm and hours of work are considered, however, the difference drops to 8 percent. Knowledge workers tend to put in long hours — 44 hours per week on average — and work more unpaid overtime than in other areas of the economy. They do not have better pension plans than other workers but do have more group registered retirement savings plans and stock options. Knowledge-industry workers are more likely to be covered by insurance, medical, dental and family support plans than other workers, but they are less likely to have access to workplace child care. They are less often unionized and consequently have less access to formal grievance systems. Knowledge workers are more often involved in self-directed workgroups (52 percent) than workers in other industries (41 percent). But some workers in knowledge-based workplaces report being over-educated, and some are not necessarily more satisfied with their pay (Drolet and Morissette, 2002: 50, 52).

More generally,

> a substantial portion of "knowledge workers" is made up of subprofessionals (e.g., teachers, health care workers, and social workers) whose defining trait (relative to the ideal of what constitutes a true professional) is an inability to exercise control over their work. Even the activities of most full-fledged professionals and scientists are shaped by the dictates of their bosses. Unlike most employees, however, persons holding these kinds of jobs do exercise varying degrees of control over the process but not over the purposes of their labour. (Rinehart, 2001: 108)

So there are good and bad aspects to knowledge jobs, and there are good and bad jobs being produced by the New Economy. Along with economic and social polarization, we see employment polarization in the NE.[2]

The Dot.com Crash

The economic collapse of New Economy stocks — "the dot.com crash" mentioned in the Introduction and in Chapter 1 — is a significant chapter in the NE story. Statistics Canada researchers Beckstead and Brown (2005: 1) say: "With dramatic increases in stock prices, output and employment, new economy industries in the 1990s established themselves as important drivers of economic growth. Seemingly as dramatic has been their decline, symbolized by the collapse of stock prices in 2000 on the high-tech laden NASDAQ exchange." In Canada, "the value of the ICT sector plummeted over most of 2001, entirely on the manufacturing side" (Bowlby and Langlois, 2002: 9). Considering employment in the computers and telecommunications (CT) sector, Bowlby and Langlois (2002: 10) tell us that from March to October 2001, CT employment tumbled by 61,000 jobs, or by 9 percent. They also note that employment in the CT sector contracted more sharply during the 1990–92 recession than in the economy overall, suggesting that CT employment is more vulnerable to booms and busts. Instability in the CT sector continued after the 2001 bust, with Statistics Canada (2004b: 1) reporting in January 2004: "Since November 2002, the number of manufacturing jobs has declined by 82,000 (-3.5%). Almost all of the decline in manufacturing occurred in Quebec and Ontario. The industries hardest hit were computer and electronic products and electrical equipment and appliance manufacturing."[3]

Beckstead and Brown (2005: 4, 1) tell us that ICT employment levels remain below their 2000 peak, and ask "whether the decline in the ICT sector reflects a short-term downturn or a long-term structural shift." To answer this question, they examine entry and exit patterns of investment in ICT industries over the 1998 to 2003 period, before and after the ICT downturn, based on a product life cycle model that includes the stages of (1) slow growth, (2) high growth, (3) market maturity and (4) declining sales as consumers switch to newer products. Beckstead and Brown (2005: 7) note that entry and exit rates throughout the period remained above those of businesses in general, and that "even during the period of retrenchment, considerable investments were being made in new establishments by new and incumbent firms within the ICT sector." They go on to suggest signs of an ICT recovery but make only brief mention of the fact that this might be a case of jobless economic growth: "For both ICT manufacturing and ICT services, entry rates remained relatively high throughout the study period. For ICT manufacturing, this was true even in 2002 and 2003, *years in which*

ICT manufacturing employment fell" (Beckstead and Brown, 2005: 8, emphasis added). The less optimistic conclusion for workers is that the ICT sector is extremely volatile and is tied to a general pattern of global restructuring that does not encourage growth of more and better jobs.

The ICT downturn revealed a couple of labour market trends that we have highlighted above. "During the CT boom of 1997 to 2000, employee growth (52%) was stronger than that of self-employment (28%). However, in 2001, the entire drop occurred among employees (down 42,000 or 7%). In fact, the number of self-employed CT workers rose (up 7,000 or 10%)" (Bowlby and Langlois, 2002: 12). This is consistent with the globalization and NE practice of externalizing costs by contracting out. The CT bust also revealed the gendered character of the New Economy. "In the last quarter of 2001, almost two-thirds of all CT workers were men, much higher than the proportion outside the CT sector (53%). Even so, in 2001 the CT employment decline affected women (-20,000) more than men (-14,000)" (Bowlby and Langlois, 2002: 12).

Despite the relatively small numbers employed directly in New Economy industries, and the dot.com crash of 2001, the overall impact of the New Economy on Canadian workers has not been insignificant. New Economy technologies have increasingly been applied to "old economy" industries, often increasing productivity significantly so that more work can be done by fewer workers, thus contributing to unemployment. In addition, application of the new technologies is often tied to restructuring of labour processes and management structures. So, to repeat a point made in Chapter 1, just because the statistical impact of NE investment and employment is not great, the idea of a New Economy can still be significant. Indeed, claims that we need to improve our competitiveness and productivity because we are inevitably part of globalization and the New Economy can have a widespread social impact.

Knowledge Work and Productivity

It is with the rhetoric about globalization and the New Economy that workers find themselves on an accelerated productivity treadmill. In his "postcapitalist society" treatise, management guru Peter Drucker (1993: 82) makes a claim typical of New Economy authors: "The new challenge facing the post-capitalist society is the productivity of knowledge workers and service workers. To improve the productivity of knowledge workers will in fact require drastic changes in the structure of the organizations of postcapitalist society, and the structure of society itself." Noting that three-quarters to four-fifths of the workers in developed countries are employed in the service sector, Drucker (1993: 83) exclaims: "Their productivity, rather than the productivity of the people who make and move things, is *the* productivity of a developed economy. It is abysmally low [and] may actually be going down rather than going up" (emphasis in original). For Drucker, "the lowest level of productivity occurs in government employment," and the main hindrance to productivity growth is due to "strong labor union opposition to anything that would give the worker a 'managerial attitude,' let alone 'managerial responsibility'" (Drucker, 1993: 84, 92). According to Drucker, having a managerial attitude and responsibility is critical to increasing the productivity of knowledge and service workers.

Drucker (1993) promotes two methods in vogue for increasing knowledge and service workers' productivity — teamwork and outsourcing. He also gives more credence to the Scientific Management principles of Taylorism than most observers: "Concentration on job and task is the last prerequisite for productivity in knowledge and service work" (Drucker, 1993: 90). He argues for getting rid of any tasks that sidetrack or divert workers: "Eliminating such work may be the single biggest step toward greater productivity in both knowledge and service work." Using the case of health sector work, Drucker argues for an extreme division of labour by getting nurses, for example, out of everything but patient care. They should be relieved of all paperwork and housekeeping duties, according to Drucker, and such work should be outsourced to specialized companies.

Drucker (1993: 93, 95) refers to the practice of outsourcing to increase service workers' productivity as "revolutionary," stating: "Outsourcing is necessary not just because of the economics involved. It is necessary because it provides opportunities, income, and dignity for service workers." Drucker (1993: 95) says that the managers of outsourced companies "are willing, even eager, to do the hard work needed to improve productivity. Above all, they take the people who do such work seriously enough to challenge them to take the lead in improving their work and its productivity." But following Drucker's own description, this sounds like the old "speedup" tactic, which has been shown in case studies that also reveal that much of this outsourced service work is poorly paid and insecure, and provides little opportunity or dignity to the workers involved (Menzies, 1996; Vosko, 2000). Drucker himself defines this work as low paid and low skilled and suggests that we need to narrow the gap between high-paid, high-status knowledge work and low-paid, low-status service work to avert "a new class conflict." But this is too often done by lowering the pay and status of previously high-status work — sometimes creating more casual labour, other times extorting unpaid overtime from workers (Broad, 2000).

While noting the Taylorist notion of manufacturing work, that the worker serves the machine, Drucker asserts, although there is much evidence to the contrary:

> In knowledge work, and in practically all service work, the machine serves the worker. The task is not given; it has to be determined. The question, "What are the expected results from this work?" is almost never raised in traditional work study and Scientific Management. But it is the key question in making knowledge workers and service workers more productive. (1993: 85)

This signals a significant problem in applying the standard notion of productivity to service work, especially that of human services. Drucker's formulation is not very fruitful here, because he tends to conflate quality with quantity, ultimately focusing on the drive to increase the work done in a given hour, as with the standard definition of productivity. This suggests Drucker is not envisioning a qualitatively different post-capitalist society, despite his book's title.

Huws (2006) reminds us that the historical process that creates demand for new skills is a complex one that results in the need for certain groups of highly skilled workers. She highlights the importance of Doeringer and Piore's (1971) work on dual labour markets, with the two categories of "primary" or "internal" corporate labour markets favouring highly skilled knowledge workers, and "secondary" or "external" labour markets for lower skilled jobs. This analysis was subsequently found too simplistic and was expanded by other researchers into segmented labour market theory. We can see the continuing process of labour market segmentation unfolding with application of ICTs in the New Economy. Opportunities are created for some highly skilled workers, but some observers have forecast the end of jobs as we know them.

However, employers are moving toward having no responsibility to their workers. Salaries, pensions and employee benefits and worker education and training will become things of the past. Workers, defined as individual businesses, will be on their own, in a sink-or-swim market. Bridges asks, with great enthusiasm:

> How about policies on leaves of absence, vacations, and retirement? Leaves from what? Vacations from what? Retirement from what?... the post-job worker is going to be far more likely to be hired for a project or for a fixed length of time than a jobholder is today. Working and leisure are no longer governed by the calculus of constant employment. Without the job, time off from work becomes not something taken out of job time but something sand-

wiched into the interims between assignments or between project contracts. (Bridges 1994: 161)

In short, the benefits that workers and their unions have fought for will be obliterated in the post-job organization. Finlayson (1996: 78), who opposes this trend, argues that in the future, "virtually everyone will be self-employed, carrying their skills in a kit-bag to be deployed when and if an employer has a 'task' to be discharged, and packed up again when the assignment has been completed."

Many companies are well on their way to achieving this type of organization. However, rather than the rosy vision put forward by post-job enthusiasts, the situation for many workers is bleak. Laxer (1998: 181) explains:

> Those in the secondary workforce move in and out of it as jobs are created and lost, and often subsist on part-time incomes when they would prefer full-time work. Over the past several decades, the proportion of the population unable to earn a living has steadily increased. Taken together, these developments have pushed a very large number of people into marginalization and, in many cases, outright poverty.

Overall, critical researchers posit New Economy labour market conditions that are not favourable to the welfare of most workers. Rather than creating stimulating knowledge work for all, the New Economy is as much about manufacturing "McJobs."

Manufacturing McJobs

The expansion of part-time and other casual employment has resulted in a new dictionary definition. The *Oxford English Dictionary* defines a "McJob" as "an unstimulating, low-paid job with few prospects, esp. one created by the service sector." Released in July 2003, the eleventh edition of the *Merriam-Webster Collegiate Dictionary* added the term "McJob," defined as "a low-paying job that requires little skill and provides little opportunity for advancement." This prompted a letter of protest from McDonald's Chairman and CEO Jim Cantalupo, who called the definition "completely inappropriate and absolutely demeaning" to the 12 million US teens "getting their first employment experiences, parents supporting families, and seniors supplementing their income" from these jobs (Finn and Shaker, 2004: 40). But is it the definition or the McJobs that are demeaning? Moreover, it is not just part-time and other casual employment that have the characteristics of McJobs. Ironically, the various forms of underemployment have grown in recent years alongside overwork, with more full-time workers reporting longer hours (Morissette and Sunter, 1994), a trend to which Schor (1992) drew attention in her studies of "the overworked American." Thus both part-time and full-time work have been taking on McJob characteristics. This trend prompted Mies et al. (1988) to refer to the "housewifization of labour" — flexible and always on call, subservient and preferably wageless, ergo the expansion of the informal economy.

So, despite the rhetoric of skill shortages and the growth of knowledge work, it is in the McJobs field that work has been most readily available. In the drive to increase productivity, the New Economy is manufacturing McJobs in both goods and services production (Menzies, 1991, 1996; Reiter, 1995). Menzies (1991: 31) has noted that "many jobs are becoming part time or temporary. Even if they are full time, they're referred to as 'turnstile' jobs because people exit at the same level they entered." What is significant about the McJob is that it is becoming the most plentiful of the types of jobs being created by the technology of the so-called post-industrial information age. "The McJob is... symbolic of people's relation to the technology on the job.... Increasingly, computers determine the work to be done, which means control is being transferred to the computer and those who control and programme it" (Menzies, 1991: 31), making human labour more and more disposable. This view is, of course, contrary to that of management gurus like Drucker who claim that, for knowledge and service workers in the New Economy, the machine serves the worker. Part-timers at McDonald's and in the proliferating call centres would likely beg to differ.

Employers call the McJob approach "flexible labour." To business, flexible labour appears to mean low-cost labour. This is, in fact, the stated reason many employers use part-timers (Comfort et al., 2003). Indeed, it is also obvious that many businesses see casual labour as disposable labour. A recent management book on flexible labour makes this apparent with its list of "frequently asked questions":

1: What exactly is "flexible working"?
2: How much will it save me?
3: What are my liabilities? Can I be sued if I casualize all my staff?
4: Do I have to pay minimum wages for non-standard staff? Do they enjoy full protection and rights?
5: Can I lay off staff and insist that they work when it suits me?
6: How can I get the best out of my staff who are only here on a casual basis?

7: How do I go about getting the most from my resources?
8: What activities can be put out to flexible working?
9: What attitudes should I adopt towards flexible workers?
10: How much will it cost me? (Pettinger, 2002: 117–18)

The casualization of labour is intimately tied to both the degradation of work and the feminization of work, all of which figure prominently in current economic restructuring. As noted above, even the Economic Council of Canada, hardly an institution given to criticizing the prevailing capitalist economic system, found more "bad" than "good" jobs being created, in terms of both skill content and wages. The prospects for many workers appear to be for casual, at best semi-skilled work, and a declining standard of living.

Regardless of their promise, the new technologies tend to be applied to the goal of increasing output, in both goods and services production, often displacing workers in the process. We have seen this on assembly lines, where computers and robotics have increased output while decreasing the need for workers. We have also seen it in the computerization of office work, which has resulted in, for example, the disappearance of skilled secretarial pools. Meanwhile, too many of the jobs created in the New Economy are low-skilled data-entry work or high-stress but low-paid call centre work. A common complaint by workers regarding use of the new technologies in workplace restructuring, as with the Japanese notion of "kaizen" (continuously striving for greater productivity), is that their efforts on work teams are rewarded by management reducing the number of workers as output increases (Schenk and Anderson, 1995, 1999).

As for theories of work and the labour market, many discussions in the late 1960s and early 1970s based on the thesis of post-industrial society postulated shorter working hours, higher wages and expanded leisure time as the norm. However, given a life of unemployment for some, casualization of labour for others, and lengthened working days for yet others, the post-industrial society thesis would seem to be incongruous with present facts. The evidence better supports a thesis of increasing alienation and exploitation of labour through degradation, de-skilling and segmentation of work and workers. As new skilled knowledge jobs appear, employers look for new management strategies and ways to automate jobs and de-skill the work — whatever serves to control labour. The use of new technology to further de-skill and segment work, the continued internationalization of capitalist production, the drive to cheapen labour through both globalization and erosion of labour's strength ("union busting"), and the casualization of work all serve to disorganize labour. The fact that most new jobs are being created in a service sector that can be staffed by an already less unionized female labour force is a propitious circumstance for employers. But the casualization and "housewifization" of work in its various forms is not restricted to women or the service sector.

Some observers have argued that the new technologies of the Information Age have helped capital to emancipate itself from labour (e.g., Sivanandan, 1990, 1997). As noted above, advances in communications and transportation mean that capital can now roam the globe in search of cheap, docile labour. De-skilling and segmentation of work, combined with use of robotics, means that business needs smaller numbers of more easily replaceable workers. And despite all the talk of new human resource strategies, the key goal of managers is to get more work from workers. The process we see unfolding includes the creation of a global reserve army of knowledge workers for the New Economy. Huws (2006: 32–33) reminds us:

> The purpose of a reserve army is not to take over all the work but to act as a disciplinary force. The actual number of jobs being relocated overseas is tiny compared with the normal "churn" in national labor markets. National employers still need skilled workers in their home territory.... The most powerful effect of offshoring is not to eliminate jobs in the United States or in Europe, it is to cheapen them.

The impact of globalization, neoliberalism and the New Economy is not found so much in the discrete empirical detail as in the overall goals of the transformation process. "Just the possibility that the job *might* move is enough to destroy [workers'] security and workers' bargaining power" (Huws, 2006: 33, emphasis in original).

If standards of life and work are not to further erode, there is much work to be done by trade unions and social justice activists. Subsequent chapters will examine how, in capital's attempt to reboot the accumulation process, workers are constantly shoved into and out of the labour market through industrial restructuring, new management strategies and neoliberal public policy. Contributors will also discuss what might be done by workers and their communities to counter the negative effects of capitalism's New Economy.

Notes

1. For more on the OECD *Jobs Study*, see Chapter 8.
2. The issue of quality of work in the New Economy is further addressed in a number of chapters below.
3. This data does not present a perfect picture of ICT industries because ICTs are aggregated with non-ICT manufacturing.

CHAPTER 3

Managing Change

Organizational and Managerial Responses to the New Economy

Janice Foley

The New Economy that has emerged as a result of advances in information and communication technologies was to bring about huge increases in prosperity and productivity, reduced unemployment and inflation levels, and shorter business cycles. But as earlier chapters have shown, there is little or no evidence that these benefits have accrued, or if they have, they have gone mainly to multinational corporations whose profits have skyrocketed (United Nations, 1999: 32), and to the top five percent of income earners.

Despite rising corporate profit and productivity levels, real average wages have been relatively flat in Canada since the early 1980s and have been declining in the US since 1987. Incomes and working conditions have also polarized. Even the highly skilled knowledge workers have no guarantee of job security, and the situation is worse for the rest. While the former can capitalize on their skills if they lose their jobs, earning higher incomes as contract workers (Guest, 2001), the remainder hold their jobs at the employer's sufferance unless a collective agreement exists. The least fortunate have joined a new army of non-standard workers. All employees, regardless of union or job status, must now constantly upgrade and market their skills to current and potential employers in order to stabilize their employment situations. The prospect of unemployment is very real in the New Economy and has more serious ramifications than ever as the social safety net crumbles. Youth, women and the less-educated have been the major victims of these trends, starting in the 1990s. Compounding the problem is that the New Economy has severely eroded the power of organized labour (see Chapter 7). Because employers can now recruit globally and freely move production, many highly paid, unionized jobs have disappeared. In addition, national labour has been supplanted by foreign-trained, less expensive labour.

As a result, the employer is in a stronger position vis-à-vis employees and organized labour in the New Economy. Increasingly, employers are making unilateral decisions about wages, working conditions and job arrangements. While this arrangement is highly satisfactory for employers, some of these decisions can have a negative impact on job quality and employee well-being. Nevertheless, it is notable that the employer response has not been uniform and many new human resource management practices have been introduced that could improve the quality of employees' work lives. Unfortunately, the introduction of any practices that benefit employees has largely been extra-contractual, which therefore means that they can be abandoned if employers no longer find them desirable.

Contemporary Organizational and Managerial Practices

In responding to the pressures of the New Economy, many firms have adopted new organizational and managerial practices. Despite the rhetoric of proponents of the New Economy, the consequences for employees have not been uniformly positive.

One common strategy has been to extend hours of operation in an effort to provide better customer service. These weekend and evening hours are generally filled on a part-time basis, which can be helpful to students and to workers with family or other responsibilities. But these jobs tend to be poorly paid and only rarely are employee benefits provided. This can be a significant problem, for example, for single parents whose sole income derives from this type of employment.

Many of the new managerial practices also stress cost-cutting and productivity improvement. Downsizing, which has been very popular, both reduces payroll costs and increases productivity by reducing the number of employees in a work unit and increasing workloads. However, it may raise employees' stress and accident levels (see Chapter 5). In addition, new computer or communications technology has been introduced into many workplaces to streamline how the work is done. Outcomes for employees can include job loss, higher skill requirements to qualify for newly created jobs, further de-skilling of lower-level jobs and fewer job opportunities for those with less formal training. Further examples of contemporary managerial practices will be presented and critiqued later in this chapter.

Proponents of the New Economy argue that these practices are necessary to keep companies competitive, and that they therefore protect jobs in the long run and enable employers to offer higher salaries, better benefits and more challenging and interesting work. However, the high-calibre jobs promised by New Economy proponents are not commonplace even among the highly educated. College and university graduates have reported feeling underemployed for the past two decades. The problem may be particularly acute within the public service (Lowe, 2001), and for women and younger employees (Kelly et al., 1997). This is a serious concern in the New Economy because firms are increasingly being forced to acknowledge that they must fully utilize the capabilities of their employees if they are to succeed.

Documenting Emerging Managerial Practices

Understanding how managerial practices have changed in the New Economy, and especially how they have affected employees, has only recently become a priority. One important survey of existing private sector practices, the *Human Resource Practices Survey*, was conducted in 1993 by a group of academics from Queen's University (Betcherman et al., 1994). Another, the *Workplace and Employee Survey* pilot study, examined private sector organizational and management practices in Canada between 1993 and 1996. It was the first survey ever conducted in Canada that collected responses from employers and their employees, linking workplace practices and employee outcomes (Picot and Wannell, 1997; Statistics Canada and HRDC, 1998). That survey was redistributed in slightly modified form in 1999 (Statistics Canada, 2001) to a nationally representative sample of private sector employers and employees. These three national surveys together provide the most useful data on how private sector organizational and managerial practices have changed in recent years.

Public sector data on contemporary organizational and managerial practices was collected as part of the Human Resources Government Project, begun in 1996 by researchers with the Canadian Policy Research Networks (Lowe, 2001). In addition, a study of non-standard employment in the federal public service from 1981 to 1997 was published in 1999 by the Public Service Commission (1999). Finally, a study of innovation and technological change was conducted in 2000 that compared the public and private sectors (Earl, 2002).

High Road and Low Road Approaches to Productivity Improvement

Taken as a whole, these surveys confirm the existence of some of the hallmark practices associated with the New Economy. They include "increases in non-standard employment, a shift toward the employment of knowledge-based and highly-skilled workers, changes in production systems and the organization of work, flatter organizational structures, [and] leaner workforces" (Chaykowski, 1997: iii).

New human resource management (HRM) strategies are being pursued to help companies achieve higher productivity and improve competitiveness. Some of the new practices benefit both employees and employers, enhancing employees' commitment and job satisfaction and increasing their willingness to work toward organizational goals. Enticements include opportunities for training, for information-sharing, for participation in decision making and for jobs that provide high levels of autonomy and responsibility. Achieving productivity by offering these types of benefits is considered the "high road" approach.

A "low road" approach is also evident. This path to higher productivity brings gains to the employer while subjecting employees to increasingly oppressive working conditions. Most commonly, to extract maximum worker effort, technology is employed to control work pace and facilitate employer monitoring of employee actions. This technology frequently reduces the skilled component of jobs so that dissatisfied workers can be easily replaced, obviating the need for training. An alternative strategy is to make workers responsible for the production process and require them to find ways to continuously improve it, even if it means fewer workers will be needed. This "low road" approach to productivity improvement is geared toward controlling costs rather than encouraging employee commitment to organizational goals and generates few benefits for workers.

The Private Sector

The 1993 survey (Betcherman et al., 1994) identified three major strategies in use in the four industries studied (wood products, fabricated metal products, electrical and electronic products and business services.) The first strategy concentrated on reducing labour and non-labour costs, and was typically found in smaller, non-unionized firms and in traditional rather than high technology sectors. Seventy percent of establishments adhered to this strategy, which placed a low priority on human resources.

The second focused on process improvements through work reorganization, the introduction of new technology, the establishment of labour-management committees, and the training of employees to broaden their skills. This strategy was most common among larger, unionized companies. The third strategy, also common among larger companies, emphasized the development of new products and markets. Regardless of size, there were recurring concerns related to technological change, quality, productivity, efficiency and cost containment.

The most important finding from the 1993 survey was that while there was a lot of rhetoric about the value of treating employees as a competitive advantage, few establishments had made HRM practices a priority. By far the most common approach was to hiring non-standard workers, frequently in term or part-time positions, as a means to cut costs. Job redesign was fairly common, with 37 percent of establishments reporting that employees were being rotated among work unit jobs or given additional tasks of a similar or a more managerial nature. Flexible scheduling was introduced by 32 percent of establishments, usually in the form of flexible hours. The majority of establishments made no accommodation for personal and family needs.

Only the larger, more technologically sophisticated establishments, such as those in the electrical and electronic products sector and those providing business services, moved away from traditional practices. In some cases financial incentives were introduced. Pay was linked to performance in 22 percent of establishments, usually in the form of profit-sharing. Alternatively, employees were given a "voice" by way of employee suggestion programs, problem-solving groups or "quality circles" wherein employee volunteers met regularly to identify ways to improve production processes.

About 43 percent of establishments introduced employee participation initiatives, primarily oriented toward health and safety, quality improvement and work unit performance issues. An extreme measure, rarely implemented, was the establishment of self-managed teams whose members were completely responsible for the work process, assuming managerial and supervisory as well as production responsibilities. The more progressive establishments were more likely to provide training and job security. But only 45 percent of survey respondents reported formal training and development initiatives, and much of that was directed toward health and safety, which was legally mandated. So "high road" HRM strategies to increase competitiveness were most notable by their scarcity in 1993.

The 1996 pilot study (Statistics Canada and HRDC, 1998) revealed that 57 percent of companies remained preoccupied with cost-cutting, but they now tended to be the larger companies with more than 500 employees. Both traditional sectors like construction, and high technology sectors like communications, education and finance were in this category. Fifty-eight percent of respondents reported that HRM was moderately to extremely important within their establishments, but so was cost-cutting. HRM strategies were least common in the low-skill, low-wage sectors like retail, hospitality and transportation that are expected to generate the greatest number of jobs in the New Economy (Lowe, 1998). Two-thirds of establishments were focused on better customer and supplier service via improvements in product or service quality, but they too pursued the other strategies. These also tended to be the larger establishments, particularly those in the manufacturing and business services sectors.

It should be noted that 44 percent of establishments introduced no organizational changes in the three-year period covered by the 1996 survey, but when they did, they typically downsized or redesigned business processes. There were also attempts to train employees to perform a number of jobs. This allowed companies to more closely integrate organizational functions to reduce payroll costs, improve performance and quality, and increase organizational flexibility. The adoption of new technology was commonplace between 1993 and 1996, with 42 percent of establishments, affecting 60 percent of employees, adopting new technology. In contrast with the findings of the previous survey (Betcherman et al., 1994), training levels were higher and were intended to facilitate organizational change. The majority of establishments that adopted technology or introduced organizational change offered training to help employees deal with it.

The follow-up study conducted in 1999 (Statistics Canada, 2001) revealed that re-designing work processes was still in vogue. Although downsizing was not as prevalent, it still ranked second to work process redesign in terms of the number of workers affected. Flexible job design, the adoption of flexible hours, reliance on part-time workers and increased use of overtime remained popular strategies. The integration of organizational functions was still underway, with 15 percent of establishments deciding to increase their flexibility by training employees to perform a number of jobs so they could be moved around as required. The tendency toward flexible job design was most evident in small establishments, but organizations of all sizes adopted flexible hours. In general, large firms introduced more organizational changes.

By 1999, practices such as sharing information with employees and establishing employee suggestions programs were more prevalent than the pilot study had indicated. This suggests that interest in less traditional HRM practices had increased, particularly in larger establishments. Self-managed work groups, fully responsible for production processes and any associated administrative tasks, were more common but still fairly rare. Similarly, innovation was more common than technology adoption over the one-year survey period, with 48 percent of establishments introducing at least one innovation, 26 percent introducing computer-based technology and 17 percent both innovating and adopting technology. Some of the industries where these changes most commonly occurred were manufacturing, finance and insurance, and information and cultural industries.

The Public Sector

The surveys reveal few differences between the public and private sectors. Non-standard employment was less common in the public than in the private sector, but it increased more rapidly in the public sector during the 1990s (Public Service Commission, 1999). According to Lowe (2001), flexible job design also became more prevalent. Fifty-nine percent of unit managers in 1998 reported their employees were being trained to handle a number of jobs, and 48 percent reported the use of self-managed work teams. This contrasted sharply with the 31.9 percent of private sector establishments that had adopted flexible job design, and the 10.3 percent that had adopted self-managed teams in 1998/99 (Public Service Commission, 1999). Other popular public sector practices included the use of flexible work hours, overtime and contract employment.

Overall, organizational change was more common in the public than the private sector throughout the 1990s (Earl, 2002; Lowe, 2001). Between 1998 and 2000, 79 percent of public sector enterprises introduced organizational change and 85 percent introduced technological change (Earl, 2002). Comparable figures for the private sector were 38 percent and 44 percent respectively. Training to support these changes was also more common in the public than private sector. Ninety-eight percent of public sector establishments offered training following the introduction of technological change, and 80 percent did so following organizational change. Comparable figures for the private sector were 72 percent and 74 percent respectively (Earl, 2002). Downsizing rather than work process redesign was the dominant strategy in the public sector through the 1990s. Between 1990 and 1997, 58,700 federal public service jobs were cut (Lowe, 2001), along with thousands of jobs in the provincial and municipal public sectors.

The Impact of Changing Practices on Employees

These emerging private and public sector practices can be categorized into two types: (1) those that increase employers' staffing or "numerical flexibility," allowing them to meet fluctuating customer or production demands through, for example, the use of overtime, non-standard employment and downsizing; and (2) and those that increase their employees' task or "functional flexibility" for example by training them to perform many jobs, letting them participate in organizational decision making, and redesigning work processes to give them more supervisory and managerial responsibilities. The latter practices are intended to enhance employee competence and commitment to organizational goals by making jobs more interesting. To that extent, increasing functional flexibility might be considered a "high road" strategy to improved productivity.

There has been considerable research on the impact of these innovative organizational and managerial practices on employees. Many of these studies have produced inconsistent results (Godard, 2001; Guest, 1999; Ichniowski et al., 1996; Kochan and Osterman, 1998; Wood, 1999). Still, some key trends can be discerned with respect to the impact on jobs and employees of the strategies and practices emerging from the New Economy. There is little doubt that there are potential disadvantages as well as benefits to both numerical and functional flexibility with respect to employee job satisfaction, morale and general well-being.

Numerical Flexibility Practices and Outcomes

Of all the strategies to achieve numerical flexibility, the ones that have been most studied are downsizing and non-standard employment. While male, blue collar workers were traditionally the ones most affected by downsizing, in the 1990s white collar, managerial and technical employees increasingly experienced its effects (Fallick, 1996). Statistics Canada figures show that close to three million people were permanently laid off from 1993–1998. They tended to be men, youths and workers with lower levels of education (Galarneau and Stratychuk, 2001).

The most common effect of downsizing on its victims appears to be long-term income reduction (Fallick, 1996), as well as loss of confidence and self-esteem (Foley, 2001). In general, labour force participants who are already vulnerable, such as those who are older, lower-skilled, or in imperfect health, seem to bear the brunt of displacement because they find it exceedingly difficult to find secure jobs afterwards (Foley, 2001; International Labour Office, 1998). The level of trauma associated with job loss is deemed second only to the death of a loved one (Appelbaum, Close and Klasa, 1999).

Survivors of downsizing generally show increased anxiety about further cutbacks and increased stress levels, as well as reduced morale, motivation and trust in management (Cascio, 1993; Laabs, 1999; Nelson and Burke, 1998). One study of the aftermath of the federal service downsizing initiative (Armstrong-Stassen, 1998) found that 65 percent of the survivors felt downsizing had an overall negative effect, particularly in terms of workload. A 1999 Public Service Employee Survey also reported that the majority of workers felt the quality of their work had suffered as a result of "having to do the same or more work now with fewer resources" (Government of Canada, 1999). The well-being of managers who oversee the downsizing initiative may also suffer, and they may ultimately leave the organization (Karambayya, 1998; Wright and Barling, 1998).

However, numerical flexibility practices can be beneficial for workers. For example, with fewer workers and managers left in the work unit following downsizing, employees have greater opportunities to broaden skills, take on new tasks and perhaps assume managerial responsibilities, all of which may better utilize their capabilities (Appelbaum, Close and Klasa, 1999; Appelbaum, Lavigne-Schmidt, Peytchev and Shapiro, 1999). Non-standard employment, the other common approach associated with numerical flexibility, can create opportunities for highly skilled workers who can contract their services to the highest bidder (Guest, 2001). Part-time, term and temporary work provides employment opportunities for those with lower-level skills or those who prefer to combine it with other responsibilities. This latter group might include mothers or students who need part-time work to support themselves while they complete their education.

Similarly, flexible hours can be beneficial to employees, particularly if they have significant non-work responsibilities. Gunderson (2002) found that benefits can arise in the forms of increased job satisfaction and productivity, and in improved work-life balance. But non-standard workers tend to experience higher levels of stress than do regular workers (European Foundation, 2002; Quinlan et al., 2001). Also, placing non-standard workers in jobs where they work side by side with regular employees can strain relations between employees as well as between employees and employers (Davis-Blake et al., 2003). The negative aspects of non-standard work tend to be borne disproportionately by women, youth and recent immigrants (Crompton and Vickers, 2000; Jackson, 2003).

The increased use of overtime may have positive or negative effects, depending on whether the hours are paid or unpaid, and whether the employee has a say in accepting or rejecting them (Sparks et al., 2001). In the New Economy, managerial and professional employees may feel compelled to work voluntary, unpaid overtime to demonstrate their commitment to the organization. Overtime hours pose a potential health risk because fatigued employees are more prone to injury and accidents (Ertel et al., 2000; Sparks et al., 1997). They also make it difficult to balance work with other aspects of life.

Numerical flexibility strategies are introduced primarily to reduce labour costs and give employers the flexibility to respond to ebbs and flows in customer and product demand. By their very nature, therefore, they generally result in jobs that provide low levels of security, are poorly paid and offer no employee benefits (Broad, 2000; Grenon and Chun, 1997). This is particularly problematic for the growing numbers of employees who would prefer to work full-time but cannot find suitable jobs, and who therefore end up holding down several non-standard, low-paying jobs that do not fully utilize their skills (Betcherman and Chaykowski, 1996). Also, as employers' rather then employees' needs have dictated the move to non-standard work and flexible hours (Godard and Delaney, 2000; Lipsett and Reesor, 1997), any benefits employees derive may be purely coincidental and short-lived.

Functional Flexibility Practices and Outcomes

Functional flexibility practices are primarily intended to change employees' skills, authority and the scope of their jobs. They frequently involve the redesign of work processes and jobs, the introduction of new technology and/or production techniques that minimize the use of labour and employee participation initiatives. The outcomes associated with these changes, similar to those associated with numerical flexibility, can be both positive and negative for employees.

The positives are usually identified as more opportunities for employees to satisfy their higher-order human development needs by participating in decisions about how their jobs are done, or to develop their skills as their jobs become more challenging (Argyris, 1960; Burchell et al., 2002; Guest, 1999; Gunderson, 2002; Leckie et al., 2001; Skorstad, 1994; Varma et al., 1999). While it is true that these positive outcomes may arise from some of the emerging functional flexibility practices, there are no guarantees that they will (Babson, 1995; Bacon, 1999; Marchington, 2001). Changes may be largely procedural rather than substantive, leading simply to more, rather than to more challenging, tasks to complete (Wood, 1999). Worse yet, some of these practices may disempower workers, increasing employers' control in the workplace (Guest, 1999; Marchington, 2001).

Technology, for example, can make work more interesting but it also has the potential to de-skill jobs and raise stress levels (Hughes et al., 2003; Lowe, 2000). One reason this may occur is because adequate training is not always provided, particularly in smaller firms (Earl, 2002). According to Statistics Canada data (Williams, 2003), having to learn computer skills can be a powerful stressor for older workers and those in low-skilled jobs. Technology can also blur the line between work and home life (Lowe, 2000), which is particularly stressful for women (Hughes et al., 2003) but which also affects men. Cell phones, pagers, laptop computers and the like enable or even oblige employees to be in constant contact with their workplaces. Many employees feel that being available 24 hours a day, seven days a week is necessary for career advancement, which makes it very difficult to devote time to family and other non-work pursuits.

Similarly, team production can make jobs more satisfying but may also "trap" workers into doing managerial work without being compensated for it, as occurs when self-managed work teams are established (Parker and Slaughter, 1988, 1994). Another problem with team production, particularly when compensation is tied to team output, is that work may intensify as the team strives for constantly rising production targets. A poor working environment may also result if the team assumes responsibility for disciplining tardy, absent or less productive members (Geary and Dobbins, 2001; Heller et al., 1998; Marchington, 2001; Smith, 1997). In a similar vein, adding managerial responsibilities to jobs to make them more interesting and implementing lean production techniques can make jobs more intense and stressful. This is especially the case if the requisite amount of training is not provided or must be undertaken outside regular working hours, again adding to work-family conflict (Bacon and Blyton, 2001; Lewchuk and Robertson, 1996).

"Management by stress" (Parker and Slaughter, 1988, 1994) occurs when an employer gives employees more responsibility without more control. Holding a work team to its production quotas without making allowance for equipment failure, inventory problems or other factors beyond the team's control is one example of this. Under the new workplace arrangements, there is a great deal of evidence that management by stress is becoming more common (Allan et al., 1999; Burchell et al., 2002; Lewchuk and Robertson, 1996; Rinehart, 1995; Yates et al., 2001). Employees are often required to master more tasks, do more work and take on additional responsibilities whether they want to or not, and without sufficient training. The fear of job loss compels them to work harder and longer and to at least appear to whole heartedly support organizational goals. But they have no input into decisions that may result in their department, division or work unit being closed down, or even in their organization's ultimate demise. Ultimately, as one author has noted, rather than improving jobs, many of the New Economy's innovations may simply yield "high costs, high turnover, [and] cynical and rebellious workers" (Carter, 1999: 133).

The differences in perspective regarding the impacts of functional flexibility practices arise in part because there are variations in the level at which these initiatives are introduced. For instance, the more rudimentary forms of employee participation, such as employee suggestion programs, are much more common than the establishment of self-managed work teams (Leckie et al., 2001). Only the latter would have the potential to truly empower workers and fundamentally change their influence in the workplace.

Similarly, jobs can be redesigned in a variety of ways. In some cases, additional job duties may be added or defined more broadly so employees can be moved from work station to work station. In others, jobs may be "enriched" by adding supervisory and managerial responsibilities, or by providing opportunities for growth and skill development. In the first instance, jobs may become less boring but only in the latter case may they become more intrinsically satisfying.

Another factor contributing to inconsistent outcomes is the way in which new practices are implemented (Farias and Varma, 1998). With respect to the outcomes of downsizing, it id well known that *how* the process is introduced fundamentally affects outcomes (Band and Tustin, 1995; Labib and Appelbaum, 1993, 1994; Nelson and Burke, 1998). Similarly, work teams may or may not be given much control over work processes even where they are made fully responsible for outcomes. Needless to say, the latter case can be extremely stressful for team members (Smith, 1997). Lean production systems can have different effects depending on how the technology associated with it is implemented (Jackson and Mullarkey, 2000) and on how much "voice" employees are given (Fairris and Tohyama, 2002).

Implementation procedures may matter primarily because they affect employee's perceptions of whether their needs or only their employer's needs are being met by the new measures. Functional flexibility can be implemented in "harder" or "softer" ways. The softer approach tries to entice employees to co-operate with management by ensuring mutual gains (Burchell et al., 2002; Storey, 2001; Tomer, 2001), while the harder approach coerces employees into co-operating to avoid losing their jobs (Drago, 1996; Godard, 2001). The harder approach is likely to elicit employee resistance because it is seen as exploitative (Hudson, 2002; Solomon, 2002; Vandenberg et al., 1999).

To some extent, employee perceptions will be affected by how they rank their multiple needs (pay, decision making, time off, collegiality and so on). Employer efforts to get employees more involved in their jobs may create more stress unless the employee needs or wants encouragement (Riipinen, 1997). Employee characteristics like age, family status and educational background will have some impact on their needs. Furthermore, it seems reasonable to assume that employee perceptions will be affected by whether or not they feel their extra efforts to improve productivity are being suitably recognized and rewarded (Bacon and Blyton, 2001; Hudson, 2002; Osterman, 2000). Thus, the particular practices introduced, and how they are introduced, are critical to outcomes.

Rising Worker Vulnerability in the New Economy

One observer noted that in the 1990s "companies... learned more brazenly to fire long-term employees, outsourcing and subcontracting their jobs, replacing their traditional workforces with contingent and contract workers, and shifting core employment to a smaller New Economy cohort" (Tabb, 2001: 20). Overall, workers today are feeling insecure and overworked, and are fearful of what might happen if they lose their "standard" Old Economy jobs. There has never been a greater need for strong trade unions and other institutions to protect workers' interests.

But while unionization rates in Canada have remained fairly steady over the past decade, they have declined in many other countries (see Chapters 2 and 7). Some of this decline has been attributed to the direct relationships employers have been forging with individual employees through progressive HRM practices. Some pundits believe such practices have "captured the hearts and minds of workers" (Heller et al., 1998; Marchington, 2001; Parker and Slaughter, 1988), seducing them into believing that the employer, not the union, will protect their best interests. These practices have also made at least some workplaces sufficiently worker-friendly as to discourage unionization (Yates, 2001). As well, they have encouraged employees to compete with one another to gain employer favour, which has fed the individualist attitudes that are antithetical to unionization. The link between workers and their unions, as well as solidarity among workers, has weakened as a result (Guest, 1998; Smith, 1997). The tight employee-employer bond has also hidden the fundamental conflict of interest that lies at the heart of that relationship under capitalism, between employers' needs for cheap and productive labour and employees' needs for living wages, benefits and good working conditions.

Even where workers realize they cannot rely on employers to protect their interests, high levels of unemployment and constant employer threats to move jobs offshore if workers make too many demands (Yates, 2001) have reduced the potential for job action to enforce demands (Magdoff and Magdoff, 2004). Unions are fighting back, however, and are achieving some success, in part because many employees are extremely dissatisfied with their jobs and how their employers are treating them.

According to a recent comprehensive Canadian survey (Lowe, 2000), up to a quarter of employees believe they are either in dead-end jobs that do not allow them to take any initiative or in jobs that are extremely stressful or hectic. Only one in three believe their jobs allow them to develop their skills and abilities, or that they have received adequate training to do their jobs well. Not even a quarter of employees believe their employer treats them fairly or with respect. Other evidence of worker disenchantment in Canada comes from the 2002 Public Sector Employee Survey referred to earlier (Government of Canada, 2002). The survey showed that only 22 percent of respondents were satisfied with their career progress, attributing the lack thereof in part to work-family conflict and in part to limited access to developmental opportunities. Given the increasing number of people working more than 41 hours per week (Shields, 2000), some averaging 51 to 55 hours, it is no surprise that difficulties with balancing work and family have escalated in the past decade (Duxbury and Higgins, 2001). Nevertheless in the United Kingdom, as in Canada and the US, employers remain reluctant to introduce "high commitment" HRM practices and would opt for "non-employee-centered" strategies like non-standard employment if left to their own devices (Guest, 2001). This suggests that employees will need assistance if they are to achieve the higher quality of work life they desire. It would offer work-life balance, job security, good training opportunities and healthy working conditions (Lowe, 1998).

Worker Protection in the New Economy

A number of the emerging organizational and managerial practices could contribute to a higher quality of work life for employees. For example, removal of supervisory levels, enriching or even enlarging of jobs, establishment of problem-solving work teams and introduction of flexible hours and family-friendly policies could all promote employee well-being. But measures must be put in place to protect employees from the possible negative impacts of these practices, and to ensure that any productivity gains are equitably shared.

A revitalized labour movement could help ensure that these outcomes are achieved, enabling unions to demonstrate that they do have a meaningful role to play in the workplace, and encouraging workers to unionize. This theme will be further explored in Chapter 7. The remainder of this chapter will examine other possible avenues of protection, such as changes to labour standards and to the regulatory environment worldwide.

On the domestic front, labour standards could be strengthened to afford more protections to the growing number of workers in non-standard jobs. Perhaps such workers could be guaranteed minimum work hours and employee benefits. Eligibility levels for various social benefits, such as employment insurance, could be amended to extend coverage to this category of workers. Incentive programs could make it worthwhile for employers to pursue "high road" rather than "low road" strategies to increased productivity. This might inspire them to train and develop their employees and to implement practices to encourage employee retention. Restrictions on workloads for all employees could protect their health and well-being.

In addition, there is a need for widespread, balanced public debate in the domestic and international communities about the kind of world we wish to create and how the interests of employers, society and workers can be reconciled. Steps must be taken to ensure that all workers in developed and developing countries have access to clean air and water, and healthy and safe working conditions. At a minimum, this will require raising the labour, environmental protection and health and safety standards in Third World countries to a level commensurate with developed countries, to prevent the exploitation of workers and the environment. Additionally, enforcement of these standards must be tightened in all countries.

Restrictions are also needed on the free movement of capital because it destabilizes national economies and contributes to high levels of unemployment. A series of taxes on capital movement, a minimum residency period for capital coming into a country or an employer levy for every job moved out of a country could be instituted.

None of these changes will be achieved without a great deal of effort because the neoliberal agenda is deeply entrenched around the world. To combat it, ordinary workers will have to assert their wishes for higher-quality work lives to their elected representatives. Representatives who are not sufficiently responsive to their concerns will have to be removed from office. Citizens will also have to more actively support international movements fighting for peace, social justice, environmental protection and protection of worker and minority rights. If they work in unionized environments, they will have to become more involved in their unions so they can elect and support union leaders who will actively pursue social justice locally and internationally.

While it is undeniable that employers face an increasingly competitive environment in the New Economy, a major impediment to productivity in North America today is workers' fears that it will cost them their jobs, or demand harder work and longer hours. This type of productivity increase is not sustainable, nor can it be justified in the name of increased profits for shareholders and corporate executives. However, the majority of employers continue to pursue the "low road" to enhanced productivity, treating their employees solely as costs to be controlled as expediently as possible. Only a concerted effort on the part of all those interested in promoting social justice will rectify this situation.

CHAPTER 4

Lifelong Learning and the New Economy

Education or Ideology?

Jane Cruikshank

During the 1980s and 90s Canadians experienced tremendous economic change. While some workers have thrived in the so-called New Economy, many others have found it vicious and brutal. Everywhere we see the effects of the New Economy: a widening gap between the working rich and the working poor, more part-time work, lower wages and increasing poverty.

During the last decade, Canadian government policies supported and encouraged the shift toward part-time work and self-employment, and promoted lifelong learning as the key to success in the knowledge economy. But these policies have not been very helpful to Canadian workers. This chapter critiques Canada's lifelong learning policies, which focus on skill acquisition for the knowledge-based economy and consider lifelong learning vital for Canada's global competitiveness. However, lifelong learning policies and practices have not dealt with the issues of credentialism, de-skilling of work and underemployment of many well-educated Canadian workers.

Canada has become an increasingly polarized society. We have seen far-ranging corporate restructuring ostensibly designed to make Canada competitive in the global economy. And we have seen the emergence of a highly polarized workforce, a decline in full-time employment and a shift toward non-standard work. As Chapter 2 showed, large numbers of self-employed workers, for example, live near or below the poverty line and are self-employed out of necessity. Similarly, part-time workers find themselves clustered at the low end of the income scale and many work part-time because they, too, cannot find full-time employment. The labour market has become increasingly divided into "good jobs" that require high levels of education and skill and provide high pay and benefits, and "bad jobs" that tend to be low-paying, low-skilled, and provide few opportunities and no benefits. Wealth inequality is growing, and many Canadians find themselves in vulnerable situations (Kerstetter, 2003; Saunders, 2003). This polarization is unacceptable in a country as wealthy as Canada.

The new "flexible" workforce is built upon the supremacy of the market. However, while neoliberalism is the ideology and free trade agreements provide the framework, technology is the vehicle that companies often use to implement this ideology. Technological change involves the introduction of new equipment, mainly computers and telecommunications, that enables business to change the way work is organized (see Duffy et al.,).

Technology has enabled business to drastically restructure the workplace. The promise is to improve work. But too often companies use technology to slash jobs and turn full-time positions into part-time and temporary ones. Computers simplify and control work, making it possible for employers to replace full-time positions with part-time McJobs in all economic sectors (see Chapters 2 and 3).

Moreover, we are being told that we have no choice but to adapt to a self-employment economy, a world without jobs, where people work on short-term contracts and move in and out of the labour force at the behest of the market. Under these rules, people will work as individual "entrepreneurs" and sell themselves on a piecemeal basis.

What does all this restructuring mean for the skills acquisition and training that are not only necessary for any kind of work but for survival in the ICT-driven New Economy? In the most general terms, workers are told they must continually retrain and upgrade their skills so they can maintain a competitive edge. Working in the NE will require entirely new kinds of skills — mainly related to computerization, digitization and information technology. That "computer literacy" is now a necessity for almost any work captures this idea in a simple way. These new skills, it follows, will require more and more specialized education than has been necessary in the past. Given the revolutionary nature of the new ICTs, forms and levels of education and training of the past will simply not be adequate. Post-secondary education, for example, is becoming a necessity, not a luxury, just as a high school diploma became a necessity in the 1960s. Presumably, the new "worker as entrepreneur" will also have to learn some new social, entrepreneurial skills — those relating to networking, identifying work and job opportunities and self-marketing. In short, knowledge workers will need knowledge training.

And, as the new ICTs are themselves continually evolving and revolutionizing, workers will need to re-educate themselves continually throughout their working lives. This is not to say that every conceivable job will require high levels of education. Many jobs will not. But to get and keep good jobs, education, the means by which to maintain NE technical and social skills, will become an open-ended pursuit. Lifelong learning will be the new "name" of the education and training "game."

The Role of Lifelong Learning

To explore the issue of lifelong learning, it is important to understand the political context into which it fits. Historically, lifelong learning (under the name adult education) in Canada has had a broad base and has covered a variety of areas such as learning for civic and social purposes, as well as for skill development. The Antigonish Movement, Farm Radio Forum and the Fogo Islands Process are examples that speak to the richness of lifelong learning in Canada.

The Antigonish Movement, which began in the 1920s under the leadership of the St. Francis Xavier University Extension department, focused on the development of local study groups that helped people to analyze their needs and find solutions to community problems. Adult educators provided assistance and support using practical educational methods such as mass meetings, study groups, kitchen meetings, radio listening groups and leadership schools (Coady, 1950). The Antigonish Movement was responsible for the development of co-operatives and credit unions in small communities throughout Atlantic Canada. It "pointed concretely to the role adult education could play in the individual and collective empowerment of the marginalized and oppressed" (Welton, 1987: 18), and was considered a highly successful movement.

Farm Radio Forum, a national program that ran from 1941 to 1965 and was sponsored by the Canadian Broadcasting Corporation (CBC), the Canadian Association of Adult Education (CAAE), and the Canadian Federation of Agriculture, was designed to stimulate rural development. Farm Radio Forum was built on four adult education techniques: weekly radio broadcasts, printed study materials, local discussion groups and reports of discussion findings. Small groups across Canada would meet weekly in people's homes and to discuss a specific, predetermined topic relevant to the farming community. The groups would listen to a radio broadcast, discuss the topic using study materials and send their findings to a provincial Farm Radio Forum office (located in the extension department of a university in each province). The findings would be compiled, forwarded to the national office and aired in subsequent broadcasts, thus providing a vehicle for communication among the groups. Community projects such as rural electrification, co-operative medical services, co-operative buying clubs and stores, and community centres were thus developed and flourished in rural communities across Canada. Farm Radio Forum was internationally known, and projects based on this model "were developed in at least 44 other countries" (Selman, 1991: 103).

The Fogo Island Process, a project under the National Film Board of Canada's Challenge for Change program that ran from 1969 to 1977, focused on stimulating social change using film as the vehicle. Working in co-operation with Memorial University Extension service, a number of films were produced that focused on the Fogo Islander's perceptions of community problems and possible solutions. The films were then replayed to the community members to help them understand the problems from a variety of perspectives and work toward change (MacNeill, 1969). The Fogo Island films were nationally acclaimed as a highly effective tool to stimulate social and economic change.

These three examples show how past adult education/lifelong learning programs combined education, community development and social justice visions and worked to strengthen local communities (see Alexander, 1997; Selman et al., 1998; Spencer, 1998; Welton, 1987). It is a story that speaks to the importance and potential of lifelong learning in Canada.

With the New Economy, however, priorities have changed. Canadian lifelong learning policies have become increasingly tied to skill acquisition that will presumably enhance Canada's global competitiveness (Council of Ministers, 1999; OECD, 2001; Statistics Canada, 1999). Whereas lifelong learning could be used to promote human, social and community economic development, instead it serves the market. This shift in focus mirrors the political changes that have occurred over the past quarter-century.

Canadians are being told that lifelong learning is the key to success in the New Economy. A recent government document states:

> To remain competitive and keep up with the accelerating pace of technological change, Canada must continuously renew and upgrade the skills of its workforce. We can no longer assume that the skills acquired in youth will carry workers through their active lives. Rather, the working life of most adults must be a period of continuous learning. Having the skills and learning that employers demand can open the door to better jobs and a better standard of living. (HRDC, 2002: 37)

We are being told that we must develop new skills for the new knowl-edge-based economy and the Canadian government clearly places a high priority on this policy direction. For example, in the December 12, 2003, federal Cabinet shuffle, Paul Martin, the newly minted prime minister, an-nounced the creation of a new department, the Department of Human Resources and Skills Development, thus signalling the importance of skills and training for New Economy jobs. In a March 2004 speech, Joe Volpe, then Minister of Human Resources and Skills Development, spoke glow-ingly of the need for a highly skilled workforce.

Skilled workers are the source of innovation — the key to sustaining economic growth in the new economy. Canadian workers' capacity to capitalize on changing skills needs [sic] will underpin the productivity and competitiveness of Canadian firms in the decades ahead. (Volpe, 2004)

Volpe called skills development and lifelong learning a "national priority." A recent Industry Canada (2001: 60) report that discusses ways to address the "skills challenge" states that Canada's goal is to "develop the most skilled and talented labour force in the world."

Because of the sheer repetition of this message, workers now tend to see lifelong learning as a personal survival strategy, as a hedge against unemployment and poverty. For example, we are told that we must continually upgrade our computer skills if we hope to remain employable in our tight job market. And we are told that the alternative to this ongoing training is obsolescence and failure. However, we see a simultaneous rise in educational levels of workers, a de-skilling of work and underemployment for many well-educated workers. Even many university graduates cannot find good jobs.

Credentialism and Underemployment

Over the past three decades, the educational credential bar has been rising inexorably. Many now question the need for high levels of education for most jobs and suggest that educational qualifications are simply a way for "employers to screen out the few from the busloads of job seekers who often appear at the door for a single position" (Torjman and Battle, 1999: 24). Certainly technology is changing the nature of work, yet many jobs are restructured "to minimize the need for skills rather than to further develop the capacities of workers" (Jackson, 2002: 16).

Knowledge economy theories assume that workers will require more knowledge and skill to deal with the complexities of the new workplace, and that without this knowledge, they will be left behind. Even though Canadian post-secondary institutions provide high-quality education, the organization of work in the New Economy tends to prevent many graduates from applying their knowledge in the workplace (see Lowe, 2000). As well, technology has helped to reduce the skill requirements of workers, and many are now reduced to watching and taking commands from computer screens (Reid, 1996). For example, most technology jobs are not glamorous systems analysis jobs but rather are low-wage data entry jobs.

Yates (2003: 92) furthers this argument and says that while "neo-classical economists believe that machinery tends to raise the skill requirements of jobs… the opposite is generally the case." Because the skill aspects of jobs have been incorporated into the computer, "the more sophisticated the machinery used, the lower the skill required of the worker." For example, it takes more skill for a secretary to type on a typewriter than on a computer using a word processing program, because "the intelligence is built into the machine and the program" (p. 93).

Between 1971 and 1991, the number of jobs requiring a university education increased by 40 percent. The number of university graduates in Canada, however, increased by 140 percent (Gingras and Roy, 1998). Not surprisingly, 1.4 million or 25 percent of Canadian workers believe they are overqualified for their jobs. This perception of being underemployed was held by Canadians with college diplomas, bachelors, masters and doctoral degrees (Compton, 2002). Lowe (2000) argued that 29 percent of university graduates are working in jobs that do not require a university degree and that one in five workers with post-secondary credentials work in jobs that require only a high school diploma. The problem, then, is that Canada has a "highly educated workforce chasing fewer and fewer jobs that actually demand high levels of qualifications" (Jackson and Robinson, 2000: 48).

The Canadian economy seems unable to generate enough skilled jobs to match the rising educational levels of workers. For Lowe, the crux of today's employment problem is job quality. The mismatch between educational credentials and job requirements reduces the quality of life for many well-educated workers and "represents squandered human capital" (Lowe, 2000: 116). Because of the continued focus of lifelong learning as a survival strategy in the New Economy, the underemployment of skilled workers will most likely increase.

While university graduates may have better job prospects than those without degrees, many Canadians are forced to work in jobs that are unrelated to their training. Raising educational levels will not create new jobs, nor will it keep people from sinking into poverty. Between 1981 and 1997, the number of Canadians with post-secondary certificates, diplomas and degrees who were living in poverty rose dramatically. In fact, in 1997, 33 percent of poor families and 31 percent of poor unattached individuals in Canada held a post-secondary certificate, diploma or degree (Ross et al., 2000). A recent study on post-secondary funding issues in Ontario states that in 1998, the median salary of 25–29-year-old high school graduates was $27,000. The median salary of university graduates in that age group was $36,000. However, 25 percent of the university group earned less than $25,000, which clearly was lower than that of the high school graduates (Mackenzie, 2004). Therefore, the theory that university graduates receive higher salaries than people without university degrees is not entirely accurate.

Jackson (2005: 1, 2) argues that the real wages of young workers aged 15 to 24 "have fallen to just 75 to 80% of the real wages earned by young workers a generation ago, even though today's young workers are much more highly educated." Jackson holds that policy makers often mistakenly believe that young workers will move to higher-paying jobs once they have gained experience. In fact, 47 percent of Canadian workers who were low-paid and full time in 1996 failed to move up by 2001. For women, this number was an astounding 72 percent (Saunders, 2005). The chances of moving up during the 1996–2000 period were no better than in 1985–89 (Saunders, 2005).

Policy and the Skills Debate

Labour market trends seem to run counter to public policy. Canadian policy makers place a great value on training and skill enhancement. They believe firmly that Canadian competitiveness is based on the good jobs associated with a highly skilled labour force. However, as shown in Chapter 2, at present, job creation is in the area of flexible, low-wage and insecure employment. Thus, there is a wide divide between the rhetoric of skill enhancement and the reality of the labour market.

One way the rhetoric for lifelong learning has been framed is through claims about a skilled labour shortage in Canada and the looming shortage when the "baby boomers" retire. For example, Jane Stewart, when she was Minister of Human Resources Development, claimed that, "a critical shortage of skilled workers in Canada could grow to one million by 2020 unless the country changes its approach to education and training" (McCarthy, 2001). The Canadian Federation of Independent Business argues that "the skills shortage among smaller businesses is already as high as 300,000" (Beauchesne, 2002: A15). However, demographer David Foot scoffs at the labour shortage scare, noting that the baby boomers "aren't retiring for at least another five years and their kids are entering the labour market" (Beauchesne, 2002: A15). Noting that Canada has an unemployment rate of seven percent, Foot says it "doesn't sound like a labour shortage to me" (p. A15). Also, with the trend toward eliminating mandatory retirement and the fact that many baby boomers do not have adequate pensions, the anticipated groundswell of retirements, particularly in the high skills jobs, may not occur.

Gingras and Roy (1998) also conclude there is no shortage of skilled labour and argue that Canadian skills compare favourably with other industrialized countries. While there will always be cyclical shortages in some skill areas, these "cannot be averted by increasing investment in training" (Gingras and Roy, 1998: 10). Canada, they claim, leads the OECD countries in the proportion of people with both secondary and university education. A recent study from Human Resources Development Canada (HRDC) acknowledges that Canada has "the highest proportion of people with post-secondary education in its working-age population" in the entire world (HRDC, 2002: 26). In 1999, "39 percent of Canadians had completed community college or university" and, because of the large number of people in the "echo" generation, HRDC predicts an enrolment increase of 20 percent by 2015. Looking specifically at Canadians in the paid workforce, in 2003, 60.7 percent of the labour force between the ages of 25 and 54 had a completed post-secondary certificate, diploma or university degree (Saskatchewan's, Chartered Accountants, 2004). In actual numbers, in 2003, 4,483,200 Canadians in the labour force had a post-secondary certificate or diploma, while 2,905,800 working Canadians had completed at least a bachelor's degree (Statistics Canada, 2004c).

Given this saturation, and the fact that one-quarter of university and college graduates are employed in clerical, sales and service jobs, it seems almost absurd to claim that Canada is uncompetitive because of a shortage of knowledge and skills. Even though Canada has one of the best-educated workforces in the world, millions of Canadians are either unemployed or underemployed, and yet the unemployed are still being told to "get an education." "At the policy level... the clarion call to 'educate, educate, educate' provides a handy catch-all solution for just about any economic or social problem imaginable: poverty, low productivity, globalization, inequality" (Stanford, 2001: 31).

Training by itself can neither prevent jobs from disappearing nor create more jobs. Barlow and Robertson (1994: 88) quote James Turk, Executive Director of the Canadian Association of University Teachers (CAUT), who sums up the problem nicely:

> More education without a change in the range and nature of jobs does not create any wealth. It merely shuffles the deck. If everyone in Canada had a PhD, we would still have a million and a half unemployed, a million underemployed, and many millions doing boring, mindless, poorly paid jobs. More education for some allows them to displace others, but it does not create new jobs nor increase the overall opportunities for the population as a whole.

It is important to ask the question, "Who benefits from the overabundance of highly skilled workers?" Clearly, employers benefit. A large pool of skilled workers seeking a limited number of jobs enables employers to pay lower wages and offer fewer benefits. It also ensures compliance in the workplace, as few workers will demand better working conditions and salaries if they know they can easily be replaced. For example, China and India have trained "tens of thousands" of computer programmers, creating a surplus of highly skilled workers (Yates, 2003: 93). Consequently, those who do find jobs tend to be paid very low wages. Many work as low-wage independent contractors and transmit their work electronically to their overseas employer (Yates, 2003), a situation that, as noted below, has ramifications for Canadian IT workers.

What is actually happening with New Economy jobs? As shown in Chapter 2, the core of New Economy jobs — the information and communications technology (ICT) industries and the science industries — make up a tiny part of employment in Canada. By 2000, employment in the ICT sector had risen to only 4 percent of all workers. Adding the science industries at 4 percent of all workers means that 92 percent of all jobs in Canada are still *not* so-called New Economy jobs (Beckstead et al., 2003). Many new IT jobs are simply part-time, low-wage call centre jobs. Yet public policy makers focus on ICT jobs as a high priority for lifelong learning policies. As well, the percentage of "knowledge workers" outside the ICT and science industries actually declined drastically, from 17 percent in 1981 to 12 percent, in 1996 (Beckstead and Gellatly, 2003).

The years since the technology "bust" of 2001 have not been kind to the computer industry. Even with the pronouncements of strong economic growth, a recent Statistics Canada (2004d) report notes that Canada lost 82,000 manufacturing jobs in 2003. Among the industries hardest hit were computer and electronics producers, the ones most associated with New Economy jobs.

Much of the New Economy/IT employment will be lost even without an economic bust. Like jobs in many industry sectors, IT companies look for low-cost workers. A Price Waterhouse Coopers study, for example, predicts that by 2010, 14 percent of Canada's current IT workforce will migrate to low-cost countries like India, China and Russia (Scott et al., 2004) which, as previously noted, have a surplus of skilled computer programmers. It predicts that by 2010, 25 percent of all IT jobs in the US also will go overseas, and claims the jobs to be relocated include those in research, development and production. The report states that "any knowledge-based function that does not require direct personal interaction is a candidate" for outsourcing (Scott et al., 2004: 2). In any IT business, the authors say, 30 percent of IT staff should be on site and close to the "users," while the remaining 70 percent can be located offshore. Given this trend, federal government policies that focus so heavily on skill training for such jobs seem doomed to fail.

So it is important to question government policies that focus so heavily on skill training for New Economy jobs. The training discourse is based on the assumption that there will be plenty of work if people develop skills that meet the changing needs of the marketplace. However, it does not matter how well trained workers are if technology is creating a world without enough good jobs to go around.

Moreover, as already noted, when organizations downsize and computerize, the remaining workers are often forced to perform more tasks. These tasks are not necessarily more challenging, because they tend to be computer-based rather than people-centred (Livingstone, 1996, 2004). With computerization, the skill requirements of many jobs have been reduced, and consequently many workers have become "mere appendages to machines" (Reid, 1996: 101). In fact, "contrary to the mythology, the advent of the knowledge society doesn't mean that all jobs require more knowledge. In many cases, less judgement is required" (Reid, 1996: 101). For example, cashiers who used to count change now press buttons called "cheeseburger" or "coffee" and watch the change come down a metal tube; factory workers and craftspeople who once produced things now push buttons and watch machines do their jobs; administrative and clerical workers who used to have some autonomy now spend much of their time taking instructions from and being monitored by computers. The examples are endless.

The promise of developing skills for the New Economy is seen by many as a hoax being perpetrated on Canadians in an attempt to deflect attention from the current job crisis. Instead of its promised benefits, the New Economy has produced job insecurity, a polarization between the rich and the poor, a shredded social safety system, and a habit of poor bashing — blaming the unemployed and underemployed for their fate (see Chapters 6 and 8).

Some authors argue that the push for increased training is part of an ideology that views unemployment as a temporary problem, criticizes the education system for failing to provide adequate training to equip people for the New Economy and blames individuals for their inadequate skills (Edwards, 1993; Dunk et al., 1996). Within this ideology, training systems need only to be revamped and the unemployed trained for the problems to be solved. In short, the responsibility rests with the individual, and unemployment becomes an individual "deficit" problem rather than a structural one resulting from neoliberal policies. This ideology creates the space to "justify coercion and 'policing' of the unemployed" (Dunk et al., 1996: 3) and opens the door to "learnfare" programs.

Like workfare, which requires welfare recipients to work, "learnfare" training programs require people receiving social assistance to take training as a condition of income support. The programs are based on the belief that people are unemployed because they are inadequately trained. Therefore, social assistance benefits are linked to training, which, in theory, will enable the unemployed to obtain jobs. However, Shragge (1997) points out, learnfare programs have not been effective in helping people obtain jobs. In fact, "they have created a large pool of very cheap, subsidized labour that has been used by private sector businesses, government institutions, and community organizations" (p. 27). In short, learnfare programs are "reminiscent of the workhouse approach to social assistance" (Shragge, 1997: 29) and are a coercive, punitive and completely inappropriate response to a structural unemployment problem (see Shragge, 1997, for a detailed discussion of learnfare). In fact, Swift (1995) argues that the best one can expect from learnfare is that it will prepare people to take "non-standard" or bad jobs and to lower their employment expectations.

This analysis clearly fits with the thrust of the 1994 OECD *Jobs Study* report, a draconian economic development strategy that was designed as a blueprint for member OECD countries, a blueprint that Canada has followed (OECD, 1995, 1996). The *Jobs Study* favoured the creation of jobs only in the private sector. It called for two distinct streams: high-skilled jobs that would have high knowledge requirements, and low-wage jobs that would "absorb significant numbers of low-skilled unemployed workers" (OECD, 1994: 33). Because there will never be enough good jobs for everyone, the main OECD strategy for reducing unemployment was to promote the growth of low-wage jobs. It described ways to ensure that workers would be desperate enough to take these jobs, such as: lowering minimum wages, reworking employment-protection legislation, lowering trade barriers and eliminating social supports.

The *Jobs Study* report gave lifelong learning a central role in increasing the skills of workers in the high-skilled, high-wage tier. However, lifelong learning was limited specifically to jobs. It was seen solely as an investment in business and in the economies of member OECD countries.

Thus, it is obvious that the growing polarization of the labour market is paralleled by a similar trend in training (Swift and Peerla, 1996). While a two-tiered job system is widening the gap between the working rich and the working poor, the same phenomenon is happening with lifelong learning. Under the name of human resource development, lifelong learning is used to increase the skills of a small number of core workers in the high-wage and high-knowledge tier. At the same time, under the name of learnfare, lifelong learning forces welfare recipients into dead-end "training" programs, which keep them trapped in poverty. Thus, lifelong learning, which should be used to enhance the lives of Canadians, has instead been used to create two very distinct classes of workers.

The Role of Training Ideology

Why, despite all the evidence to the contrary, do people persist in believing that more training will bring them better employment opportunities and job security? Why don't we have more opposition, more rebellion from university and college graduates who find themselves unemployed and underemployed? Why are they not publicly challenging the skills training rhetoric? Why do many academics and trade union leaders believe the rhetoric around training as a way of helping workers and reducing poverty?

Bouchard (1998: 137) argues that the only way to promote the training agenda is to couch it in a "carefully constructed ideology." Ideology has been the driving force behind recent efforts to "hard sell" skills training and to convince people that continuous training and retraining is "normal." The idea of "training-as-cure-all," Bouchard argues, is an attempt to construct a neoliberal view of the economic order as reality. In doing so, the ideology of training also serves to legitimize the existing power structure.

This ideology has been the focus of a massive corporate public relations strategy in Canada over the last quarter century. There have been extensive media campaigns crafted in large part by conservative think-tanks such as the Fraser Institute to garner consensus on the neoliberal view of the economy (see, for example, Laxer, 1993; Marchak, 1991; McQuaig, 1993, 1995, 1998). Training is an integral part of this ideology and of these media campaigns, which have been so effective that a significant proportion of the public "now believe that their interests lie in supporting the market agenda" (McQuaig, 1998: 28). As well, some people who have achieved a high level of education have thrived in the New Economy — including many academics and trade union leaders. Thus, the seeming credence of the promise that education is the key to the "good life" can be difficult to challenge, given the intensity of these campaigns.

While the Canadian media airs other viewpoints, "the chorus of (neoliberal) voices simply overwhelms, not because of the force of their arguments, but through their sheer numbers and the prominence they are given" (McQuaig, 1995: 13). This constant bombardment simply becomes "clatter in people's heads." "Through sheer repetition — like the monotonous, incessant banging of plates — it lodges in our heads, becoming a dull background noise, a kind of invisible yet inescapable fact of life" (McQuaig, 1995: 13). This ideology is seen as "the way of the world" and people who challenge it are ridiculed as "living in the past."

What Can We Do?

Despite the clatter about training, lifelong learning has a significant social justice history and potential. Ettore Gelpi, who was responsible for lifelong education (a European term for lifelong learning) at UNESCO from 1972 to 1993, says we need to begin with the premise that "lifelong education policies are not neutral" (Gelpi, 1979: 2). For Gelpi, lifelong education can go in either of two directions: it can emancipate and encourage democratic participation, or it can control and repress. That is, lifelong education can either reinforce the power structure or it can be an agent of social change.

Lifelong learning must go far beyond its current focus of high skills development for the New Economy. The International Commission on Education for the Twenty-first Century called for a rethinking of the term "lifelong education." Its report says:

> Not only must it adapt to changes in the nature of work, but it must also constitute a continuous process of forming whole human beings — their knowledge and aptitudes, as well as the critical faculty and the ability to act. It should enable people to develop awareness of themselves and their environment and encourage them to play their social role at work and in the community. (Delors, 1996: 21)

The Delors report states that education throughout life is based on four pillars: *learning to know*, which involves the acquisition of knowledge; *learning to do*, which involves training for work; *learning to be*, which develops one's personality, judgement and personal responsibility; and *learning to live together*, which develops an understanding of other people, of values of pluralism, mutual understanding and peace. While the formal education system tends to emphasize *learning to know*, Canada's lifelong learning policies tend to focus exclusively on the *learning to do* pillar. The Delors Commission argues that lifelong education must be based on all four pillars.

An even broader interpretation of lifelong learning sees it as a "democratization of education" and "rooted in the community" (Ireland, 1978: 20). This conception goes much further than the Delors Commission's and embodies a broader, collective vision, one that was strong in past Canadian adult education work but is now in marked contrast to Canada's skills development focus. In this view, lifelong learning should question and critique:

"lifelong education is based on a dialectical theory. It is not an absolute. It must itself be subject to unceasing criticism. Its declared foundations must be subject to challenge, and studies should help to redefine its theory and its practice" (Gelpi, 1979: 21).

We need to step back and look at what is happening to the concept and practice of lifelong learning in Canada. Just as many have jumped on the neoliberal bandwagon, where the market is the ruler of the universe and people subservient to its dictates, so too has the concept of lifelong learning changed. It has moved from being an agent of change to simply reinforcing the power structure.

We must question the rhetoric of the so-called "knowledge society" and challenge the ideological underpinnings of Canada's current lifelong learning policies. We need to advocate for policy changes, and to do this we must work at both the national and the community levels. We have to ask "what will we do with labour that is simply not needed in the conventional wage economy?" (Reid, 1996: 194–195). Reid sees this as a moral question. Some people are benefiting from the New Economy, but many are losing. The question, he asks, is how do we share the benefits?

In fact, there are a number of ways to share the benefits, such as the four-day work week, job-sharing, a guaranteed annual income, paying people to work in the voluntary sector and providing sufficient pay for part-time work for everyone (Broad, 2000; O'Hara, 1993; Rifkin, 1995). While it is easy to critique the different visions, proposals for the redistribution of work are being recognized in a number of countries (Livingstone, 1996; Hayden, 1999).

Duffy et al. (1997: 242) suggest that the short-term nature of many jobs might push people to mobilize politically, and progressive groups might "challenge not simply the nature of employment but also the broader economic structure that sustains the crisis." This is consistent with Gelpi's understanding of lifelong learning. Lifelong education should raise awareness of these issues and their importance to people's lives. As always, those in power will try to quash opposition, and because of this, lifelong education "becomes a struggle requiring the co-ordination of grassroots activities into new systems and cultural movements; and this cannot be separated out from activity on the much greater political scale" (Gelpi, 1979: 4).

We must get free of the yoke of skills development for the New Economy and look at lifelong learning from a broader perspective. We should develop political education strategies at both the national and local levels to counter the massive media campaigns of the right-wing think-tanks and to advocate for policy changes. It is important that a broad segment of the community be included in this process, which was historically integral to adult education practice. As Gelpi (1979: 6) says:

> Community groups, workers, their co-operative and trades union movements, craftsmen, architects, artists, scientists either organized or independent, the different age groups — all provide both the context and the actual promoters of cultural activities and the most authentic learning.

It is important to look at workplace issues, such as workplace reform, work redistribution, worker empowerment and new forms of work, as well as parallel systems, such as co-operatives and community economic development activities. We have much to learn from past practice in Canada (see Alexander, 1997; Fairbairn et al., 1991; Welton, 1987), and also from progressive groups who live in Third World countries (see Lappe, 2002; Yates, 2003).

Conclusion

Lifelong learning is important to Canadians, but it is wrong to say it is essential to our competitiveness in the global economy.

> Our economy needs dishwashers and janitors and labourers and secretaries and cashiers and manufacturers and waiters and drivers — in fact we need more of them all the time. Further education may be extremely valuable for these Canadians, but they don't need it to do their jobs well, and it won't guarantee them a better standard of living. (Stanford, 2001: 3)

A democratic society requires balance. The so-called New Economy is a lopsided economy that supports business, often at the expense of workers. For many, the New Economy promotes economic insecurity, and more and more people are finding themselves trapped in contingent jobs. Similarly, many highly skilled workers are seriously underemployed.

It is important to look at the types of work that are being created in the New Economy. We must challenge its current focus and the way that lifelong learning policies have been shaped to fit into it. We need to move from what Susan George (1997) calls an "Age of Exclusion" to one of "Inclusion," and to explore alternative perspectives of the economy, perspectives that treat people as citizens, not consumers. We should explore the many benefits that lifelong learning can bring and not focus so narrowly on our global competitiveness. We must work toward promoting lifelong learning policies that benefit the whole person, the workplace and the community.

CHAPTER 5

Stresses and Strains

Workers' Health and the New Economy

Michael Polanyi

Technological developments, intensified international competition and neoliberal deregulation have combined to stimulate fundamental changes in work systems, employment relations, organizational structures, and the labour market experiences of workers in North America and other industrialized countries.

The liberalization of trade and finance has resulted in significant growth in the exchange of goods and services and the flow of money across international borders. Meanwhile, technological advancements in computers, telecommunications and transportation have increased the mobility of physical and financial capital as well as goods and services. Improvements in technology have allowed firms to produce goods more quickly and cheaply, saturating domestic markets and exacerbating competition. Technological advancements have also reduced the time it takes to develop new products, thus reducing the shelf life of goods and forcing firms to constantly innovate. Furthermore, technology advancements have given consumers fuller access to information about products and the capacity to change brands more readily, again pressuring firms to innovate or reduce prices to retain customers.

Following suit, labour market norms and structures have also changed. For example, workers are no longer laid off solely in response to a downturn in the economy, but also to rationalize operations in thriving markets. Unionization has decreased in many developed countries as has labour-market regulation (see Chapters 2 and 3). Social safety net programs such as employment insurance have also been eroded in many cases (see Chapter 6). These transformations have vast repercussions: the nature and distribution of jobs is changing, new relationships between workers and employers are being forged and new kinds of workplace injuries and illnesses are arising. What remains uncertain, and at times contested, is the nature of the impacts of new work arrangements and structures on the health and well-being of individuals, communities and societies (Frenkel et al., 1999; Milkman, 1998).

There is a glowing optimism to much of the discussion of the New Economy; the dark underside is seldom acknowledged. Government leaders, such as former Canadian Prime Minister Paul Martin (2000), extol the virtues of the New Economy, citing its "technological breakthroughs" and "cascade of new industries," which "hold the potential to create many more new jobs and many more new opportunities than was ever possible in the past."

But this is more than an "economy of innovation" (Martin, 2000). Faced with the pressures of intense competition (Reich, 2001), firms are also seeking to minimize production costs, and we are only starting to grasp what this drive for flexibility means for the health of workers and their communities.

In this highly competitive environment, many firms have adopted flexible strategies of production. Two primary forms have emerged: "functional flexibility" and "numerical flexibility" (see Chapter 3). Flexible production strategies have both direct and indirect implications for the health and well-being of labour force participants.

There is much debate as to the impacts of the New Economy. Certainly, some are benefiting, as is shown by the rise of incomes of high-skilled workers in information-driven sectors. But our research points to four inter-related trends that merit concern and attention: the spread of computer usage, the intensification of work, the growth of job and employment insecurity and the polarization of market incomes.

This chapter aims to explore the health impacts of these experiences in the New Economy. Based on this analysis, we outline a framework for healthy work and for policy directions to promote healthier work in Canada and other industrialized countries.

The Evolving Health of Workers in the New Economy

Recent economic and workplace transformations have been accompanied by positive and negative changes in workers' health. The number of work fatalities and work-related injury and illness claims have decreased substantially over recent decades in Canada and other developed countries (Marshall, 1996; Mustard et al., 2001).

However, Canada still has the highest work-related mortality rate of all OECD countries, and is fourth highest in workplace injuries (Osberg and Sharpe, 2003). While this may be attributable, in part, to different classification criteria and the resource-based nature of the Canadian economy, Canada also has made comparatively little progress in reducing its fatality rate over a 21-year period (achieving only a 6.6 percent reduction, compared to Italy's 60 percent decrease), and has had only modest success in reducing work-related injuries (six other countries achieved greater reductions) (Osberg and Sharpe, 2003).

"Workers," of course, do not constitute an undifferentiated group. There are important variations in work-related health outcomes by gender, race and class. For example, a major longitudinal study of British civil servants found a stepwise gradient of decreasing health status exists as one moves down the occupational hierarchy (Marmot et al., 1991). In Canada, those lower on the occupational hierarchy have been found more likely to report ill health in subsequent years (Mustard et al., 2003).

Gender differences in worker health are complex and varied. While women in Canada appear to experience higher rates of work stress, disability days and musculoskeletal injuries than men, men experienced more than twice as many time-loss injuries in 1996 (Federal, Provincial, Territorial Advisory Committee in Population Health, 1999). Walters et al.'s (2002) analysis of Canadian data found few gender differences in health. For health problems that were more likely to be experienced by women, such as stress, migraines and arthritis, they found that neither work or non-work exposures, nor greater individual vulnerability explained differences. Indeed, Klumb and Lambert's (2004) extensive review of studies on women's work experience and health concluded that engagement in paid employment has no overall adverse effect on women's health. On the other hand, Strazdins and Bammer (2004) did find that exposure to repetitive and poorly designed work, as well as less time to relax at home, were factors in women's greater experience of musculoskeletal injuries in developed countries.

Racial differences in work-related health outcomes have received less attention; although given the increased exposure to unhealthy working conditions and jobs, people of colour appear more likely to experience poor health outcomes (Das Gupta, 1996; Jackson, 2002). Empirical studies from the US have found that Blacks are at a higher risk of fatal work injuries, but that the effect of race on non-fatal injuries is inconsistent or weak (Oh and Shin, 2003).

It has long been known that peoples' lives are profoundly affected, positively and negatively, by their work. Work provides us with income, it is a source of social networks and support, it offers us a sense of identity, and it gives our lives challenge and purpose. The health impacts of the physical demands of work and exposures to occupational health and safety hazards have long been documented. More recently, however, increased attention has been paid to the way that psychosocial conditions at work influence the health of workers.

For example, employee job control and decision latitude can moderate or reduce job strain. Robert Karasek, an American labour sociologist, developed the "job strain model" of work and health during his doctoral studies at the Massachusetts Institute of Technology in the early 1970s. The model grew out of his observation that jobs with high demands did not always incur negative impacts on workers, and sometimes had positive impacts. For example, demanding jobs seemed to lead to personal growth and active engagement outside of work when workers had a high level of control or latitude in their jobs. He therefore postulated that a worker's degree of control over her or his work was central in determining whether high demands had healthy or unhealthy impacts.

Today, decision latitude, or the ability to organize one's own tasks, take breaks and use a range of skills, is considered central to reducing the strain and stress caused by jobs. Where decision latitude is greater, psychological demands are less likely to pose a major health risk (these are so-called "active jobs," that lead to well-being, learning and personal growth). But where decision latitude is limited, and demands are high, job strain results, with associated ill-health effects (de Lange et al., 2003; Karasek and Theorell, 1990; Van Der Doef and Maes, 1999).

Fairness has also emerged as a core element in understanding the relationship between working conditions and health. In the early 1980s, medical sociologist Johannes Siegrist interviewed young German heart attack patients (Research Institute for Psychology and Health, 2004). He was surprised to find that most of them were not overweight and did not have high blood pressure. Indeed, many of their doctors were at a loss as to why they had suffered heart attacks. Through his interviews, Siegrist discovered that many had been working 70 to 80 hours a week and also had experienced negative events related to their occupations, such as being fired or not being accepted for promotion. Siegrist hypothesized that an *imbalance* between what workers invest in their work and what they receive in return might be a catalyst for heart disease, since reciprocity in social exchanges is a deeply rooted human expectation. When reciprocity is violated, people experience emotional distress. Hence, Siegrist developed his "effort-reward imbalance" model (Siegrist, 1996). He undertook as to whether an imbalance between the perceived level of effort put into a job (e.g., the amount of pressure from deadlines, the level of responsibility and amount of overtime work) and the perceived level of reward (in terms of pay, promotion opportunities and status) led to negative health outcomes. In more than 40 studies the verdict was clear: effort-reward imbalance was associated with coronary heart disease and other negative health outcomes (Peter and Siegrist, 1999).

In brief, there are five potential pathways through which these adverse labour-market experiences may influence health: (1) stress-induced physiological changes, such as increased cholesterol (Kasl et al., 1998); (2) changes in the nervous, immune and endocrine systems that may have long-term negative health consequences; (3) increased risky health behaviour, such as decrease in physical activity and increase in smoking, drinking and unhealthy dietary habits (Morris et al., 1992); (4) loss of social support (Gore, 1978); and (5) inadequacy of income.

Below, we discuss the evidence of negative health implications of expanded computer use, the intensification of work, rising levels of job, employment and income insecurity and increased polarization of income.

Increased Computer Use and Health

There is debate as to how the rising prevalence of computer use is affecting the health and well-being of workers. Concerns over computer usage have shifted over time, from a focus on electromagnetic emissions to a focus on musculoskeletal disorders due to the physical demands of repetitive keyboarding, to a broader concern about the human stress implications of computer use and its impacts on work-life balance. Smith et al.'s (1999) review concluded that computer tasks can produce stress reactions (e.g., changes in heart rate, blood pressure), but that the health impacts of computer use depend on the strategy used to implement computer technology and the presence of other adverse characteristics of jobs (high demands, limited control, excessive task difficulty with inadequate skills, lack of variety or repetitiveness of tasks, poor supervisory relations, technology problems and job insecurity — many of the other factors explored in this chapter). In fact, most Canadians say that computers make work more interesting and even more secure (Lin and Popovich, 2002). For example, only 18 percent of Canadians indicate that learning to use computers causes stress, while 44 percent point to excessive workload as a source of stress. Hence technology such as computers is not *necessarily* a problem per se, but it can become one if healthy work organization and design features are not in place.

Health and Intensification of Work

From a health standpoint, research as far back as the 1950s has established that quantitative work overload may cause biochemical changes, specifically, elevations in blood cholesterol levels. Numerous medical studies have found that coronary heart disease and heart attacks are related to work overload, for example, by working more than 60 hours a week, holding down two job, and forgoing vacations (Ivancevich and Matteson, 1980). Overload has also been linked to the problem of escapist drinking, which in turn is linked to both health and performance difficulties.

Recently, there is evidence of negative health impacts experienced by workers who continuously operate at high speeds. European data shows that individuals who work at high speed or to tight deadlines report roughly twice the rates of stress, injuries and back, neck and shoulder pain compared to individuals who never work under these pressures (European Foundation for the Improvement of Living and Working Conditions, 2002).

High levels of psychological demand at work — such as having a hectic job, or facing conflicting expectations — also contribute to job strain, which is associated with a range of ill health outcomes, including coronary heart disease (CHD), mental illness, musculoskeletal injuries and cancer (Dunham, 2001; Jones et al., 1998; Schnall et al., 1994).

Life away from work is also affected by heavy work demands. One Canadian worker in three now experiences conflict between work and family (Duxbury and Higgins, 2001), with evidence of similar conflict in the US (Ferber and O'Farrell, 1991), the United Kingdom (Franks, 1999) and Europe (Fagan, 2003). Long hours of work have been directly linked to negative physiological and psychological health symptoms, as well as to family relationship difficulties (Sparks et al., 1997; Landsbergis, 2003). Disturbed relaxation ability, correlated with elevated blood pressure and coronary heart disease, is linked to working more than 50 hours per week (Ertel et al., 2000). A Dutch study found that "leisure sickness" on weekends and holidays, characterized by headaches, sore muscles, fatigue and nausea, is common among employees who are perfectionists, carry large workloads and feel very responsible for their work (Burrell, 2001).

Non-standard hours of work (e.g., rotating shifts, compressed work weeks and irregular hours) have also been linked with ill health (Martens et al., 1999). However, there is conflicting evidence on the health impacts of non-standard, or "flexible," work hours (Sparks et al., 2001). The key seems to lie in whether employees can choose and are satisfied with their hours and schedules (Ala-Mursula et al., 2002; Sparks et al., 2001). Long hours at work may be more detrimental to the health of those workers (most often women) with heavy domestic workloads. The inability to balance work and family, which is exacerbated by long or unpredictable work hours, has also been directly linked with increased stress and ill health (Duxbury et al., 1994; Ertel et al., 2000; Frone et al., 1997).

Precarious Work Arrangements and Health

Working arrangements have undergone a profound transformation in most if not all industrialized countries. In particular, there has been a significant increase in the proportion of the workforce holding part-time or multiple jobs, working at home or in remote locations, and in casual, temporary or short-term positions (Broad, 2000).

Michael Quinlan, a professor at the University of New South Wales in Australia, has been researching regulatory aspects of employment for over 20 years. Noting the significant growth in non-standard work over the past two decades, he has become concerned that there has been little consideration of the health effects of such arrangements. His work suggests that labour market changes — outsourcing, downsizing, the growth of small business and increases in temporary and part-time work — are having negative impacts on worker health due to increased work demands, inadequate health and safety management and lack of enforcement of labour standards (Quinlan et al., 2001).

The specific reasons that many non-standard workers experience poor health are complex and require further study. Such workers may face more difficult working conditions and experience higher levels of job insecurity, lower levels of control over their working conditions and arrangements, a poorer quality of social interaction or particularly heavy demands associated with their employment arrangements (Lewchuk et al., 2003).

Non-standard employment also perpetuates income disparities in society, lengthening the distance between the "haves" and "have-nots" — those with paid, extended healthcare and dental benefits and those without; those with employer-funded pension plans and those without; those with disability coverage and those without. Health researchers are increasingly convinced that inequality in society is associated with worsened health outcomes — for all citizens (Wilkinson, 1996). Hence the polarization of the labour market is of grave concern.

The rise in non-standard work arrangements has increased perceived job insecurity. Jane Ferrie at the University College of London is a leading researcher on the health implications of job insecurity. Over the last 10 years, Ferrie has studied British civil servants who have undergone a program of restructuring that involved repeated periods of job insecurity (Ferrie et al., 1999; Ferrie, 2001). Ferrie has found a consistent impact of perceived job insecurity on psychological health, and growing evidence of a relationship between job insecurity and self-reported ill health. Perceived job insecurity also has negative effects on workers' marital relationships, parenting effectiveness and their children's behaviour (Nolan et al., 2000).

Workers experience job insecurity in response to potential corporate closures, mergers and downsizing, and as a result of working in jobs that are short-term. Downsizing has been linked to increased workplace fatalities, workplace accidents, musculoskeletal injuries and psychiatric disorders (Landsbergis, 2003; Probst and Brubaker, 2001). A study conducted in a

Finnish town found that downsizing results in changes in work, social relationships and health-related behaviours.

Downsizing can lead to a condition called "post-downsizing stress syndrome," or survivor's syndrome, bringing on symptoms of anxiety, guilt, paranoia, mistrust and feelings of hopelessness that spill over into the personal lives of workers (Littler, 2000; Shore, 1996). Turnover and absenteeism rates as well as stress-related disorders increase after downsizing (Appelbaum et al., 1999). Cohen (1997) found that employees who had become disabled after experiencing downsizing took substantially longer to recover. If the downsizing trend continues, the costs associated with employee stress, currently estimated at $200 billion annually in the US (Carter, 1999), will only increase.

The health effects of job insecurity appear to be moderated by the prevailing level of labour market opportunity (Mohr, 2000; Turner, 1995). In other words, job insecurity can be less harmful when there are other employment opportunities available to workers. Indeed, there is a large body of literature exploring the mental and physical ill-health impacts of unemployment (Jahoda, 1982; Warr, 1987). As noted above, emerging research suggests there are also negative health impacts of underemployment, although more research is needed in this area (Dooley, 2003).

The health impacts of employment insecurity and inadequacy are in turn affected by the perceived adequacy and security of income. Price et al. (2002) found that "financial strain" explains a significant portion of the relationship between employment status and subsequent depression. In general, income inadequacy, or poverty, has been clearly established as a predictor of ill health (Raphael, 2001).

Polarization of Income and Health

Income insecurity — and ill health — are not equally distributed. Women and people of colour are more likely to work in low-income jobs, less likely to have benefits and more likely to live in poverty (Jackson, 2005; Maxwell, 2002). Although women increasingly participate in the paid workforce, they are disproportionately represented in part-time or temporary employment (Cranford et al., 2003). Typically, those jobs pay low wages. For instance, of Canadian lone parents who reported wages for 2000, 62.4 percent were earning less than $10 an hour, with 42 percent earning below $8.50 an hour (Campaign 2000, 2003). And single, employed mothers with dependent children are at particular risk of poor psychosocial health (Macran et al., 1996).

Immigrant women are also concentrated in the lowest paid jobs in the service and clerical sectors of the economy — as office cleaners, domestics, workers in food processing factories or the hospitality industry. These jobs are low-status, marginal, unsafe and poorly paid. They often do not correspond to workers' areas of expertise or training since official recognition of foreign credentials remains a serious barrier, as does the inability to converse in an official language. They face stress related to societal discrimination and racism in the workplace (Hajdukowski-Ahmed et al., 1999). In sum, the economic gaps between immigrants and all other Canadians have widened, and people of colour who were born and educated in Canada still have lower earnings than comparable other Canadian workers (Jackson, 2002, 2005).

The pursuit of equity is a moral imperative. However, it is also a concrete pragmatic concern, given emerging evidence that regardless of actual incomes the degree of income inequality at the local and national levels is predictive of poorer health outcomes (Wilkinson, 1996). Hence, the polarization of incomes associated with flexible labour markets is a health concern.

In summary, there is reason to believe that stress or "strain" in today's flexible economy is related not just to the worker's job, but to the worker's experience of the broader organization and arrangements of employment. Further quantitative and qualitative research is needed on the health impacts of cost-cutting and high productivity strategies. However, there is now enough evidence to initiate action to reduce the negative health effects of neoliberal, flexible employment strategies, and to promote the adoption of healthier — and more authentically productive — workplace practices and labour market conditions.

There is compelling evidence that the social organization of work matters profoundly to health. Further research will help to develop a better understanding of the specific dimensions of healthy and unhealthy jobs, and to build support for particular interventions to improve working conditions. Since increasing productivity, not promoting health, is the ultimate aim of economic enterprises in capitalist society, research is also needed to better demonstrate the costs of unhealthy working conditions to businesses and societies in general.

Toward "Healthy Work" in the New Economy

Given the focus on work in contemporary capitalist societies, it is astounding how little attention has been paid to the development of broadly shared policy goals with respect to work. In Canada, government committees and commissions have periodically considered aspects of work (Advisory Committee on the Changing Workplace, 1997; Advisory Committee, 1997; Human Resources Development Canada, 1994), but there has been no broad-based public consultation on the desired future role and nature of work, perhaps because of the neoliberal climate of deregulation.

However, there is reason to believe that such a shared vision may be achievable among workers. There is some consistency in what employees, as a group, want from work: jobs that are interesting (something they like to do), jobs that provide opportunities to develop their abilities, and jobs that allow them to decide how work is done (Lowe, 2000; Polanyi and Tompa, 2004). Some organizational theorists and employers also recognize that providing employees with opportunities for involvement in decisions, training and development, and meaningful work actually increases commitment and economic success, at least in the longer term (Ichniowski et al., 2000; Wood and de Menezes, 1998).

Research on work-related health conditions and productive organizations suggests five interrelated dimensions of healthy and productive work: *availability* and security of work; *adequacy* of income and benefits from work; *appropriateness* of work arrangements and job demands; *active* participation and engagement of workers; and the *appreciation* or support of workers by supervisors and co-workers (see Figure 5.1).

Figure 5.1 Pillars of Healthy Work

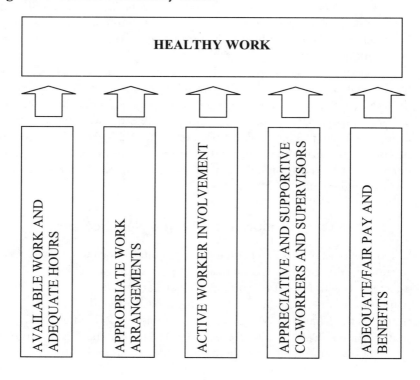

Available Work

Work is central to human existence, fulfilment and well-being. It is not surprising, then, that unemployment and "job creation" have been central public concerns and important agenda items for politicians and social organizations.

What *kind* of jobs should be promoted? Should we support only high-paid, full-time, permanent jobs, as unions often suggest (e.g., Dagg, 1997)? Or should we accept that the provision of high-paid, full-time jobs to all is perhaps neither possible nor desirable, and that a range of work arrangements needs to be promoted? Or, more radically, should we accept that there may no longer be enough paid work for all of us, and instead focus on creating conditions of income security — increasing the viability and highlighting the social value of a range of citizenship roles (e.g., parenting, caregiving and volunteering as well as paid work)?

It may be necessary to emphasize the importance of paid work. However, there has been some rethinking of the relative importance of paid work, versus unpaid work, in recent years. This is partly due to the co-existence of chronic unemployment on one hand, and unaddressed social and community needs on the other. Some observers question whether it is right that paid work is highly rewarded while unpaid family, community and civic contributions go largely unrewarded (Brown and Lauder, 2001). The growing awareness of the importance of early childhood development and social and citizen participation to population health suggests a need to rethink the relative importance and rewards given to waged employment as opposed to broader social and civic participation.

Renewed attention has also been directed towards the idea of a basic income policy over the last decade in Canada (Lerner et al., 1999), the US (Aronowitz et al., 1998) and Europe (Brown and Lauder, 2001; Gorz, 1999). There are difficulties with this approach, including its affordability. However, it does bring attention to the need to radically reform income support programs to help people get and keep work (Battle and Torjman, 2000), and to support a broader conception of work and participation in society. A number of promising attempts have been made to combine labour force adaptability and a solidaristic welfare system, notably by the Danish approach of "flexisecurity" (European Foundation for the Improvement of Living and Working Conditions, 2002b).

Increasing income security would enable workers to refuse jobs that are unsafe and underpaid (see Chapter 6). It would also afford them greater choice and control over their work content, work conditions and work arrangements. At the same time, firms would gain a greater degree of flexibility as workers and their representatives became less economically dependent on long-term job security and more open to a range of different work arrangements. Unfortunately, businesses are slow to support this approach, given that an insecure labour force and unemployed "industrial reserve army" also exert downward pressures on wages, and weaken labour's bargaining position, which meets the profit needs of business in the short term (Magdoff and Magdoff, 2004).

Providing a greater degree of income security will not necessarily change the fact that bad jobs continue to be disproportionately allocated to women, people of colour and people with less education and of a lower socio-economic class. Indeed, socio-economic conditions before working life (childhood and adolescence) and outside of work (social networks, education, employability and financial independence) shape workplace experiences and, thus, levels of health. Hence, a key consideration in all these dimensions of work is to reduce inequalities in the distribution of quality work by gender (Reskin and Padavic, 1994), class (Johnson and Hall, 1999) and race (Das Gupta, 1996).

Adequate Income and Benefits

Most people would agree that those who work should earn an income adequate to their needs. However, minimum wages have stagnated and fallen in Canada and the US, to the point where full-time employment at minimum wage often leaves individuals and families below the poverty line (Maxwell, 2002).

Many authors in Canada and the US call for increases in, and better still, an indexing of minimum wages for both social and economic reasons (Bluestone and Harrison, 2000; Goldberg and Green, 1999; Saunders, 2005). Minimum wages in four of 10 Canadian provinces are currently set so low that a full-time, year-round worker ends up living in poverty (National Council of Welfare, 2004). Workers in Canada need to be paid at least $10 an hour to be safely above the poverty line.

There is also widespread consensus on the need to extend and enforce adequate wages, benefits and rights for non-full-time workers. Books and government reports from both the US (e.g., Herzenberg et al., 1998; Skocpol, 2000) and Canada (Betcherman and Lowe, 1995; Advisory Committee, 1997) recommend the extension of pro-rated benefits, pensions and health insurance to part-time workers. Others suggest that temporary workers should be treated more like permanent workers by their placement agencies (European Foundation, 2002a, 2002b), and that temporary agencies should be obliged to provide benefits (King et al., 2000).

Requiring employers to provide pro-rated benefits to part-time workers would reduce the fixed costs associated with hiring new workers, which currently lead employers to demand overtime work that is often unpaid, rather than spreading the work to more workers (Advisory Committee, 1997). Finally, it should be made easier for workers to transport their pensions from employer to employer (so-called "portable pensions") (Advisory Committee, 1997; Herzenberg et al., 1998).

Appropriate Work Arrangements

Contemporary work and family (or home) lives are highly interdependent as workers — especially women — increasingly combine paid work with family and home responsibilities. We have already seen the health importance of ensuring a fit between the demands of paid jobs and non-work interests and responsibilities. Along with promoting gender balance in household responsibilities, it is essential to increase workers' control over their paid work time — how much they work, when and where.

A first step to increasing worker control over hours is to ensure that even the lowest-paid workers make a living wage (Schor, 1992). A second step is to increase the rights of workers to choose and control their hours of work. This can be achieved by providing them with the option of taking time off in lieu of overtime pay, increasing vacation entitlement and parental and care-giving leave, making it easier for them to change from part-time to full-time and vice versa, and giving them the right to voluntarily reduce work time (Duxbury and Higgins, 2001). Again, enhancing income security by providing a basic income would ensure that workers are in a better position to negotiate and enter into working arrangements that fit their non-work lives (Gorz, 1999).

Providing appropriate work also means linking it to workers' interests, and ensuring it is meaningful and encourages learning and growth (Polanyi and Tompa, 2004). Here again, the importance of increasing worker choice over work content is central.

Active Work

New efforts are needed to ensure that workers are actively contributing members of workplaces. If there are to be more open and flexible legal frameworks surrounding employment arrangements, "the role of workers in decision-making and the need to review and strengthen the existing arrangements for workers' involvement in their companies will also become essential issues" (European Commission, 1997). Proposals for improving democratic voice in companies include electing voluntary single- or multi-employer worker committees, mandating employee participation councils, and enabling greater worker, consumer and community representation on company boards (Herzenberg et al., 1998; Vail et al., 1999). There is an economic rationale for increasing worker participation as well, as there is strong evidence of a positive impact of direct worker participation on quality, cost reduction and increased output (Sisson, 2000). In general, participation programs that have clear and focused aims, a long-term plan, top management commitment, are based on values that are acceptable to both managers and workers, and support training for employees are most likely to succeed (Sagie and Koslovsky, 2000).

Appreciative and Supportive Work Environments

Social support and good social relations make an important contribution to health in various settings (Marmot, 2003). Social support in the workplace refers to overall levels of positive social interactions. Johnson and Hall's (1988) research shows that such support may mitigate the negative health impacts of high psychosocial demands and low job control. Marmot (2003) writes that reducing social inequalities, designing social settings to increase interaction and avoiding actions that devalue or denigrate individuals or groups, for example through prejudice or discrimination, all help to improve levels of social support.

In summary, a range of policy directions seem to offer the possibility of creating social and economic conditions conducive to improved worker health. However, it is important to recognize that different workers in fact want different kinds of jobs, working conditions and arrangements, depending on their interests, life situations and responsibilities, skills, values, personalities and so on (Polanyi and Tompa, 2002). Workers may be more or less able to deal with difficult working conditions, depending on their level of social support, financial independence, employability and education outside of work. This is not to excuse poor working conditions for people who have minimal skills or awareness of other opportunities. Rather, it is to say that workers must have the opportunity to choose and engage in work that fits their desires, interests and needs.

Conclusion

Work is complex and people are diverse, so it is difficult to identify all the desirable dimensions of work. At this point, the specific policies are less important than the need to generate a broad-based dialogue on policy options conducive to healthy and productive work. Stakeholders must work together to articulate a shared vision of work and a program to achieve it. There are promising methodologies for engaging stakeholders in visioning processes (e.g., Polanyi, 2001).

Policies are also influenced by and reflective of the power distribution among various groups in society. Given that neoliberal labour market changes have reduced the power of workers and unions in many places, we need to focus on strategies to rebalance power in workplaces. This could be done by expanding opportunities for representation among high-skilled and autonomous workers, and by developing new forms of representation, such as sector-based systems and multi-employer bargaining systems for smaller service sector firms (Advisory Committee, 1997; Herzenberg et al., 1998).

In part, the task of changing power relations requires changing the structures of decision-making and the opportunities that are provided to influence decisions in various social institutions. We have already spoken of the importance of creating increased opportunities for worker participation at the workplace level. However, there is also a need to broaden opportunities for democratic participation in social and political institutions (government, media, schools, community-based organizations). There is good reason to believe that enhancing democratic participation will lead to more equitable decisions, build social cohesion, increase social support and develop a greater sense of power and capacity among citizens — all of which are essential to good health.

CHAPTER 6

From Welfare to Workfare

Public Policy for the New Economy

Garson Hunter and Dionne Miazdyck-Shield

The modern welfare state in Canada is being redesigned to accommodate employers' needs for economic restructuring in the so-called New Economy. More specifically, in refashioning welfare funding structures and program delivery, modern welfare states have moved from needs-based eligibility, social entitlement and labour market exclusion programs to models that emphasize selective entitlements, active programming and maximum participation in wage labour (Theodore and Peck, 1999: 488). "Active" welfare programming implies that national, standardized programs for welfare have been replaced by local experiments in delivery. This shift, in our view, is not fundamentally new, contrary to the claims made by New Economy public policy analysts that theirs is a *new* approach to public, specifically welfare, policy. We propose that this shift in vision and functioning of welfare programming is designed to meet the needs of the economy and employers, thus conforming to a historic capitalist socio-political dynamic.

In the US, the active welfare programming model is viewed as the "work-first approach" (Peck, 2001; Theodore and Peck, 1999) or "third way neo-liberalism" (Platt, 2003: 21), and in Britain the model is viewed as "Third Way" policy making (Holden, 1999; Jordan and Jordan, 2000; Callinicos, 2001). Welfare change in Canada is a hybrid Third Way policy that combines both the features of US policy and the welfare ideology of Britain (Hunter and Miazdyck, 2003). In this chapter, we refer to the current changes to the modern welfare state as either Third Way public policy or New Economy public policy.

To fully comprehend the effects of the New Economy on the modern welfare state requires an understanding of the relationship between governments and business in Western industrialized nations. A clear definition of the welfare state is crucial to understanding development of social and public policies in capitalist economies. This applies whether the economy is labelled as industrial, post-industrial or New.

"Social policies" are the activities and principles that guide the way the groups that make up a society intervene in and regulate the relationships between individuals, groups, communities and institutions to generally determine the distribution of social resources and the level of well-being of citizens (Barker, 1995: 355). "Public policies" are, more specifically, created by governments and the state, and they most often reflect compromises in the conflicts between different groups in society as represented by political parties and social and political interest groups. "That is, social reforms have been defined and administered as national programs; they have represented the political compromise between a national capitalist class and resistance to its particular forms of exploitation by sections of a national working class or social movements; and they have depended partly on the kind and degree of political alternatives that have evolved in particular nations" (Teeple, 1995: 18). These compromises are unstable situations that are always open to change due to the power shifts among (unequal) groups. This chapter is concerned mainly with public policy, and more specifically with welfare policy or that set of policies and practices that is often called the welfare state.

What is referred to as a welfare state is defined here as the welfare effort, or legislatively sanctioned and publicly or quasi-publicly administered spending on welfare benefits (health, education, social assistance, unemployment, pensions, et cetera) (Hicks, 1999: 168–69). The modern welfare state (often referred to as the Keynesian welfare state[1] refers to a pattern of expansion and development of public policies and services within particular industrialized nations since World War II. The modern welfare state refers to political and policy development in only certain industrialized nations, as not all industrialized nations indeed have a welfare state.[2] Welfare states exist in countries with capitalist economies where "the welfare state can also be seen as a capitalist society in which the state has intervened in the form of social policies, programs, standards, and regulations in order to mitigate class conflict and to provide for, answer, or accommodate certain social needs for which the capitalist mode of production in itself has no solution or makes no provision" (Teeple, 1995: 15).

This is in contrast to, say, a fully functioning socialist economy. In such an economy, where there is no distinct inequality based on owning the means of production, there would be no need for a welfare state. In a society where fundamental social differences do not form the basis for social and political inequality, the provisions made to the populace would not change in response to the labour needs of capital. In addition, services would not fluctuate in response to economic cycles nor reflect the power imbalances that exist between capital and labour and other social groups.

International research has indicated that a key factor in the early development of a welfare state is the degree of working-class mobilization. Hicks (1999: x), for example, concludes "that labor organizations and their politics built the welfare state by exploiting — sometimes quite fortuitously, sometimes most deliberately — the political opportunities offered to them." Therefore, central to the development of a welfare state is an industrialized economy with some history of working-class mobilization. The development of a modern welfare state within a structure of industrialized capitalism and organized labour should therefore more accurately be referred to as "welfare capitalism," and its policies as "capitalist public policy" rather than "public policy."

In this chapter, we will consider whether the approach to the welfare state, and public policy more generally, now common in the NE is actually all that new. Third Way or NE welfare policy, as we said, emphasizes selective entitlements, active programming, and maximum labour market participation. We contend that these are mainly surface changes and that their fundamental purpose is to meet the needs of employers in the NE. Interestingly, and in a seemingly contradictory way, proponents of Third Way welfare policy argue that theirs is a new approach because welfare policy must now conform to the economic and labour market dictates of the (new) economy. As we will see, welfare policy for the past several centuries has had the same goal. In deconstructing the changes they advocate and have wrought, we will show that they are not new because they serve the interests and needs of capitalist employers (and not those of disadvantaged and other citizens).

In analyzing recent welfare changes to determine what is "new" in the New Economy, it is useful to look at the history of industrialized countries. The interplay of public policy and labour predates the Industrial Revolution of the 1780s and the consolidated capitalist economy of the 1850s. Therefore, we examine public policy under the (mercantilist) economy that preceded a consolidated capitalist economy and public policy within semifeudal economies for any overall similarities in their intent. Covering the past 700 years, ours, however, must be only a cursory examination of the history of welfare/public policy.

A Brief History of Public Policy and the Economy

During pre-Elizabethan times (prior to the mid-sixteenth century), before the development of the English *Poor Law*, religious Canon Law stressed the innocence of poverty (Golding and Middleton, 1982; Himmelfarb, 1984). The destitute were not seen as morally inadequate. "Those who were blessed not with poverty but with riches had the sacred duty of charity, the obligation to sustain the holy poor and to relieve the misery of the unholy" (Himmelfarb, 1984: 4). However, the obligations to the poor (i.e., the majority) would end at the point where they interfered with the well-established and powerful class of landed interests who dominated the institutions of power at that time.

The fourteenth century Black Death pandemic wiped out perhaps a third of the population of Europe, including England, leaving the remaining labourers in a position of some power. The existing state, to the benefit of the landed class, introduced the [First] *Statute of Labourers* legislation in 1349, the precursor of 400 years of English *Poor Law* (Dolgoff and Feldstein, 2000: 43).

Under the emerging mercantile system, and as a result of land enclosure, the labour organization of England was regulated by the *Poor Law* and the *Statute of Artificers* (Polanyi, 1957: 86). Commenting upon the intent of the poor laws, Ziegler (1998: 256–57) writes that through these measures the government restricted the rights of labourers to seek higher wages and leave their place of employment, made the giving of alms to the able-bodied unemployed illegal and codified wages. The thrust of the public policy, as exemplified in these laws, was to restrict the rights of labourers in favour of the interests of the landed class. The landed class of England judged all persons poor if they did not have an income that could keep them in leisure (Polanyi, 1957). "Poor" was synonymous with what was known as the "common people," and the common people were made up of all but the landed classes. "Hence the term 'poor' meant all people who were in need and all the people, if and when they were in need. This, of course, included paupers, but not them alone. The aged, the infirm, the orphans had to be taken care of in a society which claimed that within its confines there was a place for every Christian" (Polanyi, 1957: 87).

Separate from those not expected to work were the able-bodied and the paupers; the least deserving among the poor being the paupers, who were able to perform manual work. Beggary among this group was to be severely punished, and repeated vagrancy was a capital offence (Piven and Cloward, 1971: 15). The burden of providing relief (currently referred to as welfare or social assistance) fell upon the parish, which taxed householders to pay for it. This taxation was not looked upon favourably by the landed class, who pressed to have control over those they supported.

> The Poor Law Act of 1601, the famous "43 Elizabeth," consolidated earlier legislation.... [I]t regulated relief for the impotent poor, employment for the able-bodied and correction for the wilfully idle. These triple aims of work discipline, deterrence and clas-

sification became the purpose of poor law policy for two centuries, until the institutions it created could no longer support the massive poverty and distress its inadequacies produced.... Patrician concern for the poor touched by Christian morality now acquired the sharper flavour of the taxpayers' more pragmatic demands. (Golding and Middleton, 1982: 11)

In addition to the landed interests, public policy (poor law) was also being adjusted to serve the needs of the emerging and growing business community.

The economic system of the time, a developing mercantilism coupled with an emerging industrial capitalism, produced a new class of merchants, bankers and industrialists who demanded changes to public policies to serve their particular interests (Saville, 1994). The increasing power of this new capitalist class, especially from the growth in international trade and later in industrialization, was such that the ruling class of landowners realized that some sharing of power was inevitable.

The eventual emergence of industrial capitalism (early 1800s) and its new economic arrangements necessitated reforms to the *Poor Laws*, which were ushered into place in 1834. The historian E.P. Thompson (1968: 295) viewed the *Poor Law Act* of 1834 as perhaps the most sustained attempt to impose an ideological dogma, in defiance of the evidence of human need, in English history. Writing on the *Poor Law* of nineteenth century England, Titmuss (1968: 189) commented:

> The essential, though financially reluctant, role of the poor law was to support industrialism and the attempt in the nineteenth century to establish a completely competitive, self-regulating market economy founded on the motive of individual gain. It has had to create a great many rules of expected behaviour; about work and non-work, property, savings, family relationships, cohabitation, men-in-the-house, and so forth.

Documenting the transition to capitalism in early nineteenth century America, Katz (1989) also links social welfare policy for the unemployed to the redefinition of poverty as an errant moral condition. Katz (1989: 14) suggests that the redefinition of poverty "served to justify the mean-spirited treatment of the poor, which in turn checked expenses for poor relief and provided a powerful incentive to work." This moral definition of poverty helped to ensure a supply of low-cost labour for the market economy.

During the latter decades of the nineteenth century and early twentieth century, some governments began to introduce old age pensions, such as Germany in 1889, England in 1908 and Canada in 1927. The programs were extremely selective, benefiting only a small group of the unemployed and/or poor. Depressions during the 1880s and 1890s highlighted the limited ability of private charities to deal with unemployment and poverty. The depression of 1893 saw work introduced as a type of welfare program in the form of public works projects, such as street cleaning, street paving, construction, rather than mandating it as a condition of receiving welfare (Katz, 2001: 63).

In sum, several centuries of economic and political development show a clear pattern. Various forms of governments enacted legislation and developed welfare programs that did provide some level of benefits to poor and working people. However, more importantly, these programs, from the British *Poor Law* through to the public works programs of the 1890s, were more designed to respond to the needs of employers and the structure of the economy. The theme running through this history is that by ensuring that people do not have resources, they cannot significantly resist the employer-imposed discipline of the labour market.

Creation of the Modern, Keynesian Welfare State

Following the depression of the 1930s and the rise of labour militancy, governments introduced a number of social programs (for example, the New Deal in the US) to alleviate the threat of further social disruption. Again, the inability of private charity to deal with poverty and misery was evident. Public works projects appeared again, similar (although much larger in scope) to those of the depression of 1893. The main contribution of the New Deal, however, was "to assert the primacy of government in the field of social welfare" (Katz, 2001: 142).

The New Deal was not, in fact, about subsuming economic policy within social policy but rather rescuing capitalism "run rampant." While having the government assume the primary role for overseeing social welfare during the New Deal may have mitigated the extremes of poverty and misery, it also, and more importantly, protected the legitimacy of the market system during a time of social militancy. An important theme of public policy is that, even when it is introduced in response to social agitation, it will be framed to best reflect the interests of the most powerful group. Noam Chomsky (1993: 16) put it in more forthright terms in paraphrasing Adam Smith in *Wealth of Nations*:

> "The wealth of nations" is no concern of the "architects of policy," who, as Smith insists, seek private gain. The fate of the common people is no more their concern than that of the "mere savages"

who stand in the way. If an "invisible hand" sometimes provided others with benefits, that is merely incidental.

At the end of the Second World War, the lessons that governments had learnt from dealing with worker militancy and social unrest during the 1930s were not lost. "All western countries (introduced) income protection programs, won in response to the political mobilization of poor and working people over the course of the twentieth century" (Piven, 2002: 19). These income protection programs took many forms, from unemployment insurance, medicare and government health insurance, and enhanced forms of social assistance to those unable to work. In general terms, these programs, often referred to as an entitlements-based approach, were based on three principles. First, they were social entitlements — that is, citizens were entitled to these protections simply by virtue of being citizens. Second, they were based on need only — that is, anyone, even the able-bodied unemployed, was eligible for funding simply by being unable to provide for oneself. Third, the programs were based on labour market exclusion — those who didn't have jobs were eligible simply because they were unemployed; looking for a job was not the basis for receiving benefits. In many important ways, this kind of welfare policy actually contributed to economic redistribution by transferring income, through the taxation and social assistance programs, from those who were comfortable and those who were well off to those who did not have enough to live on. With millions of people leaving military service and the economy expanding, governments applied these lessons from past labour militancy to creating the modern welfare state.

Based on a general consensus, during and immediately after World War II, Western governments adopted a more interventionist, or Keynesian, approach to the economy. This is the period during which "economic statism" developed, as governments took a direct role in regulating the economy. They did this by providing various kinds of incentives for business investment, including vast expenditures in military spending, especially in the US. Along with business and economic development subsidies, governments also dramatically increased spending on roads, infrastructure and the suburbanization of metropolitan areas. This pattern continued from the 1940s through the 1970s.

Moscovitch and Drover (1987: 13) suggest that Canada's state expenditures can be explained by two hypotheses: "1) the necessity of state intervention to assure continued private capital accumulation and profitability, and 2) the necessity of state social intervention, including expenditures on social welfare programs, to regulate labour in the workplace and at home by diminishing the cost to capital of a mobile, available, and appropriately educated labour force." Social expenditures therefore reduce the costs of production, which assists private capital accumulation, and the expenditures legitimize the social order. Conversely, the more stable and potentially less volatile the industrialized country, the less need for social programming. It is within the state (government, judicial and executive branches) that the struggles between big and small capital, finance and industry, rulers and the ruled are resolved, "reflecting the interests of the most powerful and dominant factions while at the same time attempting to secure the collective rule of the whole" (Jones and Novak, 1999: 114).

During these first decades after WWII, the modern, Keynesian welfare state developed to better complement the employment needs of the capitalist labour market. But the economic expansion due to government interventionist expenditures of the 1950s through the 1970s began to slow down in the mid 1970s. The next upswing of profits in the business cycle resulted from a dramatic lowering of corporate income taxes, the shedding of labour and the de-unionization of large segments of the labour force, the development of "free trade" agreements that allowed capital access to high-profit sectors in other nations, and the government advancement of the so-called New Economy.

As Chapters 1 and 2 show, a contingent, flexible workforce and free trade (the globalized economy) are tools of business in the New Economy. The New Economy welfare state reflects and supports these economic changes. Public policies of the welfare state are now being modified to adapt to the current labour force needs of capital, shifting from a Keynesian welfare approach to a neoliberal, workfare approach that modifies public policy to fit the desire of business for a "flexible workforce" (Broad, 2000). Within the current period of neoliberal dominance, wherein market interests are the major priority of nearly every government, public policy is being redefined.

Third Way Welfare Policy

Proponents of the Third Way claim that theirs is an innovative, modern approach to public policy capable of meeting the challenges of the twenty-first century New Economy. In defending changes to public policy, two arguments are used: (1) that government intervention and economic redistribution are wrongheaded; and (2) that globalization forces us to minimize government spending, accept a weaker labour position and cut back social programs. The message is that there is no alternative, we must adjust and adapt.

The Third Way and Welfare Dependency

Advocates believe a Third Way approach is needed because the entitlement-based approach has failed to acknowledge the importance of the market system in the new global economy (Callinicos, 2001). With the economic consequences of global integration, the autonomy of nation-states has been greatly reduced. Therefore, the economic statism of a particular form of entitlement-based eligibility welfare system has been rendered obsolete. Economic statism is an approach that points in the wrong direction, for the economic game has changed.

In its widely circulated brochure, *Agenda: Jobs and Growth, Improving Social Security in Canada*, the Canadian government states: "Our social security system must protect those most in need, people who can't work, low-income families struggling to get by, people who face barriers due to disability or chronic illness, and especially children" (Government of Canada, 1994a: 20). The brochure continues: "Many people spend years on social assistance — even though, with the right kind of employment and training support, they could find work. One problem is, CAP (Canada Assistance Plan) rules prevent the use of federal funding to provide the support they need. As a result, the system doesn't help people prepare for work. In many cases, it does just the opposite" (Government of Canada, 1994a: 20). The document further states:

> The social security system seems to keep people on a treadmill, instead of helping to solve their problems. People who want to get off welfare and provide better lives for their children often find the rules stacked against them. We need a system that works for people — a system that supports their efforts to regain self-sufficiency, and works better at reducing child poverty. (Government of Canada, 1994a: 8)

Social assistance, a system designed to help the resourceless unemployable, is instead now portrayed as trapping the employable on a "welfare treadmill." The federal government states: "But too many recipients spend many years on social assistance even though, with the right sort of employment and training support, they could successfully make the transition from welfare to work, from dependency to self-sufficiency" (Government of Canada, 1994b: 72). Welfare is presented as a system that has inadvertently promoted dependency among people who are actually employable.

New Economy public policy is viewed as an approach to rectify some of the mistakes of the old welfare state. Public policy during the modern Keynesian welfare state was based primarily on the concept of entitlement with little to say about responsibility, the assumption being that the state has a duty to offer assistance to citizens with no other resources or options for support. According to its Third Way detractors, the policy of entitlement was a "passive" income support that did little to stimulate employment. Today the Organisation for Economic Co-operation and Development (OECD) wishes to see what it terms an "active society," which represents a wide range of reforms that include linking cash benefits (welfare) to work-oriented incentives across a broad range of options (Gilbert 2004). Britain, Australia, New Zealand, the United States, Canada and the Scandinavian countries, have all developed work-oriented welfare policies. Along with the transition from passive to active policies, programs have moved from a "needs-based" approach (the financially destitute having a right to social benefits) to one focused on the responsibilities of recipients to find work, to be self-sufficient and to lead a productive life. Speaking from a Canadian perspective, Chris Axworthy (1999: 279), former federal member of parliament, former Saskatchewan justice minister and Third Way advocate, observes: "Not much has flowed from this [passive] approach other than entitlement to receive a cheque — no responsibility to prepare for old age, look for work, seek the skills needed for the workplace, relocate to a job, provide for our children, etc. Worse yet, there has been no empowerment." The assumption is that entitlement-based social programs of the modern welfare state create dependency among the recipients; they are passive programs that do not work.

Axworthy and other Third Way advocates see the continuation of entitlement-based public policy without responsibilities as unworkable. Canada and the rest of the world, we are told, must face and adjust to the new global economy. "Social programs must change to keep up with new realities — realities around a changing economy, around unmanageable public debt and around problems with the programs themselves" (Axworthy, 1999: 283). The public policy solution to the challenges presented by the new global economy is to give people receiving government assistance "the chance to acquire the skills inventory they need for the current workplace and the chance to be as independent as possible — a hand up rather than a handout" (Axworthy, 1999: 283).

Therefore, people should have the right to help from the community when they need it, regardless of the cause of that need. This help should be given regardless of the causes that lead to the need, but with a caveat:

> We need to take on faith their despair and their need for help from their community. But it does not, and should not, end there. We must demand and expect a real partnership. We must demand, in

return for this acceptance, for this unquestioning help, a commitment to a return to self-sufficiency (Axworthy, 1999: 281).

With respect to welfare recipients, Axworthy does not see that social-program rights should end with eligibility for income assistance. Partnered with the responsibility to become self-sufficient, social-program rights are actually expanded. "Job training, education and skills upgrading, entrepreneurial training, child care, jobs and other programs that assist Canadians to re-enter the paid workforce should be seen as rights too" (Axworthy, 1999: 281). The commitment from government welfare recipients, then, in their quest for self-sufficiency, is to become employed within the labour market. "For those able to take advantage of expanded, enhanced employment, education and training opportunities, it will be imperative that they do" (Axworthy, 1999: 283). Accordingly, work in all its forms is good, and the quality of that employment is not an issue for welfare programmers.

To be without employment, apparently, unless one is rich or disabled, is to be outside of the community. The corollary that people on welfare are excluded from full citizenship has its genesis in conservative ideology. Jones and Novak (1999: 188) comment:

> The primary aim of social inclusion and cohesion is therefore to bind the excluded back into the labour market as a solution to the problem. That this may result in their continuing poverty is conveniently overlooked, since it is their inclusion (whether self-imposed or structural) that is the problem rather than their poverty.

New Economy advocates of rights and responsibilities have not extended their analysis to members of society who benefit immensely from the tax laws and publicly subsidized loans that allow them to accumulate considerable wealth. They do not mention that group's responsibilities to the community for receiving a "hand up." Gilbert (2004: 65) comments:

> But the discourse on balancing rights and responsibilities has not concentrated on   the diverse obligations that might attend the full spectrum of benefits derived from social rights. Rather, the moral calculus of this equation has been applied almost exclusively to the unemployed poor — whose rights to social benefits are being weighted against the recipient's efforts to be financially self-supporting.

Within the logic of New Economy public policy, citizenship for individuals and families is defined as having a "job, [being] self-sufficient contributing to society with access to education, health care and security" (Saskatchewan Social Services, 1999). Typical of neoliberal states, according to Saskatchewan Social Services (1999) this is "A New Way of Doing Business." Seemingly at odds, however, with the goal of individual self-sufficiency, if the work is poorly paid, with few or no benefits, the government will offer programs that support that work, and hence, the individual or family's community integration. But neither the contradictions between self-sufficiency (i.e., the individual pursuit of wealth in a market-based society) and membership in a community, nor the additional responsibility and obligations of welfare recipients to the community are explained. Moreover, the idea that self-sufficiency is contrary to human nature is totally ignored.

We see what in essence is a shift from welfare to workfare priorities because, for New Economy public policy advocates, global changes and markets have created a need for the change. The old way of delivering programs is supposedly no longer viable and thus requires change. Anthony Giddens, a prominent British academic and Third Way advocate, observes, "The left has to get comfortable with markets, with the role of business in the creation of wealth, and the fact that private capital is essential for social investment" (cited in Callinicos, 2001: 8). According to Third Way and New Economy advocates, if state management of the economy was ever a feasible idea, it is now certainly a discredited one.

It is more than just interesting to note Giddens' claim. In his argument that the Third Way is new, he is actually saying it is not. For he is insisting that public welfare policy must conform to the dictates of the (new) economy — that we must get "comfortable with markets." But this is not new — as our history discussion above shows, public policy in capitalist society has conformed to the needs of the economy (read: capitalists and markets) for centuries. Thus, he and other Third Way proponents are really only advocating for a new face on a very old policy. Just as is argued elsewhere in this book, the New in New Economy and new public policy is fundamentally the same old capitalism.

Ultimately, what the Left has to offer to the New Economy that separates and defines it from the Right are alternate values (Callinicos, 2001: 8), through the stressing of community, opportunity, fairness and social justice. Put another way, Piven and Cloward assert that "the key to an understanding of relief-giving is in the functions it serves for the larger economic and political order, for relief is a secondary and supportive institution" (Piven and Cloward, 1971: xiii). These authors maintain that welfare policies are expanded during times of unemployment and civil disorder, but are restricted at other times to enforce work norms (Piven and Cloward, 1971:

xiii). Therefore, the main functions of welfare are to maintain civil order and to enforce work discipline, both of which serve capitalism. These priorities have become clear with New Economy public policy.

The Third Way, Globalization and Free Trade

The second reason that Third Way advocates offer for moving away from an entitlement-based welfare state is that globalization is inevitable. Opinions on the consequences of globalization are varied but the common thread in Third Way literature is that the welfare state must accommodate this new "reality." The ability of national governments to enact policies is curtailed by globalization. Commenting on public policy changes in Canada, Graham and Al-Krenawi (2001: 417) write: "As companies compete in an increasingly international marketplace, the demands upon national governments to restrict welfare may grow."

For an export-driven economy such as Canada, trade is crucial, and in the 1980s the focus of business was to maximize Canada's potential as a trading partner. McQuaig (2001: 55) argues that the impetus for a free trade agreement came from corporate leaders in the US who were set on ending government protectionism of the service industry and reducing corporate responsibility to meet "performance requirements." With very few protectionist measures in place in Canada in the first place, it was obvious that there was more at stake for business to push the 1988 *Free Trade Agreement* (FTA) between Canada and the US than simply reducing tariffs. Merrett (1996: 15) argues that the desire "to restructure the Canadian economy along neoconservative lines," that is to enshrine corporate rights, limit the power of labour and reduce the welfare state, was the real reason for originally pushing free trade with the US.

The 1994 *North American Free Trade Agreement* (NAFTA), signed by the participating governments of Canada, Mexico and the United States, allows businesses to ask their respective government to seek formal resolutions against other governments if local policies or trade decisions are undesirable to those businesses. "The treaties contain clauses used as levers to extend the agenda of [corporate] capital against state intervention, including measures to decrease or erase welfare statism" (Collier, 1997: 89). Altering domestic economic and social policies and programs to suit business interests creates a harmonization of policy within the partners' trade agreement (Swenarchuk, 2001).

With the signing of NAFTA, Canada has come under increased pressure to harmonize its social policies with the lower standards of the US and Mexico (Pulkingham and Ternowetsky, 1996a). Canada has moved away from adequate federal cost-sharing with the provinces for health care, post-secondary education and welfare leaving these programs financed mostly by the individual provinces without enforceable national standards. Consequently, the door has been opened to privatization and workfare programs. The pressure to adopt this New Economy public policy in Canada is largely a direct consequence of the business lobby that led to the creation of NAFTA. Peck (2001: 215) comments:

> For all the talk of globalization in Canada, much of the competition the country faces is originating from just south of the border. And just as the *North American Free Trade Agreement* (NAFTA) has accelerated and deepened the process of economic continentalization, so also it seems that pressures are mounting for a "downward convergence" in public policy.

While neoliberal concerns such as fighting the deficit and creating a trade and investment friendly business environment have conveniently provided an avenue for social spending, there is potential for direct legal attacks on social programs. In Chapter 12 of NAFTA, many public policy measures such as income security, social security and heath programs are relatively protected. However, countries are expected to grant the same rights to service providers from outside the country under the *Most-Favored-Nation* clause. Therefore, future trade challenges based on expropriation and compensation for increased government regulations, non-discrimination or procurement may deem a public program a trade barrier (Canadian Centre for Policy Alternatives, 2002). McQuaig (2001: 65) points out that trade challenges to public regulations and services under NAFTA "raises the issue of whether public programs could be seen as interfering with the private, profit-making rights of foreign corporations, and if so, is that an unacceptable infringement of the rights of foreign investors?" Public programs could be seen as monopolies, and therefore, services that are currently non-profit, protected or subsidized by the government could be deemed trade barriers and challenged under the Chapter 11 clause of NAFTA, particularly if those services are privatized in the US (McQuaig 2001).

However, by strategically citing the ethereal concept of "globalization" as the reason for policy change rather than trade agreements, leaders have brought Third Way public policy to Canada. The shape that this New, Third Way Economy has taken has not been benign, but has been an imposition of neoliberal policies such as deregulation, trade liberalization and privatization by those with economic power. The shift towards New Economy social welfare policy became most obvious in Canada in the 1990s.

The New Economy and Americanization
of Canadian Public Policy

The New Economy era changes to the welfare system in Canada have been similar to those in the US. The Government of Canada, in fact, acknowledges the similarities: "The US context is important because it provides a significant body of literature and similar thrust as found in Canadian reforms" (Human Resources Development Canada, 2000).

In 1996, the US replaced its entitlement-based, federal Aid To Families with Dependent Children (AFDC) welfare program with the *Personal Responsibility and Work Reconciliation Act* (PRWORA). The PRWORA decentralized the controlling influence of the federal government, with each state now being allowed to develop individual welfare delivery experiments. Funding under the new act was provided to the individual states as block grants rather than through jointly developed programs for which the federal government provides funding.[3] The act included significant cuts to existing programs and fundamentally changed the welfare system with the introduction of the Temporary Assistance to Needy Families (TANF) program (Karger and Stoesz, 1998: 273–74). Under TANF, there is no entitlement to assistance and states are free to determine which families receive help. Also federal "participation" standards on the proportion of welfare recipients in workfare programs and limits on the length of time families can receive welfare were eliminated.

Canada has followed a similar path. Under the old, Keynesian, cost-shared Canada Assistance Plan (CAP), people in need were entitled to assistance. Provincial welfare officials often violated that condition of CAP, but nonetheless it was designed as an entitlement program. Also, importantly, although provinces experimented with workfare programs, recipients did not have to participate in training or workfare programs to be entitled to assistance under CAP. In 1996, the Canadian government replaced CAP with the *Canada Health and Social Transfer* (CHST) *Act*. The CHST was established as a block-funded program transferring money from the federal government to the provincial and territorial governments. With no guidelines attached to the CHST, provinces were allowed to experiment with their own welfare delivery. Gone under the new CHST were the national welfare program standards of needs-based eligibility and the voluntary nature of training and participation in workfare programs. Since 2003, the CHST has been further divided into the Canada Health Transfer (CHT) and the Canada Social Transfer (CST). In spite of these changes, however, the combined financial investment from the federal government has not been restored to the level that it was under CAP, nor have national standards been emphasized.

The neoconservative Fraser Institute, a frankly New Economy and new public policy booster, identifies the introduction of the CHST legislation as an opportunity for provinces to experiment with welfare delivery:

> The creation of the CHST has given the go-ahead to Canadian provinces to move forward with innovative reforms and experimentation with the delivery of social assistance and social services. In doing so, provincial governments would be wise to consider the experiences of our neighbours to the south. (Schafer, Emes, and Clemens, 2001: 57)

The Fraser Institute's recommendations for Canada's welfare system, gleaned from the "best" of US experiences, include moves to: (1) end the entitlement to welfare; (2) divert potential recipients; (3) implement full-check sanctions; (4) implement immediate work requirements; (5) focus on employment, not training and education; (6) allow private for-profit welfare providers; and (7) encourage the involvement of faith-based non-profit organizations (Schafer, Emes and Clemens, 2001: 55–57).

Canada's movement towards workfare has more closely followed the example of the US than that of the UK. Unlike the UK, the US never established a national system of means-tested welfare. Individual US states opposed the implementation of a national program as an infringement on state rights, and under the federal AFDC, each state retained considerable leeway in the delivery of welfare programs (Jones and Novak, 1999: 189-90).

Individual provinces in Canada have always had the constitutional responsibility for welfare, for what we know today as social services. As the concept of entitlement developed in the Canadian welfare state, the federal government built a quasi- standardized, national welfare program under CAP to ensure universal standards. Individual provinces, however, were still responsible for administering welfare. The federal government used the CHST to cut funding to welfare while pointing to the "historic" jurisdiction that the provinces had over welfare programs, suggesting that the move was simply to devolve responsibility for the program back to the provinces. By returning responsibility to the provinces, the Canadian government succeeded in dissolving national standards and opening the door to New Economy policy changes, such as labour force attachment projects and workfare.

Local experimentation with welfare programming presents an advantage to the federal governments in the US and Canada. The advantage to a national government of decentralizing welfare standards is that reforms at the state or provincial level still allow for the advancement of a national reform agenda. Provincial experiments in individual welfare delivery have the advantage of appearing to be local responses to local labour situations without restriction from the federal government.

> It would be quite wrong, then, to dismiss local work-welfare experiments as merely local experiments. Self-evidently, they have material effects on "local people," but more broadly, they open up the political and institutional space for extralocal change. Still sensitive about U.S. imports, especially in highly charged fields like public policy, Canadian governments have set about the task of growing their own welfare-to-work programs. (Peck, 2001: 232)

For the federal government in Canada, extra-local change is facilitated by the joint federal-provincial/territorial Canada Child Tax Benefit (CCTB) program. Within the structure of the CCTB, the provinces can carry out their own localized workfare experiments under the umbrella of wage subsidy programs for low-income working families. The federal CHST program supports provincial savings in welfare expenditures due to increased federal spending going to low-wage subsidy programs for working families with children.[4] Resultantly, local welfare experimentation allows the introduction of sweeping welfare changes on a national scale. "This is certainly one of the reasons why local 'models' and policy ideas have been so effective in framing, channeling, and levering wider regulatory reform, even if in a conveniently circular fashion they are merely confirming and concretizing the predispositions of national policy makers" (Peck, 2001: 232).

In the Third Way UK and the US, there have been parallels in the federally orchestrated decentralization and localized experimentation of welfare programming. While accounting for differences between the two countries, Theodore and Peck (1999: 489) identify the common factors of eliminating federal entitlements, switching to block funding and instituting work-participation requirements. In Canada, the first two factors have been implemented by the federal government's CHST and cancellation of CAP, and the third by the provinces and their localized welfare delivery. With the cancellation of CAP, the provincial governments have been allowed to localize their welfare delivery policies and introduce their own workfare-styled programs more suited to the New Economy.

The Future of the Welfare State

New Economy public policy is changing the face of the welfare state. However, the current restructuring of welfare policy is not, in terms of the fundamental goals and effects, a qualitative break from the "old" or Keynesian welfare state and a shift to something new. Rather, New Economy public policy simply continues the pre-welfare state policy, in that, "The workfare offensive against the [Keynesian] welfare state and its rights-based benefits is an effort to construct a new system of labor regulation, to enforce work under the new conditions of casualisation, falling wages and underemployment that characterises postindustrial labor markets" (Piven and Cloward, 2001: x). The modern welfare state was developed in the decades immediately following World War II, when unemployment was relatively low and workers could expect lifelong employment from one employer and a wage that a family could live on. At that time, the welfare state served business needs by supplying a low-wage labour pool, controlling social unrest during a period of increased expectations from the citizenry, and providing a minimum living standard for those who could not work (Piven and Cloward, 1971).

With the economic restructuring that has been occurring since the early 1970s and a business community that increasingly seeks to impose "flexible employment" with low wages, no job security and little in the way of benefits, we see the income-support programs of the welfare state being adjusted accordingly. Current welfare programs are increasingly unliveable, with grossly inadequate benefits, time limits and workfare or constant work-search requirements. Essentially, they are designed to keep people off social assistance by forcing them into low-income, insecure employment that provides enough of an income supplement to disqualify families from welfare. This thereby assures business the "flexible" labour force it desires for profit especially in service sector and temporary employment. In effect, current welfare programming is subsidizing the wages for the low-income labour force. "Under conditions of falling wages, chronic underemployment, and job casualization, workfarism maximizes (and effectively mandates) participation in contingent, low-paid work by churning workers back into the bottom of the labour market, or by holding them deliberately 'close' to the labour market in a persistently 'job-ready' state" (Peck, 2001: 13–14). The welfare state in Canada has taken this direction with an increasing number of programs designed to keep workers in the labour force despite low wages, little or no job security, few if any benefits and short-term employment. And, as our brief history of welfare policy showed, the fact that Third Way, NE welfare policy serves the long-term, fundamental needs of employers is not new. Given its goals and effects, it is a substantial stretch of the imagination for NE welfare policy to be declared new.

A recent study from Statistics Canada indicated that nearly one-third of Canadian workers (1.7 million) were in low-paying jobs as of December 1996 (Janz, 2003: 4).[5] Less than one-half of those workers were able to get out of those low-paying jobs by 2001. The workers who were most likely to succeed were those who were able to move to full-time employment in large unionized firms. For those who remained at the same job, upward mobility was most likely to occur for individuals who increased their hours of work. Of the 53 percent of the workers who remained "trapped" in low-paid work, they were more likely to be working part-time for small, non-unionized organizations.

With the neoliberal rush to embrace labour-force attachment as the best social program, current changes to welfare programming beg the question: what of those who remain on welfare? As social assistance programming becomes increasingly marginalized, what of those who rely on it? These are the people with the most fragile connection to the labour force due to health, age, disability, education and the myriad other reasons for being on social assistance. Not only are they poor, but also they are the poorest of the poor in society. "To know something of that service — the treatment of the most impoverished — says a great deal about society's humanity and commitment to social justice" (Jones, 2001).

For all its faults, modern Keynesian welfare policy was a step in the right direction. Even though the fundamental goal of Keynesianism was to preserve capitalism, the labour and social movement unrest of the post-World War II era did provide, at least, a human face for capitalism. The actual policies and programs resulting from the belief that social welfare benefits are rights, not privileges to be earned, not only provided the poorest of the poor with some modicum of dignity and less-than-abject poverty. The so-called social safety net that developed in that era also benefited working people in their struggles with employers because they had less to fear from the age-old threat of unemployment. These ideas are now being attacked in theory and practice by NE welfare policies.

Canada has not gone far down the road to its own New Economy welfare state so it is difficult to predict the outcome. It is not the intent of the authors of this chapter to suggest that the modern welfare state represents the "good old days" to which we could return to solve current problems. However, the movement towards NE public policy certainly represents a significant regression in social welfare policy and programming. The Third Way, NE welfare policy changes have become a *Poor Law* for the twenty-first century (Jones, 2001).

There is no easy solution to the growing disparity between the haves and the have-nots in the New Economy welfare state. Social welfare programs should, of course, be defended and improved. The next two chapters look beyond, stressing the role of social movements in affecting fundamental social change. The only real solution is for working people and the poor to disrupt the functioning of society and struggle for something better. How, where or when such disruptions might occur is difficult to predict, but one thing is clear. While public policy is important, we must remember that social justice has never resulted from policies of the elite but from the broader social policy struggles of working people and the poor. The same will be true for advances in social welfare in the twenty-first century.

Notes

1. It is often called so because many attribute the main features of the modern welfare state to the theorizing and policy development of the British economist John Maynard Keynes.
2. The industrialized nations of Japan, South Korea and Indonesia have not developed welfare states similar to those in Scandinavia, Britain, Australia, New Zealand, Canada and, to a lesser extent, the US. Additionally, no developing country has produced a welfare state based upon the above definition. Therefore, being an industrialized nation appears to be a necessary condition for the development of a welfare state, but it is not a sufficient condition to that development.
3. Under block grants, receiving states can use the money as they see fit.
4. The National Child Benefit (NCB) program, a partnership between the federal government and the provinces and territories, is only available to low-income working families with children.
5. Low-paid workers were defined in the study as individuals with weekly earnings of less than $410.70 at the end of December 1996. A low-paid worker was considered to have "moved up" if her or his income had increased to at least $496.86 a week by 2001. The 2001 weekly rate was 10 percent higher than the 2001 Statistics Canada low-income cut-off for a family of two living in an urban area of at least half a million people.

CHAPTER 7

"Solidarity Forever" in Cyberspace?

Responses of the Labour Movement to Information and Communication Technologies

James P. Mulvale

Over the last 25 years, information and communication technologies (ICTs) have had a profound impact on paid work and workers. This chapter will highlight some of the many and contradictory effects of the ICTs, now celebrated as part of the New Economy, on paid work and workers. It will also explore the implications of these changes for the labour movement in Canada and throughout the world.

What follows is an exploratory discussion rather than a definitive analysis or set of detailed predictions or prescriptions. In one sense this is only fitting, as the applications and control of ICTs in the paid workplace are shifting and contested terrain for employers, workers and broader social forces on both sides of the labour-capital divide.

Assessing the Impacts of ICTs on Paid Work

According to Lowe (2000: 73), "Canadian evidence suggests that on balance, information technology has created more jobs than it has destroyed." However, the impact of ICTs varies across sectors of the labour force. For instance,

> Inadequate investment in technology and the accompanying skills may hinder the competitiveness of certain firms, making them vulnerable to low-cost producers in developing countries. Between 1986 and 1991, for example, 100,000 manufacturing jobs were lost [in Canada] in industries that used little information technology (for inventory control systems, product design, or in the manufacturing process itself); these were mainly fabricating and assembly

jobs — the kind of work that can be done more cheaply in Mexico and China. (p. 73)

Two general trends related to ICTs have confronted workers in Canada. First, there has been a significant shifting of jobs away from the (relatively high-paying, secure) manufacturing sector, to the (relatively low-paying, insecure) service sector (Broad, 2000; Vosko, 2000). Second, ICTs (along with neoliberal ideological campaigning on the inevitability of "globalization" and international trade agreements that serve the interests of multinational corporations) have greatly facilitated the flight of capital and jobs to poor countries, where workers are paid far less and usually lack the protections of unions, employment standards and work-related benefits such as insurance and health plans (see Chapters 1 and 2).

The increasingly central role of ICTs has also affected social relations between workers and managers/owners at the point of production in profound and multi-faceted ways (see Chapter 3). Some types of work have become more varied, interesting and autonomous for employees. But in many other cases, ICTs have enabled managers and employers to subject employees to new forms of cybernetic control and electronic monitoring. ICTs, like all forms of new technology, are subject to human choice in how they are deployed and used. They may increase the control of work by managers/owners, the de-skilling of labour and the exploitation of workers. On the other hand, it is possible deploy technology in the workplace in ways that put workers' interests and the common social good ahead of the drive for profit and the consequent degradation of work and elimination of jobs.

Such a humane and just deployment of technology will take place only if workers have a strong collective voice at the bargaining table. Unions must strive to negotiate clauses in collective agreements that ensure ready access for workers to training in new technologies, training that goes beyond "pressing the right buttons" to an overall understanding of design and operation. Strong unions and workplace activism are also required if workers are to gain a degree of control over how technology is used on the job. In the political realm, worker-friendly laws and public policies are necessary to ensure that ICTs benefit workers as well as bosses, and the increased levels of productivity that result from ICTs serve the broader social goals of equality and environmental sustainability.

The proliferation of ICTs in the workplace throughout everyday life presents a range of challenges and opportunities for labour unions. For purposes of this brief exploration, these challenges and opportunities will be discussed under two general headings, the "conceptual/strategic" level (how organized labour understands the impacts and implications of ICTs and uses this knowledge to frame their social vision and broad economic strategies), and the "practical/organizational" level (how ICTs affect the labour movement's collective bargaining goals, everyday work and prospects for membership growth). These two sets of challenges are discussed in the sections that follow.

The Conceptual/Strategic Level — ICTs and the Labour Movement's Social Vision and Broad Economic Strategy

ICTs have an impact on all aspects of life, not just on paid labour and collective organization in the workplace. Emerging commentaries and theories on the impacts of ICTs offer differing assessments and prognostications. Henwood et al. (2000: 13) point out that "contradictory claims are made for the 'information society.' On the one hand, the emancipatory potential of the greater availability of ICTs and information is celebrated; on the other hand, warnings are made about the threat to individual liberty and social cohesion."

The work of Manual Castells has influenced our understanding of the impacts of ICTs. He argues that information technologies "are reshaping, at an accelerated pace, the material basis of society." There is general polarization of the labour force in the information society into "truly indispensable" professionals and managers who control the "flows of information," and workers in back offices and personal services who are dispensable. Other analysts have also expressed concerns about the "cyberspace divide" in which the world's "information poor" and specific segments of the population (such as women) experience material disadvantages (cited in Henwood et al., 2000: 14). Brian Loader argues that "the development of the information society is not likely to be characterized by a linear technological progression, but rather through the often competing forces of innovation, competitive advantage, human agency and social resistance" (cited in Henwood et al., 2000: 15). ICTs have the potential to make workers' time and efforts on the job much more productive and to minimize aspects of work that are mundane, repetitive, unfulfilling, unpleasant or dangerous. They also have the potential, of course, to further wrest control of the labour process from workers, to narrow their sphere of influence and subject them to further surveillance, and ultimately to deprive them of their jobs.

Looking at the broad impact of ICTs on all aspects of life, it is also possible that workers and unions could begin to take advantage of their growing access to and familiarity with ICTs on the job to enhance participation in union governance and the pursuit of broader social justice goals through labour federations and social movements. ICTs can be valuable (and relatively inexpensive) tools, not just for marginalized workers but for other subordinated constituencies (such as racialized or ethnic communities, persons with alternative sexual orientations, or persons living with a disability) as they challenge various forms of exclusion and oppression, on and off the job.

The Practical/Organizational Level — How ICTs Change the Labour Movement

Labour unions have had to confront ICTs in the workplace on two important fronts. First, they have had to consider how these technologies affect work sites that are already organized and in which older forms of technology have been supplanted to a greater or lesser extent by ICTs. Such change has implications for workers' job security, job satisfaction and opportunities for advancement. Second, unions face the challenge of organizing employees in workplaces created by ICTs, where there is no history of union representation and where most of the workers have no direct personal experience with unions. This task of organizing in new ICT work sites is essential if the labour movement is to have a future. Existing unionized jobs in manufacturing, resource extraction and administration are declining and in some cases disappearing entirely, while the number of jobs in the ICT-driven segments of the labour market (which for the most part are not represented by unions) is growing, though perhaps not as rapidly as New Economy promoters suggest (see Chapter 2).

The Canadian Auto Workers union (CAW) was one of the first to address the impact of ICTs, in their case in the North American automobile industry. Starting in the 1980s, automobile manufacturers began to introduce robotics and to adopt "lean production" methods. The latter brought together new cybernetic technology with the reorganization of work, to decrease labour time, eliminate production "bottlenecks," and implement "just-in-time" scheduling that avoided the need for stockpiling unassembled parts and finished inventory. According to auto companies, lean production techniques in state-of-the-art factories using ICTs were part of "total quality management" that was supposed to grant teams of workers more autonomy and scope for decision-making in their immediate workplace. What ICTs and lean production resulted in, however, were work speed-up and intensification, greatly increased worker stress, loss of some jobs and much higher incidences of health and safety problems such as repetitive strain injuries (see Chapters 3 and 5).[1]

Notwithstanding these problems, the CAW has *not* adopted a Luddite[2] stance against all forms of technological innovation. Rather, this union has taken an overall "accepting but critical" stance on the introduction of new forms of technology in the workplace. The union felt that technological innovation (and related new forms of social reorganization of work, such as lean production) could not be prevented or reversed. The challenge, as the CAW saw it, was to ensure that these new developments were implemented in humane ways that involved and protected its members, and that did not undermine the role of the union as the independent and strong voice of workers. As the CAW's (1993) policy document on lean production says:

> Our union has always understood and been committed to an efficient and productive workplace producing quality goods and providing quality services. New technology and new work processes, we recognize, include the potential for creating a more prosperous society, more leisure time, and improvements in our standard of living.
>
> But this potential never was, and is not today, automatic. It is conditional on the ability of working people, through their unions, negotiating how these changes are implemented and how they shape our lives.

Other unions, such as the Union of Needletrades, Industrial and Textile Employees (UNITE), have taken a generally similar approach to the introduction of new forms of technology in clothing manufacturing. On their web site, UNITE (n.d.) has identified "10 Elements in Making the Implementation of Technology Successful," which include the following points:

- Educate the workforce so that they can participate equally in workplace discussions about change.
- Involve the Union and workers when the idea of new technology first comes under discussion, and throughout the process.
- Demonstrate respect for the knowledge, experience and skill that workers have by giving them first-hand exposure to new technology before it is introduced.
- Develop a communication plan that tells all those involved what the changes are going to be, how these changes are to be implemented, and what the ultimate goal is. (Workers will be willing to participate positively in the technological changes if they meet our need for safer and healthier work, more equitable workplaces and more interesting, responsible, higher skilled and rewarding jobs. But it is not only the workforce that has to

demonstrate that they want to participate in change. Management has to show their willingness to change, or else the credibility of the project is at risk.)

- Establish a consistent labour-management technology committee and avoid changing key players.

The Public Service Alliance of Canada (PSAC) consists of employees of the federal government who, for the most part, work in clerical or communications jobs in office environments that have been transformed by ICTs. PSAC represents people located in workplaces very different from auto plants and clothing factories, and who work in the public sector as opposed to the private sector. Nonetheless, PSAC takes an approach generally similar to UNITE in dealing with technological change, one that calls for consultation with, involvement of, and respect for the union when management wishes to introduce ICTs to the workplace. On its web site, PSAC (n.d.) states: "Whether or not the technology is used in the best interest of workers will depend on how and why it is introduced." In its policy on technological change, PSAC (n.d.) emphasizes the need for safeguards for workers in the language of collective agreements. These contractual guarantees should include:

- a comprehensive definition of technological change to cover both changes in work methods and the introduction of equipment that is different in nature, type or quantity from that previously utilized.
- a requirement for a minimum of six months' advance notice of the introduction of technological change. The advance notice shall include a detailed report on the change to be introduced and a detailed description of all foreseeable effects on workers.
- a provision for adequate training and career development for workers affected by technological change.

Other issues that must be addressed in the implementation of technological change, from the PSAC point of view, include:

- negotiation of health and safety matters so that appropriate working conditions are maintained.
- consideration of human needs and values in decisions regarding work organization that accompanies technological change.
- adequate education of the membership of PSAC as to the nature of the technology and its effects.

- preparation of the membership so it can contribute to the proper design of the work environment when the technology is introduced.
- continuing efforts to reduce working hours and to increase paid leave as a means of sharing the increased productivity resulting from office automation.
- undertaking research on the effects of technological change.

It is thus apparent that specific unions across the broad spectrum of the labour movement have developed carefully considered and detailed policies in response to the introduction of ICTs. Of course, the acid test for unions is whether these policies can be translated into practice. Rinehart (2001: 180–82) offers a short-term, pessimistic prognosis in this regard. He argues that "given the great imbalance of power between capital and labour, there appears to be little likelihood in the short run that technological innovations will have a liberating impact on workers." Rinehart criticizes unions for engaging in "a reactive approach to technological change" rather than taking the initiative to "challenge, influence, or veto management decisions about the character and purpose of new technology before its implementation" [emphasis in original]. Rinehart also contends that a fundamental realignment of political and economic power is necessary if unions are to effectively confront technological change, and if technology is to serve workers rather than rule them.

The next section examines the challenges faced by unions in a particular sector of the ICT-driven labour market — the call centre industry.

The Case of Call Centre Workers

Steedman (2003: 3) has provided a useful snapshot of "the changing face of the call centre industry in Canada." These centres are found in "telecommunications and electronic products, transportation, pharmaceutical and medical products, insurance, banking and financial services." They offer various services, including "handling customer complaints and inquiries," "giving technical advice," "entering orders and reservations," "acting as collection agencies," and "providing warranty and repair service." In 2000, this sector employed 570,000 workers in 13,400 call centres, with three-quarters working in small settings of less than 25 operators. This segment of the labour market has been expanding at an astonishing annual rate of 26 percent in recent years. In almost half of these settings, service is provided 24 hours a day. Steedman (2003: 5) also describes the technological evolution in this sector, predicting that "fully web-integrated contact centres will replace the call centre industry in the next 10 years" and that "the industry [will] integrate outbound calling, data entry and inbound service into one site."

According to Bain (2003: 4), technical innovation on the ICT front has enabled employers to wrest control of the labour process from workers, although there is some variation from one work site to another.

> Management has sought to establish "frontiers of control," which, in the majority of call centers, means repetitive, routinized work.... As a consequence, many call center workers experience work as intensive, target-driven and generally stressful (resulting in "burn-out"), and attribute the compulsion to meet targets as the principal source of pressure in the performance of daily tasks.

Other sources of discontent for call centre workers include "lack of time between calls, repetition and monotony of tasks, infrequency and brevity of breaks, strict interpretation of performance measurements, and the stress arising from the requirement to continuously perform emotional labour" (p. 4).

Despite the perception that call centre workers read prepared scripts and press prescribed buttons, the work can require considerable techno-logical acumen, keen social skills and the ability to "multi-task." Steedman (2003: 5) points out that "call centre work requires considerable interper-sonal skill, sales and telemarketing experience and frequently requires lan-guage skills in several languages," and that the availability of a *well educated* multi-lingual labour force" [emphasis in original] is an important factor for companies in deciding where to locate new call centres.

There is a definite gendering of call centre work. Webster (2003: 3–4) points out that, in the UK, "approximately seventy per cent of all call cen-tre agents... are female," with men tending to hold the "good" jobs in com-puter services and women mostly relegated to the "bad" jobs in financial services. Although there are advancement opportunities for women into middle management of call centres, their actual chances of rising into se-nior levels are slim (Webster, 2003: 5).

The province of Manitoba has experienced a rapid growth of call cen-tres. Only about 14 percent of call centre workers are unionized, however, despite the fact that employees represented by a union enjoy much higher rates of pay. In non-unionized centres, wages begin at the current provin-cial minimum of under $7 per hour. On the other hand, wages in unionized call centres that do "outsourcing" for other firms rise to as high as $12 per hour, and wages in "in-house call centres where unions are well established" (such as Air Canada, CN North America, CP Rail and Manitoba Telecom

Services) range from \$11 to over \$22 per hour (Guard, 2003: 9).

Organizing call centre workers into unions is a very challenging task. Bain (2003: 5) points out that "management policies... pressurize employees to remain engaged in continuously handling calls at their workstation over long periods of time. This presents unions who have gained access with the basic problem of how to communicate with both potential and existing members." Call centre employees often work "in multi-tenanted office buildings or suburban business parks — to which [union organizers] can be denied entry." Organizing is made even more difficult by "high employee turnover ('churn'), requiring unions to continually recruit simply to maintain existing levels of membership" (Bain, 2003: 5).

Unions have had few successes in organizing call centre workers in Manitoba. Guard (2003: 10) argues that this is due to a combination of the technical characteristics of ICTs and the regimen of social control used by management in ICT work sites.

> Employers' technological capacity to monitor workers down to the number of keystrokes combined with the extraordinarily strict work rules and exacting procedures that prevail throughout the industry make it easy for employers to use poor performance as an excuse to terminate workers who are involved in organizing.

In addition, "the highly mobile technology used in the call centre industry... enables employers confronted with a union to simply close up shop and move their operations elsewhere." For instance, "Marusa Marketing (re-named Teleperformance USA) and Telespectrum Worldwide (Canada) both... closed their Winnipeg operations shortly after organizing drives" (Guard, 2003: 11).

Guard argues that "while Manitoba's government has offered considerable inducements to call centre employers, it has so far failed to adequately protect the interests and rights of those who work in them." To remedy this situation, she prescribes two general approaches. The first is to improve wages, benefits and working conditions for call centre workers.

> Call centre workers who are injured on the job are not normally eligible for Workers' Compensation, because call centres are not automatically covered by WCB. Even in unionized call centres, workers typically earn between \$7 and \$12 an hour, wages that leave even full-time, full-year workers (the minority) under the poverty line. A higher minimum wage, more comprehensive employment standards legislation, and unjust dismissal legislation restricting

employers' right to terminate workers without cause would help to establish a more secure "floor of rights" for call centre workers. A more stable call centre workforce with some protection against arbitrary termination and the sense of basic entitlement that a living wage provides would also create a stronger base upon which to build organizing strategies. (Guard, 2003: 11–12)

The second general approach advocated by Guard is "increased public oversight of government policies regarding call centres." Government financial incentives to entice call centre employers should be matched by "comparable investments in protecting those workers [and] ensuring that the jobs that are created are stable, reasonably well-paid jobs rather than temporary 'McJobs.'" In this regard, it is especially important that government assume its

> responsibility to protect the most vulnerable workers — young people, women, Aboriginal workers, disabled workers, recent immigrants and people of colour — from employers who would use their vulnerability to exploit them. Evidence suggests that these are precisely the workers who are employed in the call centre industry. Even when they work full time, few of those working in private sector outsourcing call centres, which are the majority of such workers, earn a living wage. The vast majority of call centre workers are not represented by a union and thus have no job security. (Guard, 2003: 12)

In Australia, the labour movement's struggles to organize call centre workers have yielded a positive result. It was national news when the Australian Industrial Relations Commission "recognised contract call centres as a general industry rather than one linked to specialist sectors such as finance, aviation or telecommunications" (Robinson, 2003). This "landmark legal decision" meant that "thousands of people in Australia's 350,000-strong call centre industry are set to win significant improvements in pay and conditions." This decision was welcomed by the Australian Confederation of Trade Unions as part of its bid to "regulate one of Australia's fastest-growing industries." It was estimated in "call centre research... that in 10 years one in 10 jobs nationwide could be in some form of remote customer contact employment" (Robinson, 2003).

On a similar hopeful note, Bain (2003: 11) cites the British call centre workers who achieved better working conditions through collective action:

Unions can intervene in order to counter intensive target-setting and unacceptable management practices. The one-day strike by 4,000 British Telecom [BT] call center employees, in November 1999, was directed specifically at the company's insistence on strict employee adherence to targets of 285 seconds per call and, more generally, against a harsh management style perceived to be reflected in a ready use of disciplinary measures. The CWU [Communication Workers Union] succeeded in convincing BT to remove individual targets for employees, and gained a commitment that managers would adopt a more consultative and sympathetic approach to production-related problems. BT also agreed to establish a pilot scheme in which employees would be allowed to resolve customer problems without being subject to time targets.

So victories *are* possible through collective action in specific workplaces and industries of the growing ICT sector of the labour market. In the next section, we will step beyond such collective bargaining questions as wages, benefits and labour-management relations. We will examine some of the possibilities and limitations of ICTs for labour unions as they conduct their own day-to-day business, and as they engage in broader struggles for social justice in concert with other social movements.

ICTs and Getting Trade Union Work Done

Since unions aspire to be membership-driven, representative and democratic in their decision-making, ICTs are potentially very useful tools for them in conducting their own affairs. E-mail, discussion boards, chat rooms, Web pages, Web logs (or "blogs"), audio and video streaming and other features of the Internet can be used by unions to communicate within their own ranks, to manage their day-to-day activities and potentially even to organize non-union workers into new bargaining units. To what extent has the labour movement in Canada used ICTs to enhance its own efficiency, impact and reach? While no general and definitive answer can be given, there are some interesting indicators in this regard.

The organized labour movement in Canada has, for the most part, developed an elaborate and sophisticated network of Web sites and Internet-based resources of interest to members, activists in allied social movements, researchers and political decision-makers. The "Links" feature on the Canadian Labour Congress (2005) Web site contains, for example, connections to the Web sites of 91 union affiliates, 10 provincial labour federations and 34 local labour councils. One of the most highly developed Web sites of a Canadian-based union is that of the Steelworkers Métallos consisting of Districts 3, 5 and 6 of the United Steelworkers of America. The Steelworkers' Web site (USWA, 2005) has numerous features, including:

- an electronic newsletter called the *National Director's Update*
- information on how to become a member of the Steelworkers
- information on bargaining, campaigns and political action
- a collection of policies and briefing documents
- Web pages dedicated to "Women of Steel" (related to gender equality) and Steel Pride (related to issues affecting lesbian, gay, bisexual and transgendered workers)
- information on human rights issues, including action against racism, harassment and violence against women, and the promotion of ethnic, religious and national diversity
- the highlighting of "local heroes and tributes"
- video clips
- a "Steelworker store" selling clothing and other merchandise with the union's logo and slogans.

The Steelworkers' Web site also has two intranet sites. One is *Steelweb*, which is accessible to staff and participating local unions, and which contains "an internet e-mail address for each subscribing local union" and "the ability for authorized local union officers to view current local union membership information and make on-line updates." The other intranet site is *Steelnet*, which "includes sample collective agreement language, official Steelworker logos, [and] a complete full text database of Steelworker arbitrations in Canada." Other large Canadian unions, such as the Canadian Union of Public Employees <www.cupe.ca>, the Canadian Auto Workers <www.caw.ca> and the Communications, Energy and Paperworkers Union <www.cep.ca> have similarly information-rich and attractive Web sites.

Besides union-specific Web sites, there are also labour-friendly sites that provide up-to-date news and articles from a union perspective. *Our Times* is a progressive, independent and high-quality Canadian magazine that focuses on the labour movement and on issues of importance to working-class people. It makes selected full-text articles (as well as information on the contents of each issue) available on its Web site <www.ourtimes.ca>. LabourStart <www.labourstart.org> bills itself as the place "where trade unionists start their day on the net," and contains news items of interest to unions that come from all over the world and are available in several different languages. LabourStart also orchestrates regular e-mail campaigns in support of trade union causes around the world, especially ones that involve extremely unjust treatment of workers by employers or governments, human rights abuses, or the killing of union members or leaders. The *Ra-*

dio LabourStart on this Web site features downloadable "news, features and songs to fan the flames of discontent." *LabourStart.tv*, also part of the Web site, contains video clips produced by unions and television news items on labour stories from various countries. The LabourStart site also incorporates participatory Web forums on various labour issues and struggles.

There are many other attractive and interactive Web-based labour movement resources. For instance, a Web site called the *Cradle of Collective Bargaining* <www.humanities.mcmaster.ca/~cradle> details the history and culture of unions and the working class in Hamilton, Ontario. International bodies such as the International Confederation of Free Trade Unions <www.icftu.org> and the International Labour Organization <www.ilo.org> contain a huge amount of information of interest to unions and groups involved in anti-globalization and other international struggles for economic security and social justice.

The various features of the Internet are undoubtedly important tools for unions to communicate with, educate and mobilize their existing members. However, there appear to be limits to the usefulness of ICTs in organizing non-unionized workers into new unions. Derek Blackadder (2003), an organizer for the Canadian Union of Public Employees, argues that tools such as e-mail can indeed make union decision-making speedier and more inclusive, but it also puts pressure on organizers and officials to respond quickly to members' inquiries. In addition, he has learned from experience that, "in recruiting new members, nothing beats the smiling face of a workplace-based activist, someone with as much to gain or as much to lose as you have. And as a space for organizing, the Internet has yet to get even close to the coffee shop down the street" (Blackadder, 2003: 15)

Although ICTs provide the labour movement with a new tool kit, the nature of these technologies also presents unions with particular challenges when trying to organize workers in the ICT sector, such as employees of call centres. The challenges cited in the preceding section include a fast pace of work (that prevents employee-to-employee interaction and relationship-building), physical isolation in remote and sometimes small-scale work settings and high employee turnover. While these challenges are no doubt real, they are not totally different from the challenges faced by unions in organizing miners, factory workers or office clerks in the decades before the information technology revolution. At least with ICT workers, union organizers know that they are dealing with a constituency that is familiar and comfortable with cybernetic forms of communication. It is doubtful, to say the least, that employers will be receptive to the use of company-controlled ICTs for union purposes. But if ways can be found to ensure ready access for workers to the Internet at home, in union offices and in public spaces, then

ICTs may prove to be extremely effective tools in organizing and supporting workers in the ICT and various other sectors of the labour market.

ICTs and Social Movement Unionism

Aside from the use of ICTs by unions to accomplish their organizational tasks, new forms of cyber-communication open up an array of possibilities for organized labour to collaborate with other social movement organizations in broader struggles for economic security, social justice and environmental sustainability. Kelly O'Neill (2002: 323) underlines the importance of "online communities" and "websites of resistance," and argues that "in the context of economic globalization, the Internet facilitates a corresponding globalization of civil society that helps keep social and environmental issues on the international trade and development agenda."

The Internet has enabled grassroots organizations to take on the role of corporate watchdog. For instance, the Web was crucial in mounting an international campaign to protect the land of the Ogoni people against environmental damage from oil exploration by Shell Nigeria. The Web was also used to draw worldwide attention to two critics of McDonald's who were being sued by that company in the UK for distributing leaflets about the restaurant chain's "socially and environmentally harmful practices" (O'Neill, 2002: 324–26).

Although O'Neill (2002: 330–32) accentuates the positive prospects of cyber-activism, she also points out certain "disadvantages of online campaigns." These include:

- lack of access to the Internet for "economically disadvantaged individuals and organizations in both the North and South";
- the need to accommodate limited technical resources and compatibility problems (such as low-end browsers) of under-resourced groups;
- coping with information and e-mail traffic overload, including the danger that "downloading and sending e-mails" takes precedence over "original thoughts and reflection" as the basis of activism;
- distinguishing between information that is "credible and reliable" and that which is not, in the plethora of information that is readily available on the Web;
- ensuring that "electronic networking" is used as a support for, but does take the place of, "street-level education and organization characteristic of [the] most effective citizen movements."

The first high-profile and global Internet-based campaign for social justice was the mobilization, in 1997 and 1998, against the *Multilateral Agreement on Investment* (MAI). This proposed agreement, according to the Council of Canadians (n.d.) <www.canadians.org>, "would have been a 'charter of rights and freedoms' for global corporations — setting the stage for a two-tier health system in Canada, the erosion of our culture and the endangerment of our environment." Negotiations on the MAI among officials of the wealthy industrial countries were, according to Smith and Smythe (2001: 203), an example of "top-down, hierarchical, secretive, bureaucratic, technical, undemocratic, if not anti-democratic, decision-making." The cloak of secrecy around these negotiations was blown off in February 1997, however, when the draft text of the proposed MAI was posted on the Web by public policy advocacy groups in North America (Smith and Smythe, 2001: 192). The mass mobilization that ensued included a proliferation of Web sites about the MAI. Smith and Smythe (2001: Table 12.1) catalogued 16 sites devoted to the proposed MAI that were set up by trade unions. Although this figure represents only 4.6 percent of the total of 352 MAI-related Web sites, organized labour was directly represented in the diverse mix of organizations debating MAI on the Web. It can also be reasonably assumed that a large number of labour activists and unions were included in the other categories of groups that comprise Smith and Smythe's survey, such as "Public Policy Advocacy" groups and "Broad Anti-MAI Coalitions."

The Council of Canadians was an international leader in the fight against the MAI. The Council is non-partisan, independent and not formally aligned with organized labour, but several of its current board members come out of the labour movement, and its own Web site features several union homepages and labour-friendly Web sites on the "Progressive Links" page,

Although the mobilization against the MAI was unplanned, rapid and ultimately successful, other coalitions work in a more planned and sustained way to forge links and address issues. One example of this kind of coalition work at the international level, in which Canadian unions participate, is the Maquila Solidarity Network <www.maquilasolidarity.org>. It is "a Canadian network promoting solidarity with groups in Mexico, Central America, and Asia organizing in maquiladora factories and export processing zones to improve conditions and win a living wage." Another example is Common Frontiers <www.web.net/comfront>, the labour and progressive movement counterweight to the big business lobbies that have set in place the *North American Free Trade Agreement*:

> *Common Frontiers* is a multi-sectoral working group which confronts, and proposes an alternative to, the social, environmental and eco-

nomic effects of economic integration in the Americas. We do this through a combination of research, analysis and action, in cooperation with labour, human rights, environmental, church, development and economic and social justice organizations.

The dispersed, non-hierarchical structure of the Web makes it a particularly suitable vehicle for coalition work that addresses issues of economic security and social justice across huge geographical distances. The Web should prove to be a most valuable medium, as labour and other progressive social movements struggle for popular and democratic alternatives to the neoliberal vision of globalization favoured by multinational corporations.

Conclusions

In struggles to bring about a just and equal society, there are no simple or painless methods for making genuine progress. When labour unions confront ICTs in the workplace, or use them to build their numbers, to get their own work done internally or to engage in coalition work with other social movements, they deal with a wide array of possibilities and limitations. This brief exploration of how the labour movement navigates the new era of cyber-work and the new field of cyber-activism points to new and, to some extent, unknown challenges.

But the discussion in this chapter also points to continuities with the past. Previous generations of workers confronted new technologies in the workplace, such as the assembly line, and new forms of work organization, such as scientific management. Such challenges to workers and their unions in the past could be just as alienating and threatening, in their own ways, as electronic office equipment, robotic factory machinery or ICT-driven lean production methods are today. There is still a need for workers to take collective and organized action if they are to achieve fair remuneration, decent conditions of work and influence over the deployment and implementation of new technologies.

Labour unions not only give workers a collective voice and a degree of power in the workplace. They also play an important role in broader struggles for economic security, social justice and environmental sustainability (Mulvale, 1999). ICTs offer an array of tools for the labour movement, if it is to adopt the strategy suggested by Ife (2001) to "think and act both globally and locally." The labour movement has been quick to take advantage of innovative forms of information and communication technology. As we have seen, these tools can help organized labour to build its ranks, obtain a greater degree of economic security of working people, and participate in local, national, and global coalition work for social justice.

At the same time, it is imperative that labour unions remain fundamentally rooted in the everyday experiences and the flesh-and-blood struggles of their members. ICTs alone will not enable us to achieve a more just and equitable social order. But living, breathing human beings who draw upon their shared political ideals and bonds of solidarity with one another can put these new technologies to work, and in so doing might more easily achieve the goals of justice and equality.

Note

1. These problems are discussed directly by workers themselves in a CAW video entitled *Lean Production*.
2. "Luddism" is the sabotage or destruction of new technology in the workplace by workers. This extreme response has sometimes been used by workers feeling threatened that the employer's new technology will erode their skills, will weaken their control over their work, or will make them redundant and thereby take away their jobs.

CHAPTER 8

New Economy or New Society?

"A Change is Gonna Come"[1]

Dave Broad

To be sure, after systemic chaos will come some new order, or orders. But here we must stop. It is not possible to discern what such a new order would be. It is only possible to assert what we would like it to be and struggle to make it so. (Wallerstein, 1996: 243)

*****

The promises of globalization and the New Economy for improved work and social welfare are false ones. Whether discussing employment opportunities, job satisfaction, income, educational outcomes, occupational health and safety or state services for working people and their families, the story is the same. There are winners and losers in the New Economy, but apparently there are more losers than winners. Even the International Monetary Fund (IMF), one of the foremost promoters of globalization, admits that globalization may indeed hurt the poor (Prasad et al., 2003; 50 Years, 2003). Juan Samavia, Director-General of the International Labour Organization (ILO), has referred to a global "decent work deficit." "A survey of the world we work in today points to an inescapable conclusion.... There is a profound concern about a global decent work deficit of immense proportions, reflecting the diverse inequalities of our societies. Unless we tackle this deficit, the goal of social justice will remain beyond our grasp" (ILO, 2001b: 5).

Let us begin this concluding chapter by revisiting the neoliberal prescription for economic and employment growth. Later I will consider the ILO's recommendations for promoting decent work and then discuss the possibilities for creating decent work in the current global economy. I will close with some remarks on the kind of economy that would be required to address global needs for fundamentally improving work and social welfare.

145

The Neoliberal Prescription

Perhaps the most prominent global institution promoting the neoliberal prescription for economic and employment growth is the Organisation for Economic Co-operation and Development (OECD), whose positive sounding name contradicts its pro-capitalist goals. The OECD's employment agenda is clearly articulated in *The OECD Jobs Study* (OECD, 1994), which puts forth 10 criteria for its jobs strategy:

1. Set macroeconomic policy such that it will both encourage growth and, in conjunction with good structural policies, make it sustainable, i.e., non-inflationary.
2. Enhance the creation and diffusion of technological know-how by improving frameworks for its development.
3. Increase flexibility of working-time (both short-term and life-time) voluntarily sought by workers and employers.
4. Nurture an entrepreneurial climate by eliminating impediments to, and restrictions on, the creation and expansion of enterprises.
5. Make wage and labour costs more flexible by removing restrictions that prevent wages from reflecting local conditions and individual skill levels, in particular for younger workers.
6. Reform employment security provisions that inhibit the expansion of employment in the private sector.
7. Strengthen the emphasis on active labour market policies and reinforce their effectiveness.
8. Improve labour force skills and competencies through wide-ranging changes in educational and training systems.
9. Reform unemployment and related benefit systems — and their interactions with the tax system — such that societies' fundamental equity goals are achieved in ways that impinge far less on the efficient functioning of the labour markets.
10. Enhance product market competition so as to reduce monopolistic tendencies and weaken insider-outsider mechanisms while also contributing to a more innovative and dynamic economy. (restated in OECD, 1997: 4–5)

These proposals all point to the sanctity of the capitalist market economy and emphasize the neoliberal priorities of privatization, deregulation and downsizing of government.

The first item tells us that economic growth should be the beginning point for public policy, which is one of the fundamental assumptions of post-World War II modernization theory discussed in Chapter 1 above. The second item accords with a core belief of the New Economy, that technology is the key to economic growth, from which all else flows. Items 3 and 5 reflect the current neoliberal promotion of labour market flexibility with respect to working hours and wages, which includes the lower minimum wages for youth that we see in some jurisdictions, but Item 5 even challenges notions like minimum wage. Item 7 supports the shift from welfare to workfare policies that we see in many countries, as discussed in Chapter 6 above. Item 8 refers to the move away from notions of liberal education towards market-oriented skills training, as discussed in Chapter 4 above. And Item 9 reflects the assumption that state benefit programs like unemployment insurance must be "reformed" because they create "dependencies" on social welfare programming.

In its reports on implementing the jobs strategy, the OECD claims that the countries following its prescriptions have been making great headway in creating employment. The US is often held up as an example because its labour productivity has been higher and official unemployment numbers lower than most other Western countries. But as discussed in Chapter 1 above, labour productivity gains can be a simple outcome of forcing people to work longer and harder, and official unemployment statistics generally mask a lot of unemployment (Yates, 1994).

The Canadian government adopted the entire OECD jobs strategy following its social security review and budget program of 1994. Ostensibly, the review was a public consultation into the wishes of Canadians regarding public policy and social programming. But critics have argued that the review was really a front for selling the neoliberal agenda, as reflected in the OECD *Jobs Strategy*, to Canadians (Pulkingham and Ternowetsky, 1996a). The two main documents outlining the Canadian government's direction sport the banner "Agenda: Jobs and Growth" (Government of Canada, 1994a, 1994b). According to *A New Framework for Economic Policy*, the policy making setting includes economic globalization, competition from developing countries and the information economy. To address these issues, we are told: "Productivity growth is the foundation of economic progress and must therefore be the primary focus of economic policy" (Government of Canada, 1994b: 16). The government's proposed framework for achieving this objective is stated as one that will help Canadians acquire skills, encourage them to adapt to change, get government right, provide leadership in the economy and create a healthy fiscal and monetary climate. The presumption is that this will lead to innovative combinations of people, capital and ideas, which will produce stronger economic growth, resulting in more and better jobs (Government of Canada, 1994b: 36–37).

The flaw in this argument, as noted by dependency theorists discussed in Chapter 1 above, is that economic growth *per se* does not necessarily lead to the sort of social development that might include more and better jobs. If we want more and better jobs, determinants for the ingredients of a development program that might result in those jobs must be built into policy proposals from the start. One of the core arguments of this book is that economic growth in a capitalist market economy is not primarily oriented towards creating good jobs and satisfying human needs, but rather towards selling commodities at the highest possible profit to promote the accumulation of capital. One result is the decent work deficit, which, according to the evidence we have presented, is exacerbated by neoliberal policies proposed by the OECD and followed by Western governments. Meanwhile, "getting government right" has included targeting social programs for supposedly allowing workers to become dependent on social welfare, the implication being that they are lazy. So a residual policy of cuts to social programs has accompanied the trend toward fewer and worse jobs, creating yet more hardships for workers and their families.

The ILO Decent Work Agenda

"The ILO was established in 1919 in a world which was ravaged by war, threatened by revolution and haunted by the misery and poverty of working people. Its aim was to build a social framework for peace and stability within which economic processes could generate prosperity with social justice in the life of workers and in the world of work" (ILO, 1999: 4). Given the social environment in 1919, it was not a surprise that the ILO's founding charter contained the maxim "labour is not a commodity," which has been revisited at various points throughout the ILO's history (Vosko, 2000). In the wake of the Bolshevik triumph in Russia, the Western powers were very much concerned by "the threat of revolution" and by the appeal of a socialist alternative to working people in capitalist countries. Thus, it was important to have an organization with the express mandate of promoting the interests of working people. The ILO brought together representatives of trade unions, business and government for that purpose. Article I of the ILO's 1944 *Declaration of Philadelphia* was recently repeated by the current Director-General to remind us of the ILO's mandate for promoting "a fair globalization":

- labour is not a commodity;
- freedom of expression and of association are essential to sustained progress;

- poverty anywhere constitutes a danger to prosperity every-where;
- the war against want requires to be carried on with unrelent-ing vigor within each nation, and by continuous and concerted international effort in which the representatives of workers and employers, enjoying equal status with those of governments, join with them in free discussion and democratic decision with a view to promotion of the common welfare. (ILO, 2004c: 2)

Historically, the ILO's orientation has been social democratic and Keynesian in terms of public policy recommendations.

The Decent Work Program is the ILO's most recent endeavour to pro-mote improvements in the working conditions and social welfare of workers and their families. It is also the organization's program for promoting "a fair globalization." The ILO sees at least 10 criteria that must be addressed in defining decent work:

- access to employment,
- fair and equal treatment in employment,
- decent remuneration for work,
- fair conditions of work,
- a safe work environment,
- protection in case of unemployment,
- social protection and employment,
- employment and training opportunities,
- participation and motivation, and
- giving voice and collective participation. (Egger and Sengen-berger, 2001: 3–4)

The various items to be addressed in these criteria — racism and sexism, hours of work, workplace health and safety, opportunities for employment and social advancement, and vehicles for worker participation — are areas the authors of this collection say are too often lacking. The Director-Gen-eral of the ILO identifies four gaps that must be closed to reverse the decent work deficit: the employment gap, regarding quantity and quality of jobs; the rights gap; the social protection gap; and the social dialogue gap.[2]

In policy terms, the ILO advocates institutional mechanisms[3] to tackle the decent work deficit. In the neoliberal context of deregulation, the leg-islative route to promoting decent work has come under attack, but the ILO persists in promoting institutional responses to help address the decent work deficit and should be supported in this endeavour. The ILO points to evidence that shows, in addition to social benefits, there are economic benefits to creating decent work, in terms of productivity, economic growth and development (ILO, 2001b). But perhaps the ILO's most important recommendation is for "new instruments of social dialogue" to address what some social activists term "the democracy deficit." We will return to this point below, but let us first consider the ILO's prognosis for the role of New Economy jobs in countering the decent work deficit.

In its report, *Life at Work in the Information Economy*, the ILO "is guardedly optimistic on the chances for employment growth where ICTs are most in use" (ILO, 2001a: 5). The authors of the report ask: "Will the quality of work and life improve? The networking economy offers genuine potential for striking a better balance between work and family responsibilities, or work and leisure. For many work has become more rewarding in its pay and in its content" (ILO, 2001a: 11). But as discussed in Chapter 2, the ILO cautions that job losses have also resulted from technological change and increasing productivity, that ICTs can produce job ghettos and isolation for some homeworkers, and that leisure time can disappear as pressure mounts to work everywhere and all the time. What we might call a "time deficit" has added incredible stress to the lives of workers and their families (see Menzies, 2005, and Chapter 5), prompting a recent movement against overwork called Take Back Your Time <www.timeday.org>.

As for the ILO's decent work proposal for giving voice and collective participation to workers, the report says that by creating a more diversified labour market the diffusion of the new technologies renders collective organization and representation more difficult. It is sometimes argued that the new technologies provide tools for collective action, some possibilities of which are explored in Chapter 7. However, the ILO notes that fragmentation in the organization of production, and a continually changing organization of work, pose additional challenges to organizing workers in the New Economy. In its report on the New Economy, the ILO (2001a: 14) emphasizes the importance of social policy:

> A passive policy stance that leaves to markets alone the direction of change will reinforce divides. It is also the case that the quality of life and work for women and men will be exposed as much to the potential for negative outcomes as positive ones. For all these reasons, social choices and the social institutions through which such choices are moulded are essential to the digital era.

Labour *Is* a Commodity

The ILO's proposals for promoting decent work are commendable and worthy of support, because they provide a positive alternative to the neoliberal agenda. Unfortunately, the ILO itself is not immune to the "liberal virus," as Amin (2004) calls it. In its *World Employment Report 2004–05*, the ILO (2005a) clearly adopts the neoliberal policy position currently in vogue. Drawing on the old assumptions of neoclassical capitalist economics, the ILO report says our priority should be to increase labour productivity to promote economic growth, which is supposed to provide the basis for increased prosperity and better employment opportunities (a view we criticized in Chapters 1 and 2). The ILO does recognize that more and better jobs may not, in fact, automatically result from more economic growth, so it tries to square its espousal of neoliberal economic ideas with what sound like Keynesian policies for employment.

The essential problem with the ILO proposals is that, in our current global capitalist socio-economic system, labour is a commodity, despite the ILO's 1919 statement to the contrary. Labour is bought and sold in a market where capital has more power than labour. Marx and Engels explained in detail how commodification of labour was an essential component of the transition to capitalist society, and why there was the need for ready access to labour-power (Marx, 1867). For this reason labour was "freed" from feudal and other bonds to be available for production of commodities.[4] But we know that "unfree" labour has also been (e.g., slaves) and is now (e.g., casual workers and work in the informal economy) used to produce commodities (Broad, 2000; Tabak and Critchlow, 2000). The point is that capital has relied on purchase (or theft) of labour from the start, and treats it as what mainstream economists have called "a factor of production," with so-called human relations coming into play only when increased labour productivity is needed. In the most extreme case of "scientific management," labour-power is virtually disembodied, leading to its alienation in individual and social terms. Consequently, if we are to envision a really *new* economy, it will also be a new society based on decommodification of life on a global scale. Can this be done?

Promoting Alternatives Within Capitalism

Transnational corporations, in particular, own vast amounts of productive and financial assets that give them the upper hand with working people in restructuring labour processes, choosing production sites and influencing government. Trade unions and labour parties have been the vehicles through which workers and their families have gained some say over their working and welfare conditions and their employer's investment decisions. But as we have discussed in preceding chapters, it is these vehicles that employers have been trying to avoid or escape through global economic restructuring. And where geographic escape is not feasible, neoliberal policy has been used to weaken labour organizations and state institutions developed to protect workers and their families.

The Keynesian welfare state has helped bring people in Western countries out of destitution, by developing public education, public health care and social services, and instituting labour and social rights legislation. Teeple (2000) argues that the welfare state did not go far in redistributing wealth between classes, but rather amongst members of the working class. However, he does contend that important gains were made in decommodifying labour and promoting social citizenship. And it is precisely these gains that neoliberals strive to negate. They use so-called reforms to dismantle legislation and state programs that benefit workers and their families, constructing a state that is no less active than the welfare state but simply more market-oriented. Perhaps more pernicious than state cutbacks, though, is the social conservatism being promoted to induce a greater sense of individualism and, while often paying lip service to community, to undermine any sense of community that might offer alternatives to the market. Neoliberalism continues the secular trend towards "the commodification of everything" and creation of "the universal market" (Braverman, 1974; Wallerstein, 1983). Thus, not only have the most minute aspects of our daily lives been subjected to consumerism even as we produce less for ourselves, but we are doing less for others as a community. Meanwhile, having been transformed into consumers by liberal individualist ideology and capitalist advertising, we confuse needs with wants. Either consciously or unconsciously, we confront the fact that there are limits to satisfaction of both needs and wants through consumerism, which just increases individual and social alienation (Leiss, 1976; Pappenheim, 2000).

However, as capitalism is rife with contradictions, we find that there is another side to this story. While we see a global heightening of commodification, we also see that cuts to welfare programming result in a curious decommodification, as jobs disappear in health and social services and families are expected to provide the caring services formerly the responsibility of paid workers, who are now unemployed or underemployed. And of course, as in state social service employment, it is primarily women in the homes who are expected to carry out these duties. Along with this trend, we find volunteerism being promoted in public caring institutions, with the perverse twist that people are being encouraged to count such activities as work experience for inclusion on a résumé that might lead to paid employment. This would be comical if it were not for the consequence that people are expected to work for free, and are carrying out work that should be done by trained workers. Moreover, this is obviously not community service in the most altruistic sense, but in a more self-serving sense.

As an economic project, we are beginning to hear more about a "social economy," including non-commodity production of goods and services and the possibilities of reviving communities by cultivating a more altruistic volunteer sector and a socialized informal economy (Browne, 1996; O'Hara, 1993; Rifkin, 1995). There is some merit to this idea. But we must remain aware that capital has been most adept historically of exploiting the informal economy to cut costs of production and of reproducing labour power (Tabak and Critchlow, 2000). In other words, promoting the option of the social economy, as Rifkin (1995) does, without discussing the need to challenge the power structures of capital, is doomed to failure.

The best route to decommodification of social relations is through the resurrection of community which, in fact, is happening through some alternative social economy activities in the First World, and through what is more often called the informal economy in the Third World. In the *favelas* in Latin America (small squatter settlements on the fringes of large cities, of mostly recently migrated rural poor), community members are providing social services for other community members out of necessity, revealing that this work need not be done by the state or through the market. What distinguishes this from the off-loading of public services to women in the home in First World countries is that it is being done on a collective, not individual household, basis, through community kitchens, child care centres, et cetera. And even though such activities may be arising motivated by necessity, the fact remains that people need not and are not relying on the capitalist market economy to meet their need. This is also the case where production sites have been taken over by workers in situations of economic collapse, such as in Argentina (Gentile, 2004).

In their film *The Take*, Avi Lewis and Naomi Klein (NFB, 2004) document the social movement of workers and community members in Argentina that has developed in the wake of economic bankruptcy caused by neoliberalism.[5] When capitalist investors ceased production in factories because they could not get the high profits they wanted, the workers themselves began to take over operations, on a co-operative basis, to serve the local market. In addition to restarting production of goods, they have also developed co-operative social services such as health clinics for workers and their families. We must note that these activities are only the seeds of what might grow in the future. Workers' actions are generally opposed by capital and the capitalist state if they present competition or too much of an alternative to private business. This has been the case in Argentina, where workers and community members must constantly struggle to maintain their gains. To be further advanced, these activities will require greater community control of social resources, with support of progressive governments. Fortunately, there are positive signs in many Latin American countries, where leftist governments are coming to power and developing social programs and avenues of democratic participation that have historically been absent. The Bolivarian Revolution in Venezuela, for example, is a significant development, indicative of left-moving trends in other countries, and promising to end Cuba's isolation as the only socialist country in the hemisphere.[6] There is a constant struggle to maintain these processes of social transformation against local capitalist and imperialist opposition, especially from the US. But the alternative — continuing neoliberal destitution — makes the struggle worth it. This is obviously a belief held by many, for we find people around the globe engaged in struggles to improve human welfare and defend the natural environment.

Perhaps the best immediate option for labour throughout the world, as discussed in more detail in Chapter 7, is to promote social movement unionism, through which labour combines with other social movements, locally, nationally and globally, in a general struggle for social justice. This struggle brings workers together with feminists, environmentalists, peace activists, Aboriginal peoples and others to achieve a more rational and humane world order. Unfortunately, this type of solidarity is not well advanced, though there are some positive examples as labour joins others to mount a "globalization from below" against capital's "globalization from above" (Brecher et al., 1993; Brecher and Costello, 1994). Interesting examples can be found in the US-Mexico border region where transnational corporations have set up manufacturing plants to take advantage of low labour costs and lax environmental legislation. Women, in particular, on both sides of the border have combined to fight super-exploitative working conditions and environmental degradation that threatens their lives and the lives of their families. One organization working to counter the negative impacts of corporate globalization and promote social justice is the Maquila Solidarity Network.[7] There has also been increasing contact between Canadian, Mexican and US trade unionists to promote international solidarity against the exploitative corporate practices that have spread since the implementation of the *North American Free Trade Agreement* (NAFTA) in January of 1994 (see Chapter 7). Trade unionists are attempting to prevent further erosion of working and living conditions in Canada and the US, and pushing for improvements in Mexican working and living conditions. Some have also expressed solidarity with the struggles of Aboriginal groups like the Zapatista National Liberation Army in southern Mexico.

A common criticism of many current social movements is their fractured and single-issue character. And while they are playing an important role in criticizing and opposing the hegemony of transnational corporations, some authors argue that anti-globalization movements too often fail to recognize that the real problem is not just transnational corporations or certain businessmen and politicians, but rather capitalism as a system (Tabb, 1997; Petras and Veltmeyer, 2001). Without recognizing that the fundamental problem is capitalism, the anti-globalization movement is open to co-optation, as we saw with the dependency critique of developmentalism in the 1970s (see Chapter 1). In reference to the current social movements, Wallerstein (1998: 85–86) notes that "rhetoric is co-optable, even when movements resist co-optation. And movements, as we have seen, find it very difficult over time not to bend in the wind, especially if they can obtain some portion of their immediate objectives thereby." Still, we need to support the anti-globalization movement and recognize that this generation of youth activists may produce their own innovative ways of interpreting and changing the world for the better.

We should also note that the hyperbole about the potential uses of the new information and communication technologies (ICTs) is generated by the market. Television advertisements for computers and cell phones clearly show the extent to which such technology is both commoditized and wasted on the most trivial of pursuits. Meanwhile, as noted in Chapter 2, the ILO (2001a: 3) has reminded us that only six percent of the world's population has ever logged onto the Internet, mostly in the First World, and much of the world's population has no access to electricity, not to mention the basic necessities of life. So while the contributors to this volume utilize ICTs in various ways, and will likely continue to do so, we do not delude ourselves that ICTs are the cure for all of the world's ills. In fact, power outages and ice storms in recent years have shown that we may be too reliant on electricity and electronic equipment, even in non-commoditized forms. We need not be Luddites; there are some important uses for new technologies — in medicine, for example. But let's not get too enamoured of "tech fixes." Most particularly, let's not fall into the trap of believing that ICTs can enhance or replace actual human relations. For example, the notion of "virtual sex" is simply another commodity relation — an alienated relation at that — and one not immune to viruses. In fact, we could ask whether the proliferation of "spam" and computer viruses might not bring the World Wide Web crashing down completely. Regardless, we should recognize that if more and more of our time is occupied by virtual activities, we will be less active in the "real" world struggle against capitalist globalization.

More generally, against the argument that we need the new technologies to increase productivity and raise economic growth so that we will have more wealth to distribute, let us argue that economic growth and productivity are now a world problem *only* in that there are too much of both, and redistribution was never a spinoff of economic growth anyway. Thus, we should revive the human and ecological sensibility of Paul Lafargue's (1883) argument for "the right to be lazy" (cf. Darier, 1996). Let us assert that we should "work to live," not "live to work." We do not need more economic growth, but rather equitable distribution of work and world resources. Ultimately, we need to consume less and engage more in direct human relations.

Towards a Non-Commodity Society?

In recent years, we have received mixed messages about the historical trajectory of the current period. For some, with the breakup of the Soviet Union, we have witnessed "the triumph of capitalism" (Heilbroner, 1989). For others, we are now living in a post-capitalist and post-industrial society (Drucker, 1993), or a post-modern and post-Fordist society (Harvey, 1989). Whatever the label, there seems to be a growing consensus that we are in an age of transition, that we are witnessing a systemic crisis, an era of chaos in world capitalism (Hopkins and Wallerstein, 1996).

With respect to the new technologies, Davis and Stack (1993) argue that between people's needs and the immense productivity of the knowledge economy stands a system of exploitative and unequal capitalist economic and political relationships. They go on to say: "The knowledge-intensive productive forces are straining against the chains of private property relations. The qualities of knowledge, to be fully maximized, require a system based on co-operation and sharing, because co-operation and sharing generate more information and social wealth" (Davis and Stack, 1993: 12). And co-operation and sharing are the antidote to the alienation and exploitation that are not only endemic to capitalist relations of production, but exacerbated by the present neoliberal direction of economic restructuring. In short, we need to develop forms of collective ownership and co-operative control of social resources, which cannot be done without rebuilding community (Ware, 1999). Through ideological struggle, this will require co-operation, rather than the individualism and competition endemic in capitalism. We need to counter the neoliberal notion that there is no alternative to capitalism with some eutopian thinking about what sort of better society we would like to see.[8] In such a society there would be:

- Abolition of the right to exploit human labor for private profit and the end of demeaning subjection in the workplace;
- The end of alienation from one's work, work turned into creative, fulfilling labor;
- The end of male domination over the female half of humanity and recognition of women's ... needs in society;
- Full economic, political, and cultural equality to oppressed peoples ... in a cooperative world;
- Full and equal health, education, and cultural opportunities for the world's children and youth everywhere on Earth;
- Healthful and beautiful cities amid revived nature for all humanity's habitats;
- Full political empowerment to all people ruled by despots or made fools of by a sham democracy. (Zeitlin, 1996: 24–25)

Neoliberals have argued that people become too dependent on the welfare state — the "nanny state" as Margaret Thatcher called it. But the neoliberal solution is to replace the welfare state with the capitalist market, where profitable. Where not, we see the phony promotion of community and the family covering for the real purpose of subsidizing the markets (including the labour market, as has historically been done with unwaged female labour) (Mies, 1998). Capitalist society must be replaced with some kind of socialist society if we are to address human needs and promote human development. However, while we can say that we need to resurrect genuine community to counter the selfish liberal individualism of capitalist society, we cannot say with precision what that genuine community will look like or exactly how it will be achieved. The precise nature of a non-capitalist society will develop (in some unpredictable ways) within the struggle to create it, rather than from a preconceived and detailed blueprint.

Wallerstein (1998: 1–2) suggests that we engage in what he calls "utopistics":

What I mean by utopistics, a substitute word I have invented, is something rather different [from utopias]. Utopistics is the serious assessment of historical alternatives, the exercise of our judgement as to the substantive rationality of alternative possible historical systems. It is the sober, rational, and realistic evaluation of human social systems, the constraints on what they can be, and the zones open to human creativity. Not the face of the perfect (and inevitable) future, but the face of an alternative, credibly better, and historically possible (but far from certain) future. It is thus an exercise simultaneously in science, in politics, and in morality.

It is most important for our current struggles to admit that we are indeed in a period of transition, and to argue that alternatives to capitalism are possible. But it is also important to note that outcomes will be uncertain. In this sense, the transition from capitalism to another social system is inevitable, there being not only heightening global social divisions that are unsustainable, but also a growing degree of environmental destruction that threatens our place on the planet (Foster, 1999; Kovel, 2002).

Some will say that struggles to create a new society are a waste of time. First are the supporters of capitalism who will say that we cannot really make fundamental social changes, that such was tried in the twentieth century in the name of communism or socialism and did not work — ergo notions of the triumph of capitalism, or the end of history. Second are the cynics who will say that the cost is not worth it, that the struggle would be so intense, with so much destruction and loss, and with no guarantee of success, that we might as well just adapt and make the best of what we have. At best we might hope for a few reforms.

First, on the fundamentalism of capitalism, we must recognize that history has no end (Marzani, 1990) — change will come, whether through revolution or decay (Amin, 1980). Wallerstein (1998: 88) notes that "the transition period, is particularly unpredictable, but also particularly subject to individual and group input, what I have called the increase in the free will factor. If we wish to seize our opportunity, which seems to me a moral and political obligation, we must first recognize the opportunity for what it is, and of what it consists." It is obvious that the neoliberals generally have recognized the opportunity and are actively defending the capitalist system and looking for ways to sustain it. Second, as to the cynical view, we can already see that the period of transition is one of disorder, disarray, and disintegration. But keeping in mind that change will come one way or another, we must remind ourselves of something important: "Though it will be terrible to live through, it will not go on forever" (Wallerstein, 1998: 63). As the history of struggles for social justice reveals, nothing was ever gained without hard work and great effort. The real question is whether we can afford *not* to struggle for a better future. Current global conditions add new relevance to the old aphorism: socialism or barbarism (Meszaros, 2001).

Conclusion

Throughout this volume, we have suggested reforms to improve the working and welfare conditions of workers and their families. But we must admit that a social-democratic reform project is not viable, and that nothing can change fundamentally without challenging the power structures of capitalism. We must be eutopian in asserting that alternatives *are* possible (Bennholdt-Thomsen et al., 2001), that we are *not* bound by some immutable "laws of capital markets," as former Canadian Prime Minister Paul Martin has called them (Freeman, 1994). We must also be eutopian in assuming that there is more to humanity than the liberal *homo economicus* of capitalism, that given sufficient opportunity, people will aspire to and collectively work towards an equitable and ecologically sensitive world order.[9] It seems that the biggest impediment to this struggle is an ideological one, a matter of people seeing beyond capitalism to realize that a better world is possible. Currently the liberal individualism and consumerism of capitalism prevents many people from seeing that we are all better off if we work collectively to improve our world, that selfishness and the capitalist market will only continue to make things worse for the majority of humanity and the environment.

Che Guevera (1965) spoke of the paramount need in the struggle for socialism to create the new socialist human — the selfless and communitarian human being who is not alienated by capitalist ideology, and who understands that true individuality and self-interest can only be realized through transformation of society to serve the interests of all, not a rich and powerful few. Guevera knew that this is one of the most difficult struggles, and one that will continue for some time. All of the ideological institutions of the current society serve to convince people that we live in the best of all possible worlds, or at least the only possible one. People must go through a process of dis-alienation to see that a better world is possible, and to realize that their individual interests are best served through the collective struggle for human liberation. All of this may sound flowery and idealistic, but we are seeing people's hopes for humanity expressed in social justice struggles taking place every day, in all parts of the world.

Notes

1. With all due respect to Sam Cooke.
2. The various ILO publications cited in this chapter provide detailed proposals for addressing these gaps.
3. Institutional mechanisms such as labour standards, occupational health and safety and employment equity legislation.

4. Historians have documented this process of creating proletarian wage-labour (e.g., Thompson, 1968).
5. *The Take,* National Film Board of Canada, 2004. See <www.thetake.org>.
6. See recent issues of the journals *Latin American Perspectives* and *Monthly Review* for articles on developments in Latin American countries.
7. See <www.maquilasolidarity.org>.
8. I prefer the Greek term "eutopia" (a good place) to "utopia" (no place). See Simon (1985) and Broad (1998).
9. I cite the work of world-systems theorists like Wallerstein here because I find their analysis to be among the best for understanding the historical crisis and looking beyond it, and I would recommend their work to activists in current social movements (see, for example, Amin et al., 1982, 1990; Arrighi et al., 1989).

References

Advisory Committee on the Changing Workplace. 1997. "Collective Reflection on the Changing Workplace, Report of the Advisory Committee on the Changing Workplace." Ottawa: Human Resources Development Canada.

Ala-Mursula, L., J. Vahtera, M. Kivimäki, M. Kevin, and J. Pentti. 2002. "Employee control over working time: Associations with subjective health and sickness absences." *Journal of Epidemiology and Community Health* 56.

Alexander, A. 1997. *The Antigonish Movement: Moses Coady and Adult Education Today.* Toronto: Thompson Educational Publishers.

Allan, C., M. O'Donnell, and D. Peetz. 1999. "More Tasks, Less Secure, Working Harder: Three Dimensions of Labour Utilisation." *Journal of Industrial Relations* 41, 4.

Allen, S. and C. Wolkowitz. 1987. *Homeworking: Myths and Realities.* London: Macmillan Education.

Altvater, E. 2001. "The Growth Obsession." In L. Panitch and C. Leys (eds.), *The Socialist Register 2002.* London: Merlin Press.

Amin, S. 2004. *The Liberal Virus: Permanent War and the Americanization of the World.* New York: Monthly Review Press.

_____. 1994. *Re-Reading the Postwar Period: An Intellectual Itinerary.* New York: Monthly Review Press.

_____. 1980. *Class and Nation: Historically and in the Current Crisis.* New York: Monthly Review Press.

_____. 1978. *The Law of Value and Historical Materialism.* New York: Monthly Review Press.

Amin, S., G. Arrighi, A.G. Frank, and I. Wallerstein. 1990. *Transforming the Revolution: Social Movements and the World-System.* New York: Monthly Review Press.

_____. 1982. *Dynamics of Global Crisis.* New York: Monthly Review Press.

Anderson, R.B. 2005. *Aboriginal Economic Development in the New Economy.* Regina, SK: Saskatchewan Institute of Public Policy.

Anderson, S., and J. Cavanagh. 2003. *Top 200: The Rise of Global Power.* Washington: Institute for Policy Studies.

Appelbaum, S., T. Close, and S. Klasa. 1999. "Downsizing: An Examination of Some Successes and More Failures." *Management Decision* 37, 5.

Appelbaum, S., S. Lavigne-Schmidt, M. Peytchev, and B. Shapiro. 1999. "Downsizing: Measuring the Costs of Failure." *Journal of Management Development* 18, 5.

Argyris, C. 1960. *Understanding Organizational Behavior.* Homewood IL: Dorsey.

Armstrong, P., and H. Armstrong. 1994. *The Double Ghetto: Canadian Women and Their Segregated Work.* Toronto: McClelland and Stewart.

Armstrong-Stassen, M. 1998. *Reactions to the Downsizing Initiative at Human Resource Development Canada: A Summary of the Findings.* Windsor: University of Windsor.

Aronowitz, S., D. Esposito, W. DiFazio, and M. Yard. 1998. "The Post-Work Manifesto." In S. Aronowitz and J. Cutler (eds.), *Post-work: The Wages of Cybernation.* New York: Routledge.

Arrighi, G., T.K. Hopkins, and I. Wallerstein. 1989. *Antisystemic Movements.* London: Verso Books.

Auer, P., G. Besse, and D. Meda. 2006. *Offshoring and the Internationalization of Employment: A Challenge for a Fair Globalization?* Geneva: International Labour Organization.

Axworthy, C. 1999. "A Modern Socialist Approach: R and R for Social Policy." In D. Broad and W. Antony (eds.), *Citizens or Consumers? Social Policy in a Market Society.* Halifax: Fernwood Publishing.

Babson, S. 1995. "Lean Production and Labour: Empowerment and Exploitation." In S. Babson (ed.), *Lean Work: Empowerment and Exploitation in the Global Auto Industry.* Detroit MI: Wayne State University Press.

Bacon, N. 1999. "Union Derecognition and the New Human Relations: A Steel Industry Case Study." *Work Employment and Society* 13, 1.

Bacon, N., and P. Blyton. 2001. "High Involvement Work Systems and Job Insecurity in the International Iron and Steel Industry." *Canadian Journal of Administrative Sciences* 18, 1.

Bain, P. 2003. "Unions and Call Centers: The UK Experience." Paper prepared for conference on "Organizing Call Centres from the Workers' Perspective" (September 11–13), Toronto. Policies and Briefing Documents, <www.uswa.ca/program/adminlinks/docs//call_bain.pdf>.

Baldwin, J.R., and D. Beckstead. 2003. *Knowledge Workers in Canada's Economy, 1971–2001.* Ottawa: Statistics Canada.

Band, D., and C. Tustin. 1995. "Strategic Downsizing." *Management Decision* 33, 8.

Baran, P.A., and P.M. Sweezy. 1966. *Monopoly Capital: An Essay on the American Economic and Social Order.* New York: Monthly Review Press.

Barker, R. 1995. *The Social Work Dictionary.* Washington, DC: NASW Press.

Barlow, M., and H-J. Robertson. 1994. *Class Warfare: The Assault on Canada's Schools.* Toronto: Key Porter Books.

Barnet, R.J. 1993. "The End of Jobs: Employment is One Thing the Global Economy is Not Creating." *Harper's Magazine,* 287, 1720.

Battle, K., and Torjman, S. 2000. Yes, Virginia, there is a guaranteed income. Caledon Commentary, December 2000, Ottawa: Caledon Institute of Social Policy.

Beauchesne, E. 2002. "Labour Shortage Fear Unfounded." *National Post,* July 29. <www.footwork.com/post1.html>.

Beck, N. 1992. *Shifting Gears: Thriving in the New Economy.* Toronto: HarperCollins Publishers.

Beckstead, D., and M. Brown. 2005. *An Anatomy of Growth and Decline: High-tech Industries Through the Boom and Bust Years, 1997–2003.* Ottawa: Statistics Canada.

Beckstead, D., M. Brown, G. Gellatly, and C. Seaborn. 2003. *The Canadian Economy in Transition: A Decade of Growth: The Emerging Geography of New Economy Industries in the 1990s.* (Catalogue number 11-622-MIE—No. 003.) Ottawa: Statistics Canada.

Beckstead, D., and G. Gellatly. 2003. *The Canadian Economy in Transition: The Growth and Development of New Economy Industries*. (Catalogue number 11-622—No. 002.) Ottawa: Statistics Canada.

Beckstead, D., and T. Vinodrai. 2003. *Dimensions of Occupational Changes in Canada's Knowledge Economy, 1971–1996*. Ottawa: Statistics Canada.

Bell, D. 1973. *The Coming of Post-Industrial Society*. New York: Basic Books.

Bennholdt-Thomsen, V., N. Faraclas, and C. von Werlhof. 2001. *There Is an Alternative: Subsistence and Worldwide Resistance to Corporate Globalization*. London: Zed Books.

Benoit, C.M. 2000. *Women, Work and Social Rights: Canada in Historical and Comparative Perspective*. Toronto: Prentice Hall.

Betcherman, G., and R. Chaykowski. 1996. *The Changing Workplace: Challenges for Public Policy*. Ottawa: Human Resource Development Canada.

Betcherman, G., and G.S. Lowe. 1995. "Inside the Black Box: Human Resource Management and the Labour Market." In R.J. Adams, G. Betcherman and B. Bilson (eds.), *Good Jobs, Bad Jobs, No Jobs: Tough Choices for Canadian Labour Law*. Toronto: CD Howe Institute.

Betcherman, G., K. McMullen, N. Leckie, and C. Caron. 1994. *The Canadian Workplace in Transition*. Kingston: Industrial Relations Centre Press.

Bishop, A. 2002. *Becoming and Ally: Breaking the Cycle of Oppression in People*. Halifax: Fernwood Publishing.

Blackadder, D. 2003. "Talking About Organizing: Face to Face or Cyberspace." *Our Times*, 22, 6, (Dec. 2003–Jan. 2004).

Bluestone, B., and B. Harrison. 2000. *Growing Prosperity: The Battle for Growth with Equity in the Twenty-First Century*. Boston: Houghton Mifflin Company.

Bouchard, P. 1998. "Training and Work: Myths about Human Capital." In S. Scott, B. Spencer, and A. Thomas, (eds.), *Learning for Life: Canadian Readings in Adult Education*. Toronto: Thompson Educational Publishing.

Bowlby, G., and S. Langlois. 2002. "High-tech Boom and Bust." *Perspectives on Labour and Income* 14, 2 (Summer).

Braverman, H. 1975. "The Degradation of Work in the Twentieth Century." Monthly Review 34, 1 (May).

_____. 1974. *Labor and Monopoly Capital: The Degradation of Work in the Twentieth Century*. New York: Monthly Review Press.

Brecher, J., J.B. Childs, and J. Cutler (eds.). 1993. *Global Visions: Beyond the New World Order*. Boston: South End Press.

Brecher, J., and T. Costello. 1994. *Global Village or Global Pillage: Economic Restructuring from the Bottom Up*. Boston: South End Press.

Brennan, T. 2003. *Globalization and Its Terrors: Daily Life in the West*. London: Routledge.

Bridges, W. 1994. *Jobshift: How to Prosper in a Workplace without Jobs*. New York: Addison-Wesley.

Brisbois, R. 2003. *How Canada Stacks Up: The Quality of Work — An International Perspective*. Ottawa: Canadian Research Policy Networks.

Broad, D. 2000. *Hollow Work, Hollow Society? Globalization and the Casual Labour Problem*. Halifax: Fernwood Publishing.

_____. 1998. "New World Order Versus Just World Order." *Social Justice* 25, 2 (Summer).

_____. 1995. "Globalization Versus Labour." *Monthly Review* 47, 7 (December).

Broad, D., and W. Antony (eds.). 1999. *Citizens Or Consumers? Social Policy in a Market Society*. Halifax: Fernwood Publishing.

Brown, P., and H. Lauder. 2001. *Capitalism and Social Progress: The Future of Society in a Global Economy*. London: Palgrave.

Browne, P.L. 1996. *Love in a Cold World? The Voluntary Sector in an Age of Cuts*. Ottawa: Canadian Centre for Policy Alternatives.

Burchell, B., D. Lapido, and F. Wilkinson (eds.). 2002. *Job Insecurity and Work Intensification*. London: Routledge.

Burrell, D. 2001. "Weekend Woes: Working Hard can be Hazardous to your Holidays." *Psychology Today* 34.

Callinicos, A. 2001. *Against the Third Way*. Cambridge: Polity Press.

Campaign 2000. 2003. "Honouring our Promises: Meeting the Challenge to End Child and Family Poverty. 2003 Report Card on Child Poverty in Canada." Toronto: Campaign 2000. Available at <www.campaign2000.ca>.

_____. 2002. "The UN Special Session on Children: Putting Promises Into Action." Toronto: Campaign 2000. Available at <www.campaign2000.ca/rc/un-sscMay02statusreport.pdf>.

Canada, Government of. 1994a. *Improving Social Security in Canada: A Discussion Paper*. Ottawa: Human Resources Development Canada.

_____. 1994b. *A New Framework for Economic Policy*. Ottawa: Department of Finance Canada.

Canadian Centre for Policy Alternatives Consortium on Globalization and Health. 2002. "Putting Health First: Canadian Health Care Reform, Trade Treaties and Foreign Policy." Available at <www.policyalternatives.ca/documents / National_Office_Pubs/putting_health_first.pdf>.

Carter, T. 1999. *The Aftermath of Reengineering: Downsizing and Corporate Performance*. New York: Haworth Press.

Cascio, W. 1993. "Downsizing: What Do We Know? What Have We Learned?" *The Executive* 7, 1.

CAW (Canadian Auto Workers). 1993. "Work Reorganization: Responding to Lean Production." Available at <www.caw.ca/whoweare/cawpoliciesandstatements/index.aspCAW>. Policies and Statements, <www.caw.ca/whoweare/cawpoliciesandstatements/index.asp>.

Chase-Dunn, C. 1999. "Globalization: A World-Systems Perspective." *Journal of World-Systems Research* 5, 2 (Summer).

Chaykowski, R. 1997. *Fostering Human Resources in the New Economy: Challenges to the Way Ahead*. Kingston: Industrial Relations Centre Press.

Chilcote, R.H. (ed.). 2003. *Development in Theory and Practice: Latin American Perspectives*. New York: Rowman and Littlefield Publishers.

Chomsky, N. 1993. *Year 501: The Conquest Continues*. Montreal: Black Rose Books.

Clarke, T. 1997. *Silent Coup: Confronting the Big Business Takeover in Canada*. Toronto: Lorimer.

CLC (Canadian Labour Congress). 2005. "Links." Available at <www.clc-ctc.ca/

web/menu/english/en_index.htm>.

Coady, M.1950. "Mobilizing for Enlightenment." In J.R. Kidd (ed.), *Adult Education in Canada*. Toronto: Garden City Press Co-operative.

Cohen, M. 1997. "Downsizing and Disability go Together." *Business and Health* 15, 1.

Cohen, S.S., and J. Zysman. 1987. *Manufacturing Matters: The Myth of the Post-Industrial Society*. New York: Basic Books.

Collier, K. 1997. *After the Welfare State*. Vancouver: New Star Books.

Comfort, D., K. Johnson, and D. Wallace. 2003. *Part-time Work and Family-Friendly Practices in Canadian Workplaces*. Ottawa: Human Resources Development Canada.

Compton, S. 2002. "I Still Feel Overqualified for my Job." *Canadian Social Trends*. Ottawa: Statistics Canada (Catalogue number 11-008).

Council of Canadians. (n.d.) "Past Campaigns: MAI." Available at <http://www.canadians.org/browse_categories.htm?COC_token=COC_token&step=2&catid=88&iscat=1>.

Council of Ministers of Education. 1999. "A Report on Public Expectations of Post-Secondary Education in Canada." Toronto: Council of Ministers of Education.

Cranford, C., L.F. Vosko, and N. Zukewich. 2003. "Precarious Employment in the Canadian Labour Market: A Statistical Report." *Just Labour* 3 (Fall).

Crompton, S., and M. Vickers. 2000. "One Hundred Years of Labour Force." *Canadian Social Trends*. Ottawa: Statistics Canada (Catalogue Number 11-008. Spring).

Dachraoui, K., T.M. Harchaoui, and F. Tarkhani. 2003. *Productivity and Prosperity in the Information Age: A Canada-U.S. Comparison*. Ottawa: Statistics Canada.

Dagg, A. 1997. "Worker Representation and Protection in the 'New Economy.'" Collective Reflection on the Changing Workplace, Report of the Advisory Committee on the Changing Workplace. Ottawa: Human Resources and Development Canada.

Darier, E. 1996. "Paul Lafargue's The Right to be Lazy: Laziness as a Green Project?" *Socialist Studies Bulletin* 46.

Das Gupta, T. 1996. *Racism and Paid Work*. Toronto: Garamond Press.

Davis, J. 1999. "Rehthinking Globalization." *Race and Class* 40, 2/3 (March).

Davis, J., T. Hirschl, and M. Stack. 1997. *Cutting Edge: Technology, Information Capitalism and Social Revolution*. London: Verso Books.

Davis, J., and M. Stack. 1993. "Knowledge in Production." *Race and Class* 34, 3 (March).

Davis-Blake, A., J. Broschak, and E. George. 2003. "Happy Together? How Using Nonstandard Workers Affects Exit, Voice, and Loyalty Among Standard Employees." *The Academy of Management Journal* 46, 4.

de Lange, A.H., T.W. Taris, M.A.J. Kompier, I.L.D. Houtman, and P.M. Bongers. 2003. "The Very Best of the Millennium": Longitudinal Research and the Demand-Control-(Support) Model. *Journal of Occupational Health Psychology* 8, 4.

Delors, J. 1996. "Learning: The Treasure Within." (Report to UNESCO of the International Commission on Education for the Twenty-first Century). Paris:

UNESCO Publishing.

Doeringer, P., and M. Piore. 1971. *Internal Labor Markets and Manpower Analysis*. New York: Lexington.

Dolgoff, R., and D. Feldstein. 2000. *Understanding Social Welfare*. Fifth edition. Needham Heights, MA: Allyn and Bacon.

Dooley, D. 2003. "Unemployment, Underemployment and Mental Health: Conceptualizing Employment Status as a Continuum." *American Journal of Community Psychology* 32.

Drago, R. 1996. "Workplace Transformation and the Disposable Workplace: Employee Involvement in Australia." *Industrial Relations* 35, 4.

Drolet, M., and R. Morissette. 2002. "Better Jobs in the New Economy?" *Perspectives on Labour and Income* 14, 3 (Autumn).

Drucker, P.F. 1993. *Post-Capitalist Society*. New York: HarperCollins.

Du Boff, R.B. 2003. "U.S. Hegemony: Continuing Decline, Enduring Danger." *Monthly Review* 55, 7 (December).

Duffy, A., D. Glenday, and N. Pupo. 1997. *Good Jobs, Bad Jobs, No Jobs: The Transformation of Work in the 21st Century*. Toronto: Harcourt Brace.

Duffy, A., N. Mandell, and N. Pupo. 1989. *Few Choices: Women, Work and Family*. Toronto: Garamond Press.

Dunham, J. 2001. *Stress in the Workplace: Past, Present, Future*. London, WHURR Publishers.

Dunk, T., S. McBride, and R. Nelsen. 1996. "Introduction." In T. Dunk, S. McBride and R. Nelsen (eds.). *The Training Trap: Ideology, Training and the Labour Market*. Winnipeg/Halifax: Society for Socialist Studies/Fernwood Publishing.

Duxbury, L., and C. Higgins. 2001. "Work-life Balance in the New Millenium: Where Are We? Where Do We Go from Here?" Ottawa: Canadian Policy Research Networks. CPRN Discussion Paper W-12.

Duxbury, L.E., C.A. Higgins, and C. Lee. 1994. "Work-family Conflict: A Comparison by Gender, Family Type and Perceived Control." *Journal of Family Issues* 15, 3.

Earl, L. 2002 "Innovation and Change in the Public Sector: A Seeming Oxymoron." Survey of Electronic Commerce and Technology. (Catalogue Number 88F0006XIE No. 01). Ottawa: Statistics Canada.

Earle, Steve. 2002. "Amerika v. 6.0 (The Best We Can Do)." *Jerusalem*. Music CD, produced by the Twangtrust, E-Squared Productions.

Easterlin, R.A. 1998. *Growth Triumphant: The Twenty-first Century in Historical Perspective*. Ann Arbor: University of Michigan Press.

ECC (Economic Council of Canada). 1991. *Employment in the Service Economy*. Ottawa: Economic Council of Canada.

_____. 1990. *Good Jobs, Bad Jobs: Employment in the Service Economy*. Ottawa: Economic Council of Canada.

Edwards, R. 1993. "Managing Adult Unemployment in Canada and Britain: The Lack of Opportunity through Education and Training." *British Journal of Canadian Studies* 8, 1.

Egger, P., and W. Sengenberger. 2001. *Decent Work Issues and Policies*. Geneva: International Labour Organization.

References

Ellwood, W. 2001. *The No-Nonsense Guide to Globalization.* Toronto: Between The Lines.

Ertel, M., E. Pech, and P. Ullsperger. 2000. "Telework in Perspective — New Challenges to Occupational Health and Safety." In K. Isaksson, C. Hogstedt, E. Eriksson and T. Theorell (eds.), *Health Effects of the New Labour Market.* New York: Kluwer Academic.

European Commission. 1997. "Green Paper — Partnership for a New Organization of Work." European Commission [2002, 11/20/2002].

European Foundation for the Improvement of Living and Working Conditions. 2002a. "Quality of Work and Employment in Europe: Issues and Challenges." Foundation Paper. Dublin, Ireland: EFILWC. Available at <www.eurofound. eu.int/publications/files/EF0212EN.pdf>.

_____. 2002b. "Interactions Between the Labour Market and Social Protection: Seminar Report." Brussels, European Foundation for the Improvement of Working and Living Conditions. Available at <www.eurofound.eu.int/working/employment/documents/sem_prog.pdf>.

Fagan, C. 2003. "Working-time Preferences and Work-life Balance in the EU: Some Policy Considerations for Enhancing Quality of Life." Dublin: European Foundation for the Improvement of Living and Working Conditions. Available at <www.eurofound.eu.int/publications/EF0342.htm>.

Fairbairn, B., J. Bold, M. Fulton, L. Ketilson, and D. Ish. 1991. *Co-operatives and Community Development: Economics in Social Perspective.* Saskatoon: University of Saskatchewan, Centre for the Study of Co-operatives.

Fairris, D., and H. Tohyama. 2002. "Productive Efficiency and the Lean Production System in Japan and the United States." *Economic and Industrial Democracy* 23, 4.

Fallick, B. 1996. "A Review of the Recent Empirical Literature on Displaced Workers." *Industrial and Labor Relations Review* 50, 1.

Farias, G., and A. Varma. 1998. "Research Update: High Performance Work Systems: What We Know and What We Need to Know." *Human Resource Planning* 21, 2.

Federal, Provincial, Territorial Advisory Committee on Population Health. 1999. *Statistical Report on the Health of Canadians.* Ottawa: Minister of Public Works and Government Services Canada.

Ferber, M.A., and B. O'Farrell. 1991. *Work and Family: Policies for a Changing Workforce.* Washington: National Academy Press.

Ferrie, J.E. 2001. "Is Job Insecurity Harmful to Health?" *Journal of the Royal Society of Medicine* 94.

Ferrie, J.E., M.S. Shipley, M. Marmot, S. Stansfeld, and G. Davey-Smith. 1995. "Health Effects of Anticipation of Job Change and Non-employment: Longitudinal Data from the Whitehall II Study." *British Medical Journal* 311.

50 Years Is Enough. 2004. "IMF Report: Globalization May Hurt Poor." Available at <www.50years.org/cms/updates/story/21>.

Finlayson, A. 1996. *Naming Rumpelstiltskin: Who Will Profit and Who Will Lose in the Workplace of the 21st Century.* Toronto: Key Porter.

Finn, K.A., and E. Shaker. 2004. "Junk Food and Politics." *Our Times* 22, 6 (December/January).

Foley, J. 2001. "After Displacement, Who Wins, Who Loses." *Canadian Business Economics* 8, 3.

Foley, J., G. Miller, and J. Neiszner. 2003. "'Empowered?' The Experience of a Group of Federal Employees." Paper presented to the Congress of Social Sciences and Humanities, Dalhousie University, Halifax, Nova Scotia, June.

Foot, D. 1996. *Boom, Bust and Echo 2000: Profiting from the Demographic Shift in the New Millennium*. Toronto: Macfarlane Walter and Rose.

Franks, S. 1999. *Having None of It: Women, Men and the Future of Work*. London: Granta Books.

Foster, J.B. 1999. *The Vulnerable Planet: A Short History of the Environment*. New York: Monthly Review Press.

Foster, J. Bellamy, and H. Szlajfer. 1984. *The Faltering Economy: The Problem of Accumulation Under Monopoly Capitalism*. New York: Monthly Review Press.

Frank, A.G. 1981. *Crisis: In the Third World*. New York: Holmes and Meier.

_____. 1980. *Crisis: In the World Economy*. New York: Holmes and Meier.

_____ 1969. *Latin America: Underdevelopment or Revolution*. New York: Monthly Review Press.

Freeman, A. 1994. "Martin Vows to Slash Deficit." *Globe and Mail*, October 18.

Frenkel, S. 1999. *On the Front Line: Organization of Work in the Information Economy*. Ithaca: ILR Press.

Frobel, F., J. Heinrichs, and O. Kreye. 1980. *The New International Division of Labour*. Cambridge: Cambridge University Press.

Frone, M., M. Russell, and L. Cooper. 1997. "Relation of Work-Family Conflict to Health Outcomes: A Four-Year Longitudinal Study of Employed Parents." *Journal of Occupational and Organizational Psychology* 70, 4.

Fudge, J., E. Tucker, and L.F. Vosko. 2002. *The Legal Concept of Employment: Marginalizing Workers*. Toronto: Law Commission of Canada.

Galarneau, D., and L. Stratychuk. 2001. "After the Layoff." *Perspectives on Labour and Income*. Ottawa: Statistics Canada (Catalogue Number 75-001-XIE, October).

Geary, J., and A. Dobbins. 2001. "Teamworking: A New Dynamic in the Pursuit of Management Control." *Human Resource Management Journal* 11, 1.

Gelpi, E. 1979. *A Future for Lifelong Education*. Volume 1. Lifelong Education: Principles, Policies and Practices, (Manchester Monographs 13). Manchester: Manchester University, Department of Adult and Higher Education.

Gentile, G.S. 2004. "Your Factory, Under Worker Control: Lessons from Argentina." *Labor Notes* (March). Available at <www.labornotes.org/archives/2004/03/articles/i.html>.

George, S. 1997. "Winning the War of Ideas." *Dissent* Summer. Available at <www.tni.org/george/index.htm>.

Gil, D.G. 1992. *Unravelling Social Policy: Theory, Analysis and Political Action Towards Social Equality*. Rochester, VT: Schenkman Books.

Gilbert, N. 2004. *Transformation of the Welfare State: The Silent Surrender of Public Responsibility*. New York: Oxford University Press.

Gingras, Y., and R. Roy. 1998. *Is There a Skill Gap in Canada?* R-98-9E. Ottawa: Applied Research Branch, Strategic Policy, Human Resources Development

Canada.

Godard, J. 2001. "High Performance and the Transformation of Work? The Implications of Alternative Work Practices for the Experience and Outcomes of Work." *Industrial and Labor Relations Review* 54, 4.

Godard, J., and J. Delaney. 2000. "Reflections on the 'High Performance' Paradigm's Implications for Industrial Relations As A Field." *Industrial and Labor Relations Review* 53, 3.

Goldberg, M., and D. Green. 1999. *Raising the Floor: The Social and Economic Benefits of Minimum Wages in Canada*. British Columbia: Canadian Centre for Policy Alternatives.

Golding, M., and S. Middleton. 1982. *Images of Welfare*. Oxford: Martin Robertson and Company Ltd.

Golding, P. 1998. "Global Village or Cultural Pillage? The Unequal Inheritance of the Communications Revolution." In R.W. McChesney, E.M. Wood and J.B. Foster (eds.), *Capitalism and the Information Age*. New York: Monthly Review Press.

Gore S. 1978. "The Effect of Social Support in Moderating the Health Consequences of Unemployment." *Journal of Health and Social Behaviour* 19.

Gorz, A. 1999. *Reclaiming Work: Beyond the Wage-Based Society*. Translated by C. Turner. London: Polity Press.

Government of Canada. 2002. "Public Service Employee Survey." Available at <www.survey-sondage.gc.ca>.

_____. 1999. Public Service Employee Survey. Available at <www.survey-sondage. gc.ca>.

_____. 1994a. "Agenda: Jobs and Growth, Improving Social Security in Canada." A Discussion Paper. Ottawa: Human Resources Development Canada.

_____. 1994b. "Agenda: Jobs and Growth, Improving Social Security in Canada." Discussion Paper Summary. Ottawa: Human Resources Development Canada.

Government of Saskatchewan. Saskatchewan Social Services. 2003. Jobs First and Transitional Employment Allowance. Regina: Government of Saskatchewan.

Graham, J., and A. Al-Krenawi. 2001. "Canadian Approaches to Income Security." In J. Turner and F. Turner (eds.), *Canadian Social Welfare*. Toronto: Pearson Education Canada.

Grantham, C. 2000. *The Future of Work: The Promise of the New Digital Work Society*. New York: McGraw-Hill.

Gray, J. 2002. *False Dawn: The Delusions of Global Capitalism*. New York: New Press.

Grenon, L., and B. Chun. 1997. "Non-Permanent Paid Work." Perspectives on Labour and Income. Ottawa: Statistics Canada (Catalogue Number 75-001-XPE, Fall).

Guard, J. 2003. "Manitoba's Call Centre Explosion: A Preliminary Overview." Paper prepared for conference on "Organizing Call Centres from the Workers' Perspective" (September 11–13), Toronto. Available at <www.uswa.ca/program/content/951.php>.

Guest, D. 2001. "Industrial Relations and Human Resource Management." In J. Storey (ed.), *Human Resource Management: A Critical Text*. London: Thomson

Learning.

_____. "Human Resource Management — the Workers' Verdict." *Human Resource Management Journal* 9, 3.

_____. 1998. "Human Resource Management, Trade Unions and Industrial Relations." In C. Mabey, G. Salaman and J. Storey (eds.), *Strategic Human Resource Management: A Reader*. London: Sage.

Guevera, E.C. 1965. *Socialism and Man in Cuba*. New York: Pathfinder Press.

Gunderson, M. 2002. "Rethinking Productivity From a Workplace Perspective." Ottawa: Canadian Policy Research Networks Paper W/17.

Hajdukowski-Ahmed, M., M. Pond, I.U. Zeytinoglu, and L. Chambers. 1999. "We are Making a Difference. The Women's Worksite Action Group: A Participatory Action Research Project." In M. Denton. M. Hajdukowski-Ahmed, M. O'Connor and I.U. Zeytinoglu (eds.), *Women's Voices in Health Promotion*. Toronto: Canadian Scholars' Press.

Harrison, B. 1997. *Lean And Mean: The Changing Landscape of Corporate Power in the Age of Flexibility*. New York: Basic Books.

Hart-Landsberg, M. 2006. "Neoliberalism: Myths and Reality." *Monthly Review* 57, 11.

Harvey, D. 1989. *The Condition of Postmodernity: An Inquiry into the Origins of Cultural Change*. Oxford: Basil Blackwell.

Hayden, A. 1999. *Sharing the Work, Sparing the Planet: Work Time, Consumption and Ecology*. Toronto: Between The Lines.

Heilbroner, R. 1989. "The Triumph of Capitalism." *New Yorker* 64 (January 23).

Heller, F., E. Pusic, G. Strauss, and B. Wilpert. 1998. *Organizational Participation: Myth and Reality*. Oxford: Oxford University Press.

Henwood, Doug. 2003. *After The New Economy*. New York: New Press.

Henwood, F., S. Wyatt, N. Miller, and P. Senker. 2000. "Critical Perspectives on Technologies, In/Equalities and the Information Society." In S. Wyatt et al. (eds.), *Technology and In/Equality: Questioning the Information Society*. London and New York: Routledge.

Herman, E.S. 1999. "The Threat of Globalization." *New Politics* 7, 2 (Winter). Available at <http://www.wpunj.edu/~newpol/issue26/herman26.htm>.

Herzenberg, S.A., J.A. Alic, and H. Wial. 1998. *New Rules for a New Economy: Employment and Opportunity in Postindustrial America*. Ithaca and London: ILR Press, an imprint of Cornell University Press.

Hicks, A. 1999. *Social Democracy and Welfare Capitalism*. Ithaca: Cornell University Press.

Himmelfarb, G. 1984. *The Idea of Poverty: England in the Early Industrial Age*. New York: Vintage Books.

Ho, J.-H., and E.H. Shin. 2003. "Inequalities in Nonfatal Work Injury: The Significance of Race, Human Capital, and Occupations." *Social Science and Medicine* 57.

Holden, C. 1999. "Globalization, Social Exclusion and Labour's New Work Ethic." *Critical Social Policy* 61, 19 (4).

Hopkins, T.K., I. Wallerstein, et al. 1996. *The Age of Transition: The Trajectory of the World-System, 1945–2025*. London: Zed Books.

References

HRDC (Human Resources Development Canada). 2002. *Knowledge Matters: Skills and Learning for Canadians*. Ottawa: HRDC. Available at <www.innovationstrategy. gc.ca.>

_____. 1994. *Report of the Advisory Group on Working Time and Distribution of Work*. Ottawa: Government of Canada.

Hudson, M. 2002. "Flexibility and the Reorganisation of Work." In B. Burchell, D. Lapido and F. Wilkinson (eds.), *Job Insecurity and Work Intensification*. London: Routledge.

Hughes, K.D. 2005. *Female Enterprise in the New Economy*. Toronto: University of Toronto Press.

Hughes, K., G. Lowe, and G. Schellenberg. 2003. "Men's and Women's Quality of Work in the New Canadian Economy." Ottawa: Canadian Policy Research Networks Paper W/19.

Hunter, G., and F. Douglas. 2002. "Report Card on Child Poverty in Saskatchewan 2002." Regina: Social Policy Research Unit, Faculty of Social Work, University of Regina. Available at <www.campaign2000.ca/rc/pdf/SKpovertyreportnov02.pdf>.

Hunter, G., and D. Miazdyck. 2003. "Current Issues Surrounding Poverty and Welfare Programming in Canada: Two Reviews." Working Paper No. 20. Regina: Social Policy Research Unit, Faculty of Social Work, University of Regina. Available at <www.uregina.ca/spr/pdfs/working_paper_20.pdf>.Huws, U. 2006. "What Will We Do? The Destruction of Occupational Identities in the 'Knowledge-Based Economy'." *Monthly Review* 57, 8 (January).

_____. 2003. *The Making of a Cybertariat: Virtual Work in a Real World*. New York: Monthly Review Press.

Ichniowski, C., T. Kochan, D. Levine, C. Olson, and G. Strauss. 2000. "What Works at Work: Overview and Assessment." In C. Icniowski, T.A. Kochan, D.J. Levine, C. Olson and Strauss, G. (eds.), *The American Workplace: Skills, Compensation, and Employee Involvement*. Cambridge: Cambridge University Press.

_____. 1996. "What Works At Work: Overview and Assessment." *Industrial Relations* 35, 3.

Ife, J. 2001. "Human Rights, Global Citizenship and Community Development." *Canadian Review of Social Policy* 48.

ILO (International Labour Organization). 2006. *Global Employment Trends Brief, January 2006*. Geneva: International Labour Organization.

_____. 2005a. *World Employment Report 2004–05: Employment, Productivity and Poverty Reduction*. Geneva: International Labour Organization.

_____. 2005b. *Global Employment Trends Brief, February 2005*. Geneva: International Labour Organization.

_____. 2004a. *Global Employment Trends*. Geneva: International Labour Organization.

_____. 2004b. *Global Employment Trends for Women*. Geneva: International Labour Organization.

_____. 2004c. *A Fair Globalization: The Role of the ILO*. Geneva: International Labour Organization.

_____. 2004d. *Global Employment Trends for Youth*. Geneva: International Labour Organization.

_____. 2004e. "Decent Work — The Heart of Social Progress." Available at <http://www.ilo.org/public/english/decent.htm>.

_____. 2001a. *World Employment Report 2001: Life at Work in the Information Economy.* Geneva: International Labour Organization.

_____. 2001b. *Report of the Director-General: Reducing the Decent Work Deficit — A Global Challenge.* Geneva: International Labour Organization.

_____. 1999. Report of the Director-General: Decent Work. Geneva: International labour Organization.

_____. 1998. *World Employment 1998/99. Employability in a Global Context.* Geneva: International labour Organization.

IMF (International Monetary Fund). 2002. "Globalization: A Framework for IMF Involvement." Available at <http://www.imf.org/external/np/exr/ib/2002/031502.htm>.

_____. 2000. "Globalization: Threat or Opportunity?" Available at <http://www.imf.org/external/np/exr/ib/2000/041200.htm>.

Industry Canada. 2001. *Achieving Excellence: Investing in People, Knowledge and Opportunity.* Ottawa: Industry Canada. Available at <www.innovationstrategy.gc.ca>.

Ireland, T. 1978 *Gelpi's View of Lifelong Education.* (Manchester Monographs 14). Manchester: Manchester University, Department of Adult and Higher Education.

Ivancevich, J.M., and M.T. Matteson. 1980. *Stress and Work: A Managerial Perspective.* Glenview, Ill.: Scott Foresman.

Jackson, A. 2005a. "Better Educated, Badly Paid and Underemployed: A Statistical Picture of Young Workers in Canada." Research paper #33. Ottawa: Canadian Labour Congress. Available at <http://canadianlabour.ca/updir/youngworkerRevEn.pdf>.

_____. 2005b. *Work and Labour in Canada: Critical Issues.* Toronto: Canadian Scholars' Press.

_____. 2003. "Is Work Working For Women?" Ottawa: Canadian Labour Congress Research Paper #22.

_____. 2002a. "The Unhealthy Canadian Workplace." Ottawa: Canadian Labour Congress. Available at <www.clc-ctc.ca>.

_____. 2002b. "Is Work Working for Workers of Colour?" Ottawa: Canadian Labour Congress. Research paper #18.

Jackson, A., and D. Robinson, with B. Baldwin, and C. Wiggins. 2000. *Falling Behind: The State of Working Canada, 2000.* Ottawa: Canadian Centre for Policy Alternatives.

Jackson, P., and S. Mullarkey. 2000. "Lean Production Teams and Health in Garment Manufacture." *Journal of Occupational Health Psychology* 5, 2.

Jahoda, M. 1982. *Employment and Unemployment: A Social Psychological Analysis.* Cambridge: Cambridge University Press.

Janz, T. 2003. "Low-paid Employment and 'Moving Up': 1996–2001." Ottawa: Statistics Canada. (Catalogue number 75F0002MIE-No. 003).

Johnson, J.V., and E.M. Hall. 1999. "Class, Work and Health." In B. Amick et al. (eds.), *Society and Health.* New York: Oxford University Press.

References

_____. 1996. "Job Strain, Workplace Support and Cardiovascular Disease." *American Journal of Public Health* 78.

Jones, C. 2001. "Voices from the Front Line: State Social Workers and New Labour." *British Journal of Social Work* 31.

Jones, C., and T. Novak. 1999. *Poverty, Welfare and the Disciplinary State*. London: Routledge.

Jones, F., J.E.H. Bright, B. Searle, and L. Cooper. 1998. "Modelling Occupational Stress and Health: The Impact of the Demand-Control Model on Academic Research and on Workplace Practice." *Stress Medicine* 14.

Jordan, B., and C. Jordan. 2000. *Social Work and the Third Way: Tough Love as Social Policy*. London: Sage Publications.

Karambayya, R. 1998. "Caught in the Crossfire: Women and Corporate Restructuring." *Canadian Journal of Administrative Sciences* 15, 4.

Karasek, R., and T. Theorell. 1990. *Healthy Work: Stress, Productivity and the Reconstruction of Working Life*. New York: Basic Books.

Karger, H., and D. Stoesz. 1998. *American Social Welfare Policy: A Pluralist Approach*. Third edition. New York: Addison Wesley Longman, Inc.

Kasl, S.V. 1998. "Measuring Job Stressors and Studying the Health Impact of the Work Environment: An Epidemiologic Commentary." *Journal of Occupational Health Psychology* 3, 4.

Katz, M. 2001. *The Price of Citizenship: Redefining the American Welfare State*. New York: Henry Holt and Company, LLC.

_____. 1989. *The Undeserving Poor*. New York: Pantheon.

Kelly, K., L. Howatson-Leo, and W. Clark. 1997. "I Feel Overqualified for my Job…" *Canadian Social Trends*. Ottawa: Statistics Canada (Catalogue Number 11-008-XPE, Winter).

Kerstetter, S. 2003. *Rags and Riches: Wealth Inequality in Canada*. Ottawa: Canadian Centre for Policy Alternatives.

King, C.T., R.E. McPherson, and D.W. Long. 2000. "Public Labor Market Policies for the Twenty-First Century." In R. Marshall (ed.), *Back to Shared Prosperity: The Growing Inequality of Wealth and Income in America*. Armonk, NY: M.E. Sharpe.

Kivimaki, M., J. Vahtera, J. Pentti, and J. Ferrie. 2000. "Factors Underlying the Effect of Organisational Downsizing on Health of Employees: Longitudinal Cohort Study." *British Medical Journal* 320.

Klumb, P.L. and T. Lampert. 2004. "Women, Work, and Well-being 1950–2000: A Review and Methodological Critique." *Social Science and Medicine* 58.

Kochan, T., and P. Osterman. 1998. "The Mutual Gains Enterprise." In C. Mabey, G. Salaman and J. Storey (eds.), *Strategic Human Resource Management: A Reader*. London: Sage.

Kotz, D. 2003. "Neoliberalism and the U.S. Economic Expansion of the '90s." *Monthly Review* 54, 11 (April).

Kovel, J. 2002. *The Enemy of Nature: The End of Capitalism or the End of the World?* Halifax: Fernwood Publishing.

Krahn, H.J., and G.S. Lowe. 2002. *Work, Industry and Canadian Society*. Fourth edition. Toronto: Thompson Nelson.

Laabs, J. 1999. "Has Downsizing Missed Its Mark?" *Workforce* 78, 4.

Labib, N., and S. Appelbaum. 1994. "The Impact of Downsizing Practices on Corporate Success." *Journal of Management Development* 13, 7.

_____. 1993. "Strategic Downsizing: A Human Resources Perspective." *Human Resource Planning* 16, 4.

Lafargue, P. 1883. *The Right to be Lazy*. New York: Charles H. Kerr.

Landsbergis, P. A. 2003. "The Changing Organization of Work and the Safety and Health of Working People: A Commentary." *Journal of Occupational and Environmental Medicine* 45, 1.

Lappe, F.M. 2002. *Hope's Edge: The Next Diet for a Small Planet*. New York: Jeremy P. Taracher/Putnam.

Laxer, J. 1993. *False God: How the Globalization Myth has Impoverished Canada*. Toronto: Lester.

_____. 1998. *The Undeclared War: Class Conflict in the Age of Cyber Capitalism*. Toronto: Penguin.

Leader Post. 2003. "New Jobs in Lower Paid Industries." January 11: D6.

Leckie, N., A. Leonard, J. Turcotte, and D. Wallace. 2001. "Employer and Employee Perspectives on Human Resource Practices." Ottawa: Statistics Canada (Catalogue Number 71-584-MPE No. 1).

Leiss, W. 1976. *The Limits to Satisfaction: An Essay on the Problem of Needs and Commodities*. Toronto: University of Toronto Press.

Lerner, S., C.M.A. Clark, and W.R. Needham. 1999. *Basic Income: Economic Security for all Canadians*. Toronto: Between the Lines.

Lewchuk, W., A. de Wolff, A. King, and M.F. Polanyi. 2003. "From Job Strain to Employment Strain: Health Effects of Precarious Employment." *Just Labour* 3.

Lewchuk, W., and D. Robertson. 1996. "Working Conditions Under Lean Production: A Worker-based Benchmarking Study." *Asia Pacific Business Review* 2, 4.

Lin, X., and A. Popovich. 2003. "Working with Computers in Canada: An Empirical Analysis of Incidence, Frequency and Purpose, Final Report, April 2003." Ottawa: Human Resources and Development Canada, Catalogue number SP-574-05-03E.

_____. 2002. *The Effects of Computers on Workplace Stress, Job Security and Work Interest in Canada*. December. Ottawa: Human Resources.

Lipsett, B., and M. Reesor. 1997. "Flexible Work Arrangements: Evidence From the 1991 and 1995 Survey of Work Arrangements." Ottawa: Human Resource Development Canada Applied Research Branch R-97-10E.

Littler, C. 2000. "Comparing the Downsizing Experiences of Three Countries: A Restructuring Cycle?" In R. Burke and C. Cooper (eds.), *The Organization in Crisis: Downsizing, Restructuring and Privatization*. Oxford: Blackwell Publishing.

Livingstone, D. 2004. *The Education-Jobs Gap: Underemployment or Economic Democracy*. Second edition. Toronto: Garamond Press.

_____. 1996. "Wasted Education and Withered Work: Reversing the 'Postindustrial' Education-Jobs Optic." In T. Dunk, S. McBride and R. Nelsen (eds.), *The Training Trap: Ideology, Training and the Labour Market*. Winnipeg/Halifax: Society for Socialist Studies/Fernwood Publishing.

Lowe, G.S. 2001. "Employer of Choice? Workplace Innovation in Government: A

Synthesis Report." Ottawa: Canadian Policy Research Networks.

_____. 2000. *The Quality of Work: A People-Centred Agenda.* Don Mills, ON: Oxford University Press.

_____. 1998. "The Future of Work. Implications for Unions." *Relations Industrielles* 53, 2.

Mackenzie, H. 2004.. *Funding Postsecondary Education in Ontario: Beyond the Path of Least Resistance.* Toronto: Hugh MacKenzie and Associates. December. A study commissioned by the Ontario Coalition for Postsecondary Education. Available at <www.ocufa.on.ca>.

MacNeill, N. 1969. "Challenge for Change." In J.R. Kidd (ed.), 1978. *Coming of Age: Canadian Adult Education in the 1960s.* Toronto: Toronto: Canadian Association for Adult Education.

Macran, S., L. Clarke, and H. Joshi. 1996. "Women's Health: Dimensions and Differentials." *Social Science and Medicine* 42.

Magdoff, F., and H. Magdoff. 2004. "Disposable Workers: Today's Reserve Army of Labor." *Monthly Review* 55, 11.

Magdoff, H. 1982. "Measuring Productivity: The Economists' New Clothes." *The Nation* 234, 12 (March 27).

Magdoff, H., J.B. Foster, R.W. McChesney and F. Magdoff. "The Stagnation of Employment," *Monthly Review* 55, 11 (April).

Magdoff, H., and P.M. Sweezy. 1980. "The Uses and Abuses of Measuring Productivity." *Monthly Review* 32, 2 (June).

_____. 1979. "Productivity Slowdown: A False Alarm," *Monthly Review* 31, 2 (June).

Marchak, P. 1991. *The Integrated Circus: The New Right and the Restructuring of Global Markets.* Montreal: McGill-Queens University Press.

Marchington, M. 2001. "Employee Involvement At Work." In J. Storey (ed.), *Human Resource Management: A Critical Text.* London: Thomson Learning.

Marmot, M.G., G.D. Smith, et al. 1991. "Health Inequalities Among British Civil Servants: The Whitehall II Study." *Lancet* 337.

Marshall, K. 1996. "A Job to Die for." *Perspectives on Labour and Income* (Summer).

Martens, M.F.J., F.J.N. Nijhuis, M.P.J. Van Boxtel, and J.A. Knottnerus. 1999. "Flexible Work Schedules and Mental and Physical Health. A Study of a Working Population with Non-Traditional Hours." *Journal of Organizational Behavior* 20.

Martin, Paul. 2000. Speech to the Toronto Board of Trade. Toronto, Canada.

Marx, K. 1867. *Capital: A Critique of Political Economy.* Volume I. Harmondsworth: Penguin Books/New Left Review.

Marzani. C. 1990. *On Interring Communism and Exalting Capitalism.* New York: Monthly Review Pamphlets.

Mason, M. 1997. *Development and Disorder: A History of the Third World Since 1945.* Toronto: Between The Lines.

Maxwell, J. 2002. *Smart Social Policy — "Making Work Pay."* Ottawa: Canadian Policy Research Networks.

McCall, L. 2001. *Complex Inequality: Gender, Class and Race in the New Economy.* New York: Routledge.

McCarthy, S. 2001. Skills Shortage a Grave Concern. Toronto: *Globe and Mail.* February 27. Available at <http://www.nsb.com/ whatsnew.asp?i newsid =166>.

McQuaig, L. 2001. *All You Can Eat: Greed, Lust and the New Capitalism*. Toronto: Penguin Books Canada Ltd.

_____. 1998. *The Cult of Impotence: Selling the Myth of Powerlessness in the Global Economy*. Toronto: Penguin.

_____. 1995. *Shooting the Hippo: Death by Deficit and other Canadian Myths*. Toronto: Penguin.

_____. 1993. *The Wealthy Bankers Wife: The Assault on Equality in Canada*. Toronto: Penguin.

Menzies, H. 2005. *No Time: Stress and the Crisis of Modern Life*. Vancouver: Douglas and McIntyre.

_____. 1996. *Whose Brave New World? The Information Highway and the New Economy*. Toronto: Between The Lines.

_____. 1991. "Manufacturing McJobs: The Flesh and Blood of Economic Restructuring." *This Magazine* 25, 1.

Merret, C.D. 1996. *Free Trade: Neither Free Nor About Trade*. Montreal: Black Rose Books.

Merriam-Webster. 2003. *Merriam-Webster Collegiate Dictionary*. Eleventh edition. Springfield, MA: Merriam-Webster, Inc.

Meszaros, I. 2001. *Socialism Or Barbarism: From the "American Century" to the Crossroads*. New York: Monthly Review Press.

Mies, M. 1998. *Patriarchy and Accumulation on a World Scale: Women in the International Division of Labour*. London: Zed Books.

Mies, M., V. Bennholdt-Thomsen, and C. von Werlhof. 1988. *Women: The Last Colony*. London: Zed Books.

Milkman, R. 1998. "The New American Workplace: High Road or Low Road?" In P. Thompson and C. Warhurst (eds.), *Workplace of the Future*. Houndsmills, UK: Macmillan.

Mills, C.W. 1951. *White Collar: The American Middle Classes*. New York: Oxford University Press.

Mitter, S. 1986. *Common Fate, Common Bond: Women in the Global Economy*. London: Pluto Press.

Mohr, G. B. 2000. "The Changing Significance of Different Stressors after the Announcement of Bankruptcy: A Longitudinal Investigation with Special Emphasis on Job Insecurity." *Journal of Organizational Behavior* 21.

Morissette, R., and A. Johnson. 2005. *Are Good Jobs Disappearing in Canada?* Ottawa: Statistics Canada.

Morissette, R., and D. Sunter. 1994. "What Is Happening to Weekly Hours Worked in Canada?" Ottawa: Statistics Canada, Analytical Studies Branch, Research Paper Series No. 65.

Morris J.K., D.G. Cook, and A.G. Shaper. 1992. "Non-Employment and Changes in Smoking, Drinking and Body Weight." *British Medical Journal* 304.

Moscovitch, A., and G. Drover. 1987. "Social Expenditures and the Welfare State: The Canadian Experience in Historical Perspective." In A. Moscovitch and J. Albert (eds.), *The Benevolent State: The Growth of Welfare in Canada*. Toronto: Garamond Press.

Mulvale, J.P. 1999. "Defending the Past or Constructing the Future? The Role of Labour in Redefining Social Welfare in Canada." In Dave Broad and Wayne Antony (eds.), *Citizens or Consumers? Social Policy in a Market Society*. Halifax: Fernwood Publishing.

Murray, A. 2000. *The Wealth of Choices: How the New Economy Puts Power in Your Hands and Money in Your Pocket*. New York: Crown Publishers.

Mustard, C.A., D.C. Cole, H.S. Shannon, J. Pole, T.J. Sullivan, R. Allingham, and S.J. Sinclar. 2001. "Does the Decline in Worker's Compensation Claims (1990–1999) in Ontario Correspond to a Decline in Workplace Injuries?" Working Paper #168. Toronto: Institute for Work and Health.

Mustard, C.A., M. Vermeulen, and J.N. Lavis. 2003. "Is Position in the Occupational Hierarchy a Determinant of Decline in Perceived Health Status?" *Social Science and Medicine* 57.

National Council of Welfare, 2004. *Income for Living?* 120 (Spring). Ottawa: Minister of Public Works and Government Services Canada. Available at <http://www.ncwcnbes.net/htmdocument/reportIFL/IFL_e.pdf>.

National Film Board (NFB). 2004. *The Take*. Produced by Avi Lewis, Naomi Klein, and Silva Basmajian. Ottawa: National Film Board of Canada.

National Review. 2003. "Why Manufacturing Matters." Available at <http://www.findarticles.com/p/articles/mi_m1282/is_23_55/ai_n13610310>.

Nelson, D., and R. Burke. 1998. "Lessons Learned." *Canadian Journal of Administrative Sciences* 15, 4.

Nolan, J. 2002. "The Intensification of Everyday Life." In B. Burchell and F. Wilkinson (eds.), *Job Insecurity and Work Intensification*. London: Routledge.

Noreau, N. 2000. *Longitudinal Aspects of Involuntary Part-Time Employment*. Ottawa: Statistics Canada.

_____. 1994. "Involuntary Part-timers." *Perspectives on Labour and Income* 6, 3.

O'Hara, B. 1993. *Working Harder Isn't Working: A Detailed Plan for Implementing a Four-Day Workweek in Canada*. Vancouver: New Star Books.

O'Neill, K.M. 2002. "Web Sites of Resistance: Internetworking and Civil Society." In M. Pendakur and R. Harris (eds.), *Citizenship and Participation in the Information Age*. Aurora, Ontario: Garamond Press.

O'Reilly, J., and C. Fagan. 1998. *Part-Time Prospects: An International Comparison of Part-Time Work in Europe, North America and the Pacific Rim*. London Routledge.

OECD (Organisation for Economic Co-operation and Development). 2001. *Education Policy Analysis*. Paris: OECD, Centre for Educational Research and Innovation.

_____. 1997. *Implementing the OECD Jobs Strategy: Lessons from Member Countries Experience*. Paris: Organization for Economic Co-operation and Development. Available at <http://www1.oecd.org/sge/min/97study.htm>.

_____. 1996. *Implementing the OECD Jobs Strategy: Lessons from Member Countries' Experience*. Paris: OECD Publications. Available at <www.oecd.org>.

_____. 1995. *The OECD Jobs Study: Implementing the Strategy*. Paris: OECD Publications. Available at <www.oecd.org>.

_____. 1994. *The OECD Jobs Study: Facts, Analysis, Strategies*. Paris: OECD Publications. Available at <www.oecd.org>.

Oh, J.H., and E.H. Shin. 2003. "Inequalities in Nonfatal Work Injury: The Significance of Race, Human Capital, and Occupations." *Social Science and Medicine* 11.

Osberg, L., and A. Sharpe. 2003. *An Index of Labour Market Well-Being for OECD Countries*. Centre for the Study of Living Standards, CSLS research report 2003-05.

Osterman, P. 2000. "Work Reorganization in an Era of Restructuring: Trends in Diffusion and Effects on Employee Welfare." *Industrial and Labor Relations Review* 53, 2.

Ottawa (HRDC). 2000. *Reconnecting Social Assistance Recipients to the Labour Market: Lessons Learned*. Ottawa: (Catalogue number SPAH123E-03-00).

Oxford University Press. (n.d.) *Oxford English Dictionary Online*. New York: Oxford University Press. Available at <www.dictionary.oed.com>.

Palley, T.I. 1999. "Manufacturing Matters: The Impact on Productivity Growth, Wages and Income Distribution." Available at <www.aflcio.org/economicpolicy/E035.pdf>.

Pappenheim, F. 2000. "Alienation in American Society." *Monthly Review* 52, 2 (June).

Parker, M., and J. Slaughter. 1994. *Working Smart: A Union Guide to Participation Programs and Re-engineering*. Detroit: Labor Notes Books.

_____. 1988. *Choosing Sides: Unions and the Team Concept*. Boston: South End Press.

Peck, J. 2001. *Workfare States*. London: Guilford Press.

Peter, R., and J. Siegrist, J. 1999. "Chronic Psychosocial Stress at Work and Cardiovascular Disease: The Role of Effort-Reward Imbalance." *International Journal of Law and Psychiatry* 22.

Petras, J., and H. Veltmeyer. 2001. *Globalization Unmasked: Imperialism in the 21st Century*. Halifax: Fernwood Publishing.

Pettinger, R. 2002. *Managing the Flexible Workforce*. Oxford: Capstone Publishing.

Picot, G., and T. Wannell. 1997. *An Experimental Canadian Survey that Links Workplace Practices and Employee Outcomes: Why it is Needed and How it Works*. Ottawa: Statistics Canada Analytical Studies Branch (Catalogue Number 11F0019MPE No.100).

Piven, F. 2002. "Welfare Policy and American Politics." In F. Piven, J. Acker, M. Hallock, and S. Morgan (eds.), *Work, Welfare and Politics: Confronting Poverty in the Wake of Welfare Reform*. Eugene, OR: University of Oregon Press.

Piven, F., and R. Cloward. 2001. "Foreword." In J. Peck, *Workfare States*. London: Guilford Press.

_____. 1971. *Regulating the Poor: The Functions of Public Welfare*. New York: Pantheon Books.

Platt, T. 2003. "The State of Welfare: United States 2003." *Monthly Review* 55, 5.

Polanyi, K. 1957. *The Great Transformation*. Boston: Beacon Press.

Polanyi, M.F. 2001. "Toward Common Ground and Action on Repetitive Strain Injuries: An Assessment of a Future Search Conference." *Journal of Applied Behavioral Science* 37.

Polanyi, M., and E. Tompa. 2004. "Rethinking Work-Health Models for the New Global Economy: A Qualitative Analysis of Emerging Dimensions of Work."

References

Work 23, 1.

_____. 2002. "Rethinking the Health Implications of Work in the New Global Economy." Working Paper. Toronto: Munk Centre for International Studies, Comparative Program on Health and Society, University of Toronto. Available at "http://www.utoronto.ca/cphs/WorkingPapers.shtml>.

Portes, A., M. Castells, and L.A. Benton (eds.). 1989. *The Informal Economy: Studies in Advanced and Less Developed Countries.* Baltimore: Johns Hopkins University Press.

Prasad, E., K. Rogoff, S.J. Wei, and M.A. Kose. 2003. *Effects of Financial Globalization on Developing Countries: Some Empirical Evidence.* Washington, DC: International Monetary Fund.

Price, R.H., J.N. Choi, and A.D. Vinokur. 2002. "Links in the Chain of Adversity Following Job Loss: How Financial Strain and Loss of Personal Control Lead to Depression, Impaired Functioning, and Poor Health." *Journal of Occupational Health Psychology* 7, 4.

Price Waterhouse Coopers (PWC). 2004. *A Fine Balance: The Impact of Offshore IT Services on Canada's IT Landscape.* Toronto: Price Waterhouse Coopers.

Probst, T.M., and T.L. Brubaker. 2001. "The Effects of Job Insecurity on Employee Safety Outcomes: Cross-Sectional and Longitudinal Explorations." *Journal of Occupational Health Psychology* 6, 2.

PSAC (Public Service Alliance of Canada) n.d. "Policy 20 - Technological Change." Policies 20 to 40. Available at <www.psac.com/about/policies/20-40-e.shtml#pol20>.

Public Service Commission (PSC). 1999. *The Future of Work: Non-Standard Employment in the Public Service of Canada.* Ottawa: PSC Research Directorate, Policy, Research and Communications Branch.

Pulkingham, J., and G. Ternowetsky. 1996a. "The Changing Landscape of Social Policy and the Canadian Welfare State." In J. Pulkingham and G. Ternowetsky (eds.), *Remaking Canadian Social Policy: Social Security in the Late 1990s.* Halifax: Fernwood Publishing.

_____. 1996b. *Remaking Canadian Social Policy: Social Security in the Late 1990s.* Halifax: Fernwood Publishing.

Quinlan, M., C. Mayhew, and P. Bohle. 2001. "The Global Expansion of Precarious Employment, Work Disorganization, and Consequences for Occupational Health: A Review of Recent Research." *International Journal of Health Services* 31, 2.

Ransom, D. 2001. *The No-Nonsense Guide to Fair Trade.* Toronto: Between The Lines.

Raphael, D. 2001. "From Increasing Poverty to Social Disintegration: How Economic Inequality Affects the Health of Individuals and Communities." In D. Coburn and P. Armstrong (eds.), *Unhealthy Times: The Political Economy of Health and Care in Canada.* Toronto, Oxford University Press.

Reich, Robert. 2001. *The Future of Success: Working and Living in the New Economy.* New York: Alfred A, Knopf.

Reid, A. 1996. *Shakedown: How the New Economy is Changing our Lives.* Toronto: Doubleday.

Reiter, Er. 1995. *Making Fast Food: From the Frying Pan into the Fryer.* Montreal: McGill-

Queen's University Press.

Research Institute for Psychology and Health. 2004. Interviews from the fourth Dutch conference on psychology and health: Prof. Johannes Siegrist. Available at <http://pandh.fss.uu.nl/siegrist.htm>.

Reskin, B., and I. Padavic. 1994. *Women and Men at Work.* Thousand Oaks: Sage Publications.

Rifkin, J. 1995. *The End of Work: The Decline of the Global Labor Force and the Dawn of the Post-Market Era.* New York: Jeremy P. Tarcher/Putman Books.

Riipinen, M. 1997. "The Relationship Between Job Involvement and Well-Being." *Journal of Psychology* 131, 1.

Rinehart, J.W. 2001. *The Tyranny of Work: Alienation and the Labour Process.* Toronto: Harcourt Brace Jovanovich.

_____. 1995. "The Ideology of Competitiveness." *Monthly Review* October, 47, 5.

Robertson, R. 2003. *The Three Waves of Globalization: A History of Developing Global Consciousness.* Halifax: Fernwood Publishing.

Robinson, P. 2003. "Wages victory for call centre workers." *The Age* (February 11). Melbourne, Australia. Available at <www.theage.com.au>.

Ross, D., K. Scott, and P. Smith. 2000. *The Canadian Fact Book on Poverty.* Ottawa: Canadian Council on Social Development.

Roth, W. 2002. *The Assault on Social Policy.* New York: Columbia University Press.

Rynn, J. 2000. "Why Manufacturing Matters: A Production-Centered Path to Economic Growth and Social Justice." Available at <http://www.aftercapitalism. com/>.

Sagie, A., and M. Koslowsky. 2000. *Participation and Empowerment in Organizations: Modeling, Effectiveness, and Applications.* Thousand Oaks: Sage Publications.

Saskatchewan Social Services. n.d. "Building Independence — Investing in Families." Saskatchewan Employment Supplement; Saskatchewan Child Benefit; Family Health Benefits; Provincial Training Allowance; Youth Futures [Brochures].

Saskatchewan's Chartered Accountants. 2004. *Saskatchewan Check-up: Saskatchewan as a Place to Work.* Saskatchewan: Saskatchewan's Chartered Accountants. Available at <www.icas.sk.ca>.

Sassen, S. 2000. "The Demise of Pax Americana and the Emergence of Informalization as a Systemic Trend." In F. Tabak and M.A. Crichlow (eds.), Informalization: Process and Structure. Baltimore: Johns Hopkins University Press.

_____. 1998. *Globalization and Its Discontents: Essays on the New Mobility of People and Money.* New York: New Press.

_____. 1994. *Cities in a World Economy.* Thousand Oaks, CA: Pine Forge Press.

Saunders, R. 2005a. *Vulnerable Workers in Saskatchewan: Issues and Policy Options.* Presentation to the Saskatchewan Institute of Public Policy, Regina, Saskatchewan, September 23, 2005.

_____. 2005b. *Lifting the Boats: Policies to Make Work Pay.* Vulnerable Workers Series No.5, June 2005. Ottawa: Canadian Policy Research Networks.

_____. 2003. "Defining Vulnerability in the Labour Market." Research paper w/21. Ottawa: Canadian Policy Research Networks.

Saville, J. 1994. *The Consolidation of the Capitalist State, 1800–1850.* London: Pluto

References

Press.

Schafer, C., J. Emes, and J. Clemens. 2001. "Surveying US and Canadian Welfare Reform." *Critical Issues Bulletins.* Vancouver: The Fraser Institute.

Schenk, C., and J. Anderson (eds.). 1999. *Re-Shaping Work 2: Labour, the Workplace and Technological Change.* Toronto: Garamond Press.

_____. 1995. *Re-Shaping Work: Union Responses to Technological Change.* Toronto: Ontario Federation of Labour.

Schnall, P., P.A. Landsbergis, and D. Baker. 1994. "Job Strain and Cardiovascular Disease." *Annual Review of Public Health* 15.

Schor, J.B. 1992. The Overworked American: The Unexpected Decline of Leisure. New York: Basic Books.

Scott, R., T. Garner, and D. Ticoll. 2004. *A Fine Balance: The Impact of Offshore IT Services on Canada's IT Landscape.* Toronto: PriceWaterhouse Coopers.

Sears, A. 1999. "The Lean State and Capitalist Restructuring: Towards a Theoretical Account." *Studies in Political Economy* 59 (Summer).

Selman, G. 1991. *Citizenship and the Adult Education Movement in Canada.* Vancouver: University of British Columbia/ International Council for Adult Education.

Selman, G., M. Cooke, M. Selman, and P. Dampier. 1998. *The Foundations of Adult Education in Canada.* Second edition. Toronto: Thompson Educational Publishing.

Shields, M. 2000. "Long Working Hours and Health." Perspectives on Labour and Income. Ottawa: Statistics Canada (Catalogue Number 75-001-XPE, Spring).

Shore, B. 1996. "The Legacy of Downsizing: Putting the Pieces Back Together." *Business Forum* Summer/Fall.

Shragge, E. 1997. *Workfare: Ideology for a New Under-Class.* Toronto: Garamond Press.

Siegrist, J. 1996. "Adverse Health Effects of High-Effort/Low-Reward Conditions." *Journal of Occupational Health Psychology* 1, 1.

Silver, J. 1987. "The Ideology of Excellence: Management and Neo-Conservatism." *Studies in Political Economy* 24.

Simon, T.W. 1985. "Democratizing Eutopia." *Our Generation* 17, 1 (Fall-Winter).

Sisson, K. 2000. *Direct Participation and the Modernisation of Work Organization.* Dublin: European Foundation for the Improvement of Living and Working Conditions.

Sivanandan, A. 1997. "Heresies and Prophecies: The Social and Political Fallout of the Technological Revolution." In Jim Davis et al. (eds.), *Cutting Edge: Technology, Information, Capitalism and Social Revolution.* London: Verso Books.

_____. 1990. "All That Melts Into Air Is Solid: The Hokum of New Times." *Race and Class* 31, 3.

Skocpol, T. 2000. *The Missing Middle.* New York, London: W.W. Norton and Company.

Skorstad, E. 1994. "Lean Production, Conditions of Work and Worker Commitment." *Economic and Industrial Democracy* 15, 4.

Slaughter, S., and G. Rhoades. 2004. *Academic Capitalism and the New Economy: Markets, State, and Higher Education.* Baltimore: Johns Hopkins University Press.

Smith, A. 1776. *The Wealth of Nations*. London: Penguin Books.

Smith, M.J., F.T. Conway, and B.T. Karsh. 1999. "Occupational Stress in Human Computer Interaction." *Industrial Health* 37.

Smith, P., and E. Smythe. 2001. "Globalisation, Citizenship and Technology." In F. Webster (ed.), *Culture and Politics in the Information Age*. Routledge: London and New York.

Smith, V. 1997. "New Forms of Work Organization." *Annual Review of Sociology* 23.

Solomon, C. 2002. "HR's Push For Productivity." *Workforce* August.

Somavia, J. 2006. *Dealing with the Global Jobs Crisis*. Geneva: International Labour Office.

Sparks, K., C. Cooper, Y. Fried, and A. Shirom. 1997. "The Effects of Hours of Work On Health: A Meta-Analytic Review." *Journal of Occupational and Organizational Psychology* 70, 4.

Sparks, K., B. Farragher, and C. Cooper. 2001. "Well-being and Occupational Health in the 21st Century Workplace." *Journal of Occupational and Organizational Health Psychology* 74, 4.

Spencer, B. 1998. *The Purposes of Adult Education*. Toronto: Thompson Educational Publishing.

Stanford, J. 2001. "Education is Great, But It's No Guarantee of a Better Life." *CCPA Monitor* 8, 5 (October).

Statistics Canada. 2006a. *Women In Canada: A Gender-based Statistical Report*. Fifth edition. Ottawa: Statistics Canada.

_____. 2006b. "Full-time and Part-time Employment by Sex and Age Group, 2001–2005." Available at <www40.statcan.ca/l01/cst01/labor12.htm>.

_____. 2004a. "Employment by Industry and Sex, Numbers, 2003." Available at <www.statcan.ca/english/Pgdb/labor10a.htm>.

_____. 2004b. "Labour Force Survey, December 2003." *The Daily*, January 9. Ottawa: Statistics Canada.

_____. 2004c. "Labour Force Survey Estimates, by Educational Attainment, Sex and Age Group, Annual." CANSIM, Table 282-004 (18, 19).

_____. 2004d. "Labour Force Survey." *The Daily*, January 8. Ottawa: Statistics Canada.

_____. 2003a. "Year-end Labour Market Review." *The Daily*, January 24. Available at <www.statcan.ca/Daily/English/030124/d030124a.htm>.

_____. 2003b. *Earnings of Canadians: Making a Living in the New Economy*. Ottawa: Statistics Canada.

_____. 2003c. *Income of Canadian Families*. Ottawa: Statistics Canada.

_____. 2001. "Workplace and Employee Survey Compendium." Ottawa: Statistics Canada (Catalogue Number 71-585-XIE).

_____. 2000. *Women in Canada 2000: A Gender-based Statistical Report*. Ottawa: Statistics Canada.

_____. 1996. *Labour Force Annual Averages 1995*. Ottawa: Statistics Canada.

Statistics Canada and Council of Ministers of Education. 1999. *Educational Indicators in Canada: Report of the Pan-Canadian Education Indicators Program*. Ottawa: Statistics Canada.

Statistics Canada and Human Resource Development Canada. 1998. "The Evolving Workplace: Findings From the Pilot Workplace and Employee Survey." Ottawa: Statistics Canada (Catalogue Number 71-583-XPE).

Steedman, M. 2003. "The Changing Face of the Call Centre Industry in Canada." Paper prepared for conference on Organizing Call Centres from the Workers' Perspective" (September 11–13), Toronto. Available at <www.uswa.ca/program/content/950.php>.

Steindl, J. 1952. *Maturity and Stagnation in American Capitalism*. New York: Monthly Review Press.

Storey, J. 2001. "Human Resource Management Today: An Assessment." In J. Storey (Ed.), *Human Resource Management: A Critical Text*. London: Thomson Learning.

Strazdins, L., and G. Bammer. 2004. "Women, Work and Musculoskeletal Health." *Social Science and Medicine* 58.

Sweezy, P.M., and H. Magdoff. 1972. *The Dymanics of U.S. Capitalism: Corporate Structure, Infation, Credit, Gold and the Dollar*. New York: Monthly Review Press.

Sweezy, P.M., H. Magdoff, J.B. Foster, and R.W. McChesney. 2003. "What Recovery?" Monthly Review 54, 11 (April).

_____. 2002. "The New Face of Capitalism: Slow Growth, Excess Capital, and a Mountain of Debt." *Monthly Review* 53, 11 (April).

_____. 2001. "The New Economy: Myth and Reality." *Monthly Review* 52, 11 (April).

Swenarchuk, M. 2001. "Civilizing Globalization: Trade and Environment Thirteen Years On." Canadian Centre for Policy Alternatives, Briefing Paper Series: Trade and Investment, 2, 6.

Swift, J. 1995. *Wheel of Fortune: Work and Life in the Age of Falling Expectations*. Toronto: Between the Lines.

Swift, J., and D. Peerla. 1996. "Attitude Adjustment: The Brave New World of Work and the Revolution of Falling Expectations." In T. Dunk, S. McBride, and R. Nelsen (eds.), *The Training Trap: Ideology, Training and the Labour Market*. Winnipeg/Halifax: Society for Socialist Studies/Fernwood Publishing.

Tabak, F., and M.A. Crichlow (eds.). 2000. *Informalization: Process and Structure*. Baltimore: Johns Hopkins University Press.

Tabb, W.K. 2001. "New Economy... Same Irrational Economy." *Monthly Review* 52, 11.

_____. 1997. "Globalization Is An Issue, The Power of Capital Is The Issue." *Monthly Review* 49, 2 (June).

Teeple, G. 2000. *Globalization and the Decline of Social Reform: Into the Twenty-First Century*. Toronto: Garamond Press.

Theodore, N., and J. Peck. 1999. "Welfare to Work." *Critical Social Policy* 61, 19 (4).

Thompson, E.P. 1968. *The Making of the English Working Class*. London: Penguin Books.

Thomson, J.W. 1999. "Globalization: Obsession or Necessity?" *Business and Society Review* 104, 1 (Winter).

Titmuss, R. 1968. *Commitment to Welfare*. London: Allen and Unwin.

Toffler, A. 1980. *The Third Wave*. New York: William Morrow.

Togati, T.D. 2006. *The New Economy and Macroeconomic Stability: A Neo-modern Perspective*

Drawing on the Complexity Approach and Keynesian Economics. London: Routledge.

Tomer, J. 2001. "Understanding High-Performance Work Systems: The Joint Contribution of Economics and Human Resource Management." *Journal of Socio-Economics* 31, 1.

Torjman, S. and K. Battle. 1999. *Good Work: Getting It and Keeping It*. Ottawa: Caledon Institute of Social Policy.

Turner, J.B. 1995. "Economic Context and the Health Effects of Unemployment." *Journal of Health and Social Behaviour* 36, 3.

UNITE Canada (n.d.) "Ten Elements in Making the Implementation of Technology Successful." Available at <www.unite-svti.org/En/WORK_REORGANIZA-TION/Tech_Change/beststep3/beststep3.html>.

United Nations. 2005. *The Millenium Development Goals Report 2005*. New York: United Nations.

_____. 1999. *Human Development Report*. New York: Oxford University Press.

USWA (United Steelworkers of America). 2005. <http://steelworkers-metallos.ca/program/content/index.php?lan=en>.

Vail, J., J. Wheelock, and M. Hill. 1999. *Insecure Times: Living with Insecurity in Contemporary Society*. London: Routledge.

Van Der Doef, M. and M. Maes. 1999. "The Job Demand-Control (-Support) Model and Psychological Well-Being." *Work and Stress* 13.

Vandenberg, R., H. Richardson, and L. Eastman. 1999. "The Impact of High Involvement Work Processes on Organizational Effectiveness." *Group and Organization Management* 24, 3.

Varma, A., R. Beatty, C. Schneier, and D. Ulrich. 1999. "High Performance Work Systems: Exciting Discovery or Passing Fad?" *Human Resource Planning* 22, 1.

Volpe, J. 2004. "Speaking Notes to Announce Funding for 31 Sector Council Projects, Hummingbird Centre." Toronto, March 16. Available at <www1.hrsdc.gc.ca/speeches-discours/040316.shtml>.

Vosko. L.F. 2003. "Precarious Employment in Canada: Taking Stock, Taking Action." *Just Labour* 3.

_____. 2000. *Temporary Work: The Gendered Rise of a Precarious Employment Relationship*. Toronto: University of Toronto Press.

Wallerstein, I. 1998. *Utopisitics: Or, Historical Choices for the Twenty-first Century*. New York: The New Press.

_____. 1996. "The Global Possibilities, 1990–2025." In T.K. Hopkins, I. Wallerstein, et al., *The Age of Transition: The Trajectory of the World-System, 1945–2025*. London: Zed Books.

_____. 1983. *Historical Capitalism*. London: Verso Books.

_____. 1974. *The Modern World-System I: Capitalist Agriculture and the Origins of the European World-Economy in the Sixteenth Century*. New York: Academic Press.

Walters, V., P. McDonough, and L. Strohschein. 2002. "The Influence of Work, Household Structure, and Social, Personal and Material Resources on Gender Differences in Health: An Analysis of the 1994 Canadian National Population Health Survey." *Social Science and Medicine* 54.

Ware, R. 1999. "Public Moral Values, the Fabrication of Communities and Disempowerment." In D. Broad and W. Antony (eds.), *Citizens or Consumers? Social*

Policy in a Market Society. Halifax: Fernwood Publishing.

Warr, P.B. 1987. *Work, Unemployment and Mental Health*. Oxford: Clarendon Press.

Waters, M. 2001. *Globalization*. London: Routledge.

Webster, J. 2003. "Women in European Call Centres: Work, Skills and Opportunities." Paper prepared for conference on "Organizing Call Centres from the Workers' Perspective" (September 11–13), Toronto. Policies and Briefing Documents. Available at <www.uswa.ca/program/content/948.php>.

Welton, M. 1987. *Knowledge for the People: The Struggle for Adult Learning in English-Speaking Canada: 1928–1973*. Toronto: OISE Press.

Werlhof, C. von. 1988. "The Proletarian is Dead: Long Live the Housewife!" In M. Mies et al., *Women: The Last Colony*. London: Zed Books.

Wilkinson, R.G. 1996. *Unhealthy Societies: The Afflictions of Inequality*. London, Routledge.

Williams, C. 2003. "Sources of Workplace Stress." Perspectives on Labour and Income. Ottawa: Statistics Canada (Catalogue Number 75-001-XIE June).

Wood, S. 1999. "Human Resource Management and Performance." *International Journal of Management Reviews* 1, 4.

Wood, S., and L. de Menezes. 1998. "High Commitment Management in the UK: Evidence from the Workplace Industrial Relations Survey and Employers' Manpower and Skills Practices Survey." *Human Relations* 51.

World Bank. 2003. *Global Economic Prospects and the Developing Countries*. Washington, DC: The World Bank.

Wright, B., and J. Barling. 1998. "'The Executioner's Song': Listening to Downsizers Reflect on Their Experiences." *Canadian Journal of Administrative Sciences* 15, 4.

Yates, C., W. Lewchuk, and P. Stewart. 2001. "Empowerment as a Trojan Horse: New Systems of Work Organization in the North American Automobile Industry." *Economic and Industrial Democracy* 22, 4.

Yates, M.D, 2003. *Naming the System: Inequality and Work in the Global Economy*. New York: Monthly Review Press.

_____. 2001. "The 'New' Economy and the Labor Movement." *Monthly Review* 52, 11.

_____. 1994. *Longer Hours, Fewer Jobs: Employment and Unemployment in the United States*. New York: Monthly Review Press.

Ziegler, P. 1998. *The Black Death*. Second edition. London: Penguin Books.

Zeitlin, M. 1996. "In Defense of Utopia." *Monthly Review* 48, 7 (December).